No Stone Unturned

A Brother and Sister's Incredible Journey
Through the Olympics and Cancer

Jessie Garcia

In memory of our beautiful Jessi
Playful Heart
Radiant Smile
Undying Spirit
May 21, 1977–March 19, 2014

Jeff, Ruthie, and Casey,

If you are working on the epigraph you must be nearing the finish of your book. Wow, what a great accomplishment! What a beautiful tribute to Jessi and your journey with her. I thought about Bible verses for a while, and some that seemed appropriate I've shared with you below.

You and your family are in my thoughts and prayers.

Blessings,
Matt
Pastor
Blackhawk Church, Middleton, Wisconsin

1 Corinthians 13:7 "Love always protects, always trusts, always hopes, always perseveres."

Proverbs 3:3 "Let love and faithfulness never leave you; bind them around your Neck, write them on the tablet of your heart."

Ecclesiastes 3:1–6 "There is a time for everything, and a season for every activity under the heavens ...

a time to weep and a time to laugh, a time to mourn and a time to dance ...

a time to scatter stones and a time to gather them ...

a time to search and a time to give up."

Contents

Foreword by Dan Jansen

The most important and influential thing for me in my life has always been my family. I grew up the youngest of nine children and learned everything from my parents, three brothers, and five sisters. As I started to show promise in the sport of speedskating it was with their support that I finally achieved my ultimate goal of winning an Olympic gold medal.

Family values are nothing new to anyone who grew up in the Midwest and certainly nothing new to the people who were, for some reason, attracted to our sport. The Heidens, Blairs, Jansens, FitzRandolphs, and many more turned speedskating meets into family outings on cold winter weekends in Wisconsin and throughout the Midwest.

Due to the relatively small number of athletes that choose this sport, the families that were involved became, in a sense, a bigger family. My family knew the Blair family before Bonnie and I were even born. Speedskating becomes a fraternity of sorts, and very close relationships are formed early in life that still remain today.

These close bonds among the athletes and families in our sport carry on from generation to generation because everyone has an understanding of what their counterparts have sacrificed and been through to get to whatever level they have achieved, whether that be a state champion or an Olympic champion.

When I reached an elite level, I always felt it was important to offer help, advice, or assistance of any kind to the younger skaters, and I certainly always took note of the up-and-coming skaters who looked like they had a lot of potential. Somewhere around the late 1980s, I noticed one of those kids. His name was Casey FitzRandolph, and he was from my home state of Wisconsin. By the time I retired after the 1994 season, Casey had developed into someone that I knew would be the next great sprinter in a long line of world-class sprinters from the United States.

It was fun to watch him improve technically and get stronger with each passing year, and it was an absolute thrill to see him win gold in Salt Lake City in 2002. It was truly another family victory, both for the FitzRandolphs and the American speedskating family.

Fast forward eight years, and I learned that Casey's sister, Jessi, was in a fight against breast cancer. As painful as this news was, I knew one thing: The Fitz family would be there with Jessi each and every step of the way, no matter how difficult or painful those steps would be. I knew this because I knew their family, and because it's what families do—not just speedskating families but all families—and I knew theirs was strong.

In 1987 while we were competing in Germany, Bonnie Blair received a call telling her that her brother, Rob, was diagnosed with a brain tumor. I remember the uncertainty and questions we all had and our concern for Rob and for Bonnie as well. Just a few short months later, Bonnie was by my side when we heard that my sister, Jane, had been diagnosed with leukemia. After battles of different lengths, both of our siblings succumbed to their respective diseases after putting up good fights and leaving our families with everlasting memories of their strength, perseverance, and undying spirits.

I know that Jessi's fight has inspired her family as well, and I'm glad they decided to write this book. It shows that there is no one way to fight cancer, and it also confirms that the most important weapon in that fight is the love and support of a strong family.

Jessi's mother, Ruthie, says in the book that she will "catch up to Jessi one day." I, for one, believe that is true. This belief helps to bring a little peace to the things that we may never fully understand.

—Dan Jansen,
four-time Olympian,
1994 men's 1,000-meter gold medalist

Foreword by Bonnie Blair

C asey FitzRandolph, known as "Fitz", was coming into our international speedskating world as DJ and I were finishing our careers. However, I got to travel for one year with Fitz before I retired. Dave Cruikshank, who would become my husband, was still skating after I retired, and Casey and Dave went to Nagano (home of the 1998 Olympics) and roomed together quite a bit. When that happened, our close family of speedskaters and supporters grew. Mr. and Mrs. Fitz traveled to some competitions, where I got to know them. I didn't know Jessi as well, but I was aware she had been an awesome skater in her younger years before deciding to take another path in life. I also heard she was quite a soccer player. My best memories of Ruthie and Jessi were at Christmastime, when they would bring Dave and me their famous sugar cookies with icing and Christmas cutouts. To this day, my kids and I use their recipe, but I still think theirs were better.

The thing I have learned from sports is how to fight: fight through workouts, fight through races, have a goal, and do all that needs to be done to accomplish a goal. DJ's sister, who also skated, fought like crazy during her leukemia battle, as did my siblings (skaters as well), my brother Rob, who battled a brain tumor for over twenty years, and my sister Mary, who also battled leukemia. I know the three of them had that extra gear to fight, just like Jessi did in her battle, as you will see when you read this book.

As I have gotten older, I have come to know that families from all walks of life have their highs and lows. The FitzRandolphs and author Jessie Garcia take you through one family's ups and downs. I have lived through my own family's ups and downs. I know not everyone has had gold-medal highs, but I am sure we can all think of highs in our life that stand out. We might not have gone through the exact same things, but life can be a roller coaster. Jessie Garcia does a wonderful job of taking us on a ride with the FitzRandolphs. As I know from my own family, the highs are what they are, but the lows are the ones you seem to second-guess. You always wonder "what if"—what if we had done this or that, or acted sooner? Hindsight is 20-20. But the mind is a powerful tool, as I have also grown to know, and my guess is that Jessi's mind was stronger than most.

Ruthie and Jeff provided their kids with opportunities to follow their hearts, Casey by chasing his gold medal and Jessi by finding her way, which might have been a bit of a zigzag. Ruthie and Jeff were always there for both of them, maybe sometimes too much! However, what I take from their story is the never-ending love they had for both of their kids and how they would do anything for them. They might feel that hindsight would have changed things, but they really did pull out all the stops and do whatever they could for Jessi to have a longer life, probably with less pain than had she taken the conventional route of treatment for her entire bout of cancer. And with that, they should be proud of what they did in helping Fitz chase his gold and Jessi chase another day, week, month, and year. They gave their kids the tools to fight, have goals, set them, and reset them for every avenue in life, and that is a wonderful gift. For that, Mr. and Mrs. Fitz should always be proud.

—Bonnie Blair,
four-time Olympian,
five gold medals, one bronze

Introduction

In some ways, I'm not perfectly clear why I'm writing an introduction for a book about our family's amazing story. I guess I believe the events that define our lives are worth sharing, and I hope that someone might actually buy our book, read it, and possibly try some of the things we did to enhance our children's lives. If you do, I'm pretty sure they will work for you if you stick with them. Remember: persistence is a virtue. This is one motto our family abides by.

The events we are about to share, with the help of author Jessie Garcia, have taken place over a span of nearly forty years. My wife, Ruthie's, and my memories of this period are still incredibly vivid. It's as though they have been etched in stone and then splashed with a light source that seems to set still pictures and thoughts into a whirling dervish of motion. It's like having a motion picture in the back of your head that replays all the good times from the childhoods of our son, Casey, and daughter, Jessi. We recall so much motion and so many thoughts. We had so many dreams, some squashed but most realized. And more are still playing out today before our eyes.

This is definitely a labor and story of love. It's about two children who took divergent paths to adulthood, with results that at first may seem totally unfair. But as our story unfolds in these pages, I believe you will learn about a brother and sister's love for each other. You will learn about our efforts to mold them into model young adults and why that doesn't always work. You will read of our soul searching, feel our frustration, share our successes, big and small, and ultimately join us in the realization of two very different dreams: one a single success that changed a life and the other journey with many ups and downs that ultimately had a disappointing ending.

This is a story of two heroes who climbed very different mountains and defined success in two startlingly different ways. It is the story of a brother who can say that at one point in time, he was the best in the world. And it is the story of a sister who can say she wouldn't accept death as an alternative and who consequently found a quality of life through spiritual growth and a protocol of cures that our traditional medical profession does not share with cancer patients. She wasn't able to beat the demonic cancer, but her last three years were full of serenity, wisdom, and ultimately a spiritual strength that she carried with her beyond this life.

I can't promise you'll enjoy every chapter of this book. Some of our stories are not necessarily the most pleasant. But we will try to help you find your own path to dealing with your family's challenges, or at least developing some thoughts on ways you can get your family through the tough times and to the good times.

Our lives have been full of unique family experiences and the tight bond that can be forged by spending so much time together as a family unit. We have laughed and we have cried, but mostly we have been blessed with a mega-dose of good fortune during our lifetimes. This is not because we "deserved it" or because we were deeply spiritual people (although a little humility and spirituality are definitely a virtue) but instead because we never took no for an answer. Throw an obstacle in Ruthie's way and she'll crush it—if she doesn't research it to death first. Try to make me believe that something cannot be accomplished and I'll go to my grave finding a way to get it done. I believe, as much as anything, that it was this simple little premise that brought us our good fortunes: believe and you can achieve. We instilled this value in our children from the day they were born and have seen how it positively impacted their lives. We'll share anecdotes and stories of how we believed—and how we as a family ended up achieving.

You'll read about Casey's successes starting at age five and continuing, albeit with several speed bumps, until he won a gold medal in the 500-meter speedskating sprint in the 2002 Winter Olympics in Salt Lake City. You'll read about the challenges Jessi faced, from trying to establish her own identity to discovering she had breast cancer and not accepting her doctor's death sentence. Her last three years, after her doctors handed her the verdict, are a testimony to her perseverance, fight, and willingness to look to other protocols that would strengthen her body instead of poisoning it. By believing that alternative cures could do for her what the conventional wisdom of surgery, chemotherapy, and radiation could not, Jessi lived and thrived for three years after she was told she only had a few weeks or months to live.

Our story contains wonderful family times together: laughing, crying, praying, cheering, consoling, teaching, grieving, and sharing our two children's very different paths to success in their lifetimes. To say we've left no stone unturned would be an understatement.

—Jeff

CHAPTER 1

Finding a Lump

Summer 2010

I t was a week at the cabin, a place so serene they called it their slice of heaven. A log cabin laid one beam at a time, just nine hundred square feet with a great room, two bedrooms, a bath, and a tiny kitchen. It was nestled in the northern Wisconsin woods, straddling a lake with a funny name—Big Sissabagama, a word from the Chippewa Indians meaning "lake of many bays."

The FitzRandolphs were feeling calm and happy, and why not? Times were good. Their son, Casey, was eight years removed from one of the greatest achievements any mortal being can accomplish: an Olympic gold medal, won in speedskating in front of a wildly cheering American crowd in Salt Lake City in 2002. Truth be told, they weren't sure that glow would ever wear off. It was something they had fantasized about since both of their kids first put on skates. They had waited twenty-two years to see it and now hoped the ecstasy would last at least that long. Jeff and Ruthie had spent countless hours in ice rinks, driving ninety miles from their house near Madison, Wisconsin, to Milwaukee in order to be on the best oval in the state. They'd spent their kids' early years lacing up skates, serving meals, helping with homework in the car, cheering, and later volunteering to start races as the children grew. To see your own flesh and blood win Olympic gold, being the absolute best on the planet? The emotional high of that day might never go away.

Casey was married to a wonderful woman, Jenn, a first-grade teacher who fit into the family as if she had been molded for the part. The couple had two young children, a boy and a girl, both blond and feisty. Casey had started a new career in business insurance with M3, a well-respected Madison business, bought a house, and even purchased two farms he was turning into nature preserves and managing for quality wildlife habitat. He seemed to be settled in.

Jeff and Ruthie's daughter, Jessi, was also finding a rhythm to her life after a few rough years of trying to navigate her way. There were years when she probably drank a little too much, partied a bit too hard, and had a brush or two with the law. She had also been a speedskater, making her first national team at age thirteen. Many had called her the next Bonnie Blair, but she quit just a short time later. She hit some rebellious times. But now Jessi was thirty-three, dating, and embarking on a career as a graphic designer that excited her.

The kids were doing well, and Jeff and Ruthie were in what they would later call the peaceful years. It was the Fourth of July, and the weather at the cabin was pristine.

"Life is different at the lake," remembered Jeff. "Yeah, the dogs still got up at five thirty in the morning and wanted to go outside to piddle and then be fed, but after that, all options were available. Some mornings I'd look out over the lake and decide it looked like a good morning to fish. Maybe there was a slight overcast, some chop on the water, and it looked like a good walleye morning. But most mornings, I'd simply feed the dogs and fall right back into bed, knowing that I had nothing more important to worry about that day."

Most people don't stir much before eight in the north woods, and then it would be to put the coffee pot on, grab a quick shower, and have a cup of morning Joe on the front porch, as Jeff always did. He would peruse whatever Stephen King novel he was engrossed in, pausing every once in a while to glance up and watch the ducks swim by the sandy beach, standing on their heads as they dipped underwater to grab little water bugs. A loon might let out its mournful call, and occasionally a boat holding a couple of fishermen skimmed across the lake while they looked for their next hot spot. Ruthie would generally roll out of bed around nine and repeat Jeff's routine herself. Sleeping in was one of her highest priorities at the lake; the slow pace there was a welcome reprieve from her hectic schedule in Madison. That week in particular felt perfect.

"We decided to stay a couple of extra days," reflected Ruthie. "Everything was fine at home. Jessi was at our house with her dog, Kirby, watering the plants for us and feeding the fish in our saltwater aquarium."

Ruthie called Jessi to tell her they would be extending their week just a bit, and they went back to what Jeff called "just chill" time, looking across Big Siss and reliving their son's Olympic moment over and over in their heads.

"After the gold medal, I became the most contented, fulfilled, satisfied person in the world," Jeff reminisced. Quiet times like these, relaxing moments that required nothing but stillness, were about to come to an end.

Jessi FitzRandolph was lying in her boyfriend's bed when she first felt the lump. She was dating a man named Jack, a divorced dad of two who owned his own house. She hadn't found *the* guy yet, and it was too early in the process to even guess if Jack was someone she could date seriously. Plus, she knew he wasn't looking to jump into anything right after his divorce, and she herself had just finished a long-term relationship that had ended badly. Jessi and Jack were just having fun together.

That night, as they were laughing and joking like lovers do after being intimate, her hand touched her left breast. There was something there, a lump of some kind, and it was not small. *Like the size of a quarter,* she thought.

She didn't mention it to Jack. Jessi was a calm person, but she also knew instinctively, somewhere in her gut, that something wasn't exactly right. Although she tried to put the lump out of her mind and continue relaxing with Jack, a little voice said "uh-oh," and an internal warning told her she had better have it checked out if it didn't go away.

The next day, she explored the breast again, hoping that the lump might have disappeared. It was still there. The day after that, it *still* hadn't gone anywhere, and she called her doctor. When he did a closer exam on the table, he told her, "We'd better have it looked at, but it's possible that it's nothing."

Her parents were at the cabin. She stopped herself from calling them, her first thought being that she didn't want to freak them out. She knew a call would send them scurrying right home, and Jessi didn't like to be fussed over. Plus, she was trying to protect her mom and dad from the fear she knew they would have. She didn't want them worrying for the entire four-and-a-half-hour drive back to Madison.

There was nothing they, or anyone, could do until they knew the results of the tests, anyway. So she confided only in her best friend, Libby, and entered the clinical world of mammograms, MRIs, and biopsies, all in the next few days. Then she waited, the first hints of fear starting to creep in.

She tried to reason with herself. She was in her early thirties. *What could be so bad? Maybe it was benign.* But again, her gut told her otherwise.

"I kind of knew what was coming. I just had a feeling."

Jessi had recently moved back into her parents' home after breaking up with the man she'd dated prior to Jack. She was alone at their house in the morning with her dog, Kirby, the plants, and the fish when the phone rang. It was the nurse. "We got the results ... and they came back positive."

Those words are like a bowling ball crashing into the pins you thought were upright in your life. The nurse said the surgeon would be calling later to discuss things. Jessi was rattled but didn't cry. In fact, she was optimistic. Many women had overcome breast cancer. Why not her? She had been raised to believe that she could do or be anything. There were no barriers. She knew hard work paid off; she had seen it with her own eyes—her brother winning a gold medal and another Madison native, Eric Heiden, winning five. Life was supposed to bring you good things, and if it didn't, you made changes until it did. That was a basic right. She lived in a time when women could do anything; she lived in a country with the best medical care in the world. This lump in her breast would simply be a bump in the road.

"Initially, I felt it wouldn't be that bad; it would suck for a while, but I would get through it, and I would be okay," said Jessi. "It kind of goes back to how I try not to overthink things. Life goes on."

She decided to take a shower and wound up missing the call from the surgeon as the water splashed down around her. When she stepped from the steamy bathroom and called back, the surgeon was busy. Phone tag was not what she needed, so Jessi contacted Libby and tried to convince her to go to the new *Twilight* movie. Libby instead persuaded her best buddy that they would be better served staying by a phone. They went to lunch at a place known for buffalo wings, where they talked and waited. The cell phone never rang. The surgeon didn't call back that afternoon, but Jessi was going to meet with her in a day or two, so she figured she would just wait and talk to her then.

Her parents were still away and unaware of what she was going through, and Jessie decided not to mention it when her mom called to let her know they were planning to extend their stay. That night, Jessi needed an escape. She and Libby invited some people over and threw a party.

"I drank a bit. It was probably my way of coping with it. I didn't want it to consume everything. I just wanted to do my normal things."

Her biggest fear at the time was still the reaction of her parents.

Jeff and Ruthie pulled into the garage in the late afternoon. Their home was tucked into a wooded ridge on the Johnstown Moraine, which marked the maximum edge of the Green Bay lobe of the glacier's push into southern Wisconsin. The Ice Age Trail winds through the back edge of their property, which is located four miles east of the city of Verona. The landscape's uneven terrain parallels the rises and falls of their lives.

The couple unpacked the car and took the bags into the house. It had been built in the 1990s to suit their family's lifestyle and had a strategically planned view of Blue Mounds State Park some twenty-three miles to the west.

Jessi was waiting for them in the kitchen.

"Hi. I have something to tell you."

Immediately the mom alarm bell sounded.

"I'm like, whoa, this is a first," said Ruthie, knowing that her daughter, as wonderful as she was, rarely opened up to them in that way. "I knew there was a big problem."

But dad's mind was exploring more basic, everyday hiccups.

"I had just seen her car in the garage, and it had no visible dents or dings, so I figured she hadn't cracked the car up. I really had no idea."

"I'm not in trouble," Jessi reassured her parents, knowing that they might suspect that. "Can we all sit down?"

They found their way to the brightly colored stools surrounding the kitchenette table, and Jessi took a deep breath.

"I have breast cancer."

How do you react when your child springs this on you? Ruthie, a registered nurse, felt the world shifting under her feet. "I felt like I was going to pass out, like my head was spinning a little bit. I physically felt like I was going to pass out. I couldn't breathe."

"I was basically numb. It took me totally by shock," remembers Jeff. "I kind of looked at Ruthie, and I didn't know what to say. I'm not a medical person. I can deal with simpler tasks, but medical issues are out of my league. So I deferred to Ruthie and let her ask questions."

There was a pit the size of a soccer ball in his stomach. How could this be happening? He could feel the air rushing out of the family balloon that had been filled with so much happy helium back in Salt Lake City. He saw Casey on the podium accepting his gold medal, the flag raising. There were tears in all of their eyes as they screamed until they were hoarse from the stands in the cold Utah night. He saw Casey's face on national television and the front pages of newspapers. And the national anthem—just hearing it still gave Jeff chills. But now he was looking across the table at his beautiful daughter delivering a toxic punch of the most unexpected and unwelcome news.

"It was a complete opposite feeling of the elation of the gold medal. It was the lowest of lows and very hard to believe."

Jeff and Ruthie listened quietly at first. Jessi presented the case to her parents with optimism and her usual dose of practical, no-nonsense attitude.

"They both wanted to cry. I told them they couldn't cry, because if they cried, I would cry. I hate crying because it hurts, you get slobbery, and it's messy. They were actually pretty good and they didn't totally lose it. I said, 'We're all going to get through this. It's going to be okay.'"

"Right away, Jessi said, Don't worry. It's no big deal. I'm 100 percent sure I'm going to get over it." said Ruthie. Although she was a nurse, Ruthie didn't specialize in anything that could immediately help them. She didn't even work with young people. Her positions were in geriatric psychiatry and hospice. So she let her daughter take the lead.

"Jessi was so reassuring. She was so certain. She minimized it. I did too. Jeff was in denial."

But Ruthie's mind did wander back to another odd incident just a few months before.

"In April, she called me at work—and she never calls me at work—and she said, 'I think I need to go to the ER. I have terrible back pain, and it's killing me to breathe.' Off to the ER she went, where they took an x-ray and found a fracture. Why would a healthy, athletic thirty-two-year-old have a fracture? That should have sent up a red flag to her doctors."

Instead, the ER doctors told her she must have coughed wrong and sent her home to rest. The FitzRandolphs would later learn that this was a piece to the puzzle. But at this point, they didn't put the breast and the fractured rib together. Why would they? They were not cancer experts, and they were still stunned by this latest news and focused on what she was telling them that day.

"I was pretty devastated but still optimistic," said Ruthie, although she was aware of a history of breast cancer in Jeff's family. Both his mother and grandmother had it, at a much older age. Ruthie knew that there is actually a better cure rate when a woman is postmenopausal. Hormones in younger women feed the cancer cells and make it harder to control. But at that moment, they didn't have the particulars of Jessi's illness, and they still thought she might have been stage I. In that case they could get rid of the tumor and lymph nodes and be done.

Jessi still needed to inform Casey, her only sibling, and his wife, Jenn. She waited a few days until he brought his kids to their parents' house to swim in the backyard pool. Jessi sat them down the same way she had her parents and started with, "I need to tell you something." They were as floored as Jeff and Ruthie had been. Jessi was concerned about Jenn's reaction. Jenn's mom had passed away in her early fifties from brain cancer, and Jessi didn't want this latest news to break her up. Jenn's first instinct was to brainstorm how to best help her sister-in-law.

"I thought about what my mom wanted from us when she was just diagnosed. She needed us to be strong and try to keep things normal. So that's what I wanted to be for Jessi. She didn't need to be consoling us."

Ruthie had many of the same thoughts.

"I realized I had to be strong," said Ruthie. "She doesn't want to have to hold my hand and get me through it. It's got to be the other way, so I've got to be the big girl here. But I still cried myself to sleep every night."

Indeed, Jessi's family saved many of their deepest emotions for moments when they were alone.

"Casey and I cried together at home in private," said Jenn.

Jessi and Casey had gotten closer in recent years. There were times their relationship hadn't been quite as easy to define. Frankly, as his star rose, it was hard to be known as "Casey's sister." Part of that, she could admit later, contributed to her rebellion. She remembered something she overheard her father say to an acquaintance when she was just a young teenager.

"They were talking about Casey, and he said 'He's the model child.' He said that right in front of me, and that stuck with me since I was thirteen years old." Her voice trailed away a bit as she remembered this twenty years later, her eyes looking down. "I really didn't like that."

Being the sibling, or really any close relative, of a famous person—be it Olympic athlete, politician, or movie star—is not easy. It was especially hard because Casey seemed to make no mistakes.

"He was kind of the good kid, and I was the one that liked to not always follow all the rules, to put it nicely. I had my moments where I would kind of resent him, but as I got older I told myself, 'Knock that off.' He's my brother, I love him, and he's always been wonderful to me."

When Casey's two children, Sawyer and Cassidy, came into the family, Jessi took on the role of the aunt beautifully, and the brother-sister dynamic moved into a new, more adult phase.

"I spent a lot of time babysitting for the kids. I wanted to be a big part of their lives. Before that, we didn't have a lot in common, but that brought us closer."

For Casey's part, he recognized the difficult situation his sister was put in growing up, but he saw it a little differently. "I think it would have been hard, not because 'I'm Casey's sister' but because I'm Mom and Dad's other child."

Yet Jeff and Ruthie attended every high school soccer game of Jessi's after she quit speedskating. Jeff even coached the Verona soccer team during the club season opposite high school competition. Jessi was one of the team's stars. They clearly doted on both kids. Both were blessed athletically. In fact, Casey used to be envious of how healthy his sister was, perhaps more so than the Olympic gold medalist himself.

"Jessi had more talent than I did, but she chose a different road. She may have done better things in speedskating than I did. She was naturally gifted and strong and athletic. She had knee surgery—a much more significant knee surgery than mine. I still notice the pain. She doesn't even do the physical therapy exercises, but she'll go in and the therapists will rant and rave about how she's ahead of the curve."

When Jessi told her brother about the lump, he was shocked. Yet, like everyone else in the family, his immediate reaction was to think his sister was going to beat this.

"She has a very good immune system, and her body is very good at healing itself."

Jessi had successfully informed her family, as difficult as it might have been. Opening up to the rest of the world was not in her nature. She was a private person.

"I did not tell a lot of people because it's hard. Every time you tell them it brings up more emotions. I don't really like talking about it. That was the hardest part for me, having to tell all my friends, but it had to be done. It's something that has to really come from you."

Things with Jack fizzled in short order. "I'm not entirely sure why. I guess I didn't want to drag someone through cancer treatments if we didn't have strong feelings for each other."

Her close friends knew, and her boyfriend was out of the picture. Now the family tried to wrap their heads around what they might be facing: Jeff and Ruthie's independent, strong-willed, auburn-haired, gorgeous daughter was facing an uncertain cancer diagnosis. They still didn't know what stage Jessi's cancer was at, but Ruthie knew one thing.

"I kept thinking I would give anything it if were me, anything. I'm sixty years old and have had a great life. Why not me? No parent wants to hear that their child might die before them. Jessi went from having her whole life ahead of her to not knowing what her future might hold."

Ruthie worked part time at Agrace HospiceCare caring for terminally ill patients of all ages, and that particular aspect of her job was difficult to adjust to.

"I have watched many older people gradually slipping away and the loved ones grieving. I just would think to myself, this is the way it *should* be. But to lose a child, now that's another story. If you have an eighty- or ninety-year old that's passing, it still can be difficult, but one can be thankful that they have been a part of your life. We celebrate their lives."

Almost immediately, Ruthie started to have trouble concentrating at work. Her focus was on finding a cure for Jessi's cancer. It was consuming her existence.

"I had very high anxiety. I was working in a psych department at Stoughton Hospital, and the psychiatrist I worked with was wonderful. He recognized I was struggling and came up to me one day and said 'How's it going, Ruthie?' I broke down and just sobbed. We talked for a while, and I said I thought I could use a little crutch."

Within a week, she was on an ant-ianxiety medication.

"It made a big difference. I didn't tear up at the drop of a hat. I was much more in control of my emotions for the patients, who counted on me to help them."

But as they entered the early stages of their journey, no one could have foreseen what was going to come or anticipated the many changes ahead.

Casey said, "I expected a little chemo or radiation. I thought they'd remove the breast and do a little treatment and she'd be fine. Part of that was naiveté."

Jenn remembered, "I had a friend whose mom was diagnosed the summer before, and she was doing great. She hadn't even needed a mastectomy and was cancer-free now. I thought, 'Jessi will be just fine. She's young and healthy; she has to be all right.'"

Jeff said, "I've always been a glass-half-full guy. Of course, I thought, 'We're going to beat this thing, and she's going to be with us for a long time.'"

Ruthie thought, "This couldn't be happening to my baby girl. I wouldn't let anything take her from me. If I could, I would switch places with her in a moment."

Jessi herself said, "At first I thought it would probably take a year with the chemo and then I'd be done. It certainly did not work that way. It's definitely been a huge roller coaster."

The family was about to undergo a journey of fear and hope, stops and starts, misdiagnoses, mistakes, and eventually, to their shock, a total shunning from many doctors in conventional medicine. The FitzRandolphs, who had brought glory to the United States in the form of gold, would travel to two foreign countries in search of treatments not available or approved in America. They would join other pioneers in the battle against cancer, using Ruthie's medical background and their own perseverance to fight for their daughter's life. This battle would drain their savings, cause emotional distress to every member of the family, and leave them in a delicate dance between Western medicine and global alternative treatments. Perhaps someday doctors in the United States will regularly practice some of the protocols Jessi tried, but at the time several oncologists who saw her were vehemently against the family's decisions.

What the FitzRandolphs found out is that that they have an extraordinary capacity to dig deep into themselves for strength and to stand up for what they believe in. In many ways, the coming years would bring them closer together than they ever imagined. Jessi's diagnosis got worse. The cancer had already spread to her bones, but they would leave no stone unturned in finding a cure. This was, after all, their daughter, their sister. There was simply no other choice. They loved her too much.

CHAPTER TWO

A Boy and a Girl ... Perfect!

1972

To know Jessi and Casey and all that was to come for them, you must first understand their roots. Jeff and Ruthie were strong parents, very influential on their children, and always present for them. Both had wanted kids long before they met each other, but the union that produced an Olympic medalist and a cancer frontline fighter almost didn't happen. Jeff had been engaged to someone else.

He was born in 1948 in Milton, Wisconsin, the oldest of four and the only boy. Almost everyone in town either worked at Milton College or at the nearby General Motors plant in Janesville. Jeff's father, Ivan, wound up doing both. He left his role as an accountant at GM because he wanted his children to get a college education. A way to ensure this path for his family, which was always struggling with money, presented itself. He took a position teaching business administration and economics. It paid him much less money than GM, but his children's college tuition would be waived if he was a professor.

"He made $9,800 a year. I don't know that he ever got a raise, but all four us of got a free college education," Jeff recalled. If not for his father's choice, Jeff and his sisters would likely not have been able to afford a higher education. Jeff's mother, Virginia (nicknamed "Spin" because, like a top, she never stopped moving), had been a stay-at-home mom until Jeff was a teenager. At that point, she went to work at a manufacturing plant in Milton that made air conditioning ducts.

"I came from a spiritually rich but financially poor family," Jeff admitted. "But Mom made sure there were clothes on our backs, and there was always food on the table. I worked on a farm while going to high school to earn spending money. In the summer, I worked sixty hours a week and got paid fort-five dollars in cash for my efforts. I thought I was rich."

He used his four years at Milton College to major in business administration and minor in marketing. Then, in the fall of his senior year, Jeff almost made the life-changing mistake that would have veered him away from Ruthie.

It started with a road trip to Nebraska for a friend's wedding. Jeff was the best man, and a young, pretty nurse from Nebraska was the maid of honor. Her name was Melanie, and she had long, dark hair. He was smitten.

"We had a fling, and we tried to make it more. I brought her back to Wisconsin, and I proposed. In retrospect, I should not have done that."

It didn't take Jeff long to realize she wasn't the love of his life. He broke off the engagement, but it wasn't clean and it wasn't easy. Melanie decided to stay in Milton. Jeff's parents even helped her rent an apartment and furnish it.

It was time for Jeff to leave, or as he called it, "escape." He first took a job as a counselor at a Jewish summer camp in Waupaca, despite his strict Seventh-Day Baptist upbringing. But it got him away from home, and he enjoyed eight weeks overseeing his young Jewish campers. It was an eye-opening experience for a naïve, small-town boy. Working there put him outside of the fishbowl of Milton and away from the fiancée situation he had gotten himself into. When he came back, he immediately informed his family he was moving on, packed up, and made a beeline to one of the nation's most vibrant cities for young people: Madison, the home of the University of Wisconsin.

Ruthie Whitinger was born two years after Jeff in 1950, and she was brought up near the small town of Wonewoc, Wisconsin. She grew up on a farm where the family raised beef cattle and chickens. Her father, Jim, was the high school principal. Her mother, Trudy, stayed at home with Ruthie and her three siblings, tending to farm matters. But she also had a creative side as an excellent artist who had a number of paintings displayed and sold in area restaurants. Ruthie knew early on what she wanted to be. Ironically, the same profession as Jeff's first fiancée: a nurse. Ruthie had helped take care of her two younger sisters, who were five and ten years her junior. She had also been a nurse's aide in high school and was the nurturing type.

Although she excelled on the trumpet and loved music, her parents urged her into nursing, and she eventually decided they were right. Ruthie enrolled at a UW extension school and moved on to the Madison General School of Nursing in the late 1960s. She had a few wild years of her own after leaving home. It was a crazy time in Madison. Protesting was the "in thing," and the bombing of Sterling Hall on the university campus was the culmination of those riotous years. She shied away from the confrontations but found the time she was in nursing school to be exciting and invigorating compared to her youth in Wonewoc. Her path would soon cross with Jeff FitzRandolph's.

Jeff found an apartment with his lifelong friend Louis, who would later be Jeff and Ruthie's best man, and landed a great starter job as marketing director at the UW Credit Union. As sometimes happens with college buddies, Louis abruptly backed out of the lease, and Jeff was suddenly living on his own. Jeff didn't mind much because he could actually afford the rent.

"I was making $12,000 a year, already more than my dad. When I told him what I was making he said, 'Son, I'm proud of you.'"

Jeff never forgot those words. They drove him to strive for even greater success. "The power of those five words still amazes me to this day."

The new apartment had a huge picture window that looked out over the complex's swimming pool. Jeff spent a happy nine months living, working, and admiring the view out the window. Then one day fate intervened.

"I was having a barbecue with an old high school buddy of mine named Scott. Louis was invited as well but had backed out at the last moment, one of his endearing qualities. We were sitting on my deck drinking a few beers and chatting. All of a sudden in the building just down from ours, these two young ladies started hauling stuff from their cars and moving in, and we watched them for a while. I think I said to Scott, 'I kind of like the blonde. She's cute.'"

The duo noticed that the women kept opening and closing a door to get into their new apartment building, setting things down each time to deal with the door.

"So we said, 'These ladies obviously need some help.' We went over and blocked the door open for them."

Jeff thought he was being extremely considerate. Ruthie, who was indeed the cute blonde Jeff spoke of, saw it another way. Who was this jerk who came to prop open the door and left them to do all of the heavy lifting as he sat next door finishing a six pack?

"If he wanted to help," Ruthie explained, "he could have brought some stuff in. We had bricks, books, furniture and lots of small stuff. They could have said 'How can we help you?' That was not the way to win my heart. I was not terribly impressed. He never even offered us a beer!"

"I've always had trouble with first impressions," said Jeff, laughing.

Yet the forces of nature that bring two people together had now collided. It took a while for Ruthie to realize that she had met her soul mate.

"The guys I had dated were either on the UW football team, UW basketball team, in med school, going for their PhD, or absolutely, drop-dead gorgeous. I met Jeff, who is five foot six, and I couldn't take him seriously."

"I guess she was a little out of my league," Jeff reminisced.

But Jeff was sure this was a woman he had interest in. He kept trying to come up with creative ways to get to know the stunning, thin blonde with the long, 1970s free-love hair.

"When she walked by my apartment, I tried to be at the picture window to say something cute or try to impress her."

He knew she was studying for her nursing boards but still wanted to ask her out, so he got a little inventive. "I said let's go to the Arboretum [a nature sanctuary in the middle of the city] and spread out a blanket. You can study for your boards, and I'll just lie there and enjoy nature, and we'll share a bottle of wine." Jeff laughed.

They did. She studied, he drank and napped under the trees, and things were moving in the right direction.

"He was really a nice guy," Ruthie recalled. On the day of the nursing tests, "He made a little card, and it said 'Good luck on your boards.' He cut each individual letter out of a magazine and gave it to me. I thought, 'He's really very perceptive and very sweet,' although I wasn't really very physically attracted to him at that point."

"I got the idea from a ransom note message I had recently seen on TV," Jeff quipped.

To her surprise, Ruthie aced her boards. She had not been a serious student in high school and, since coming to Madison, had spent more time enjoying the nightlife than studying. She had grown up with an older brother who was incredibly intelligent and found that act difficult to follow.

"I had some teachers say, 'How come you're not more like your brother?' It gave me a low self-esteem for a while because I wasn't like my brother. Then I rebelled, as much as you could in Wonewoc when your dad was the principal, because I didn't want to be like my brother."

But now, after steamrolling the test, Ruthie was a registered nurse with new self-confidence and the sweetest, if not tallest, suitor in the world. "We were so compatible, he was so easy to talk to, and we were really good friends."

Things developed from there, rather quickly in fact. That fall, they went from friends to lovers and decided to get engaged. Wanting to surprise both sets of parents, they took the whole group to a Badger football game and brought them back to Jeff's new apartment to break the news. The entire gang was happy and congratulating one another, but Ruthie's mother, Trudy, took one look at her daughter's finger and asked: "Well, did he give you a ring?"

Oh, that. They hadn't gotten around to the ring part yet. This was 1972, when all you needed was love, not a shiny band of gold with a big diamond. Still, Ruthie's parents were a little suspicious of this Jeff character. During the courting stage, Jeff had once shown up in a bright green, 1968 Corvette convertible with Ruthie in the passenger seat. He had long hippie hair, a bandana, and blue jeans that had been cut out to bell bottoms with an American flag sewn into them.

"Her parents came out and stood on the porch of their farmhouse looking down at us. I wasn't sure how this would go," said Jeff. "I don't think [her] dad liked me at all. He was a very conservative guy. Fortunately [her mother] Trudy was more forgiving."

But Ruthie's parents didn't say anything negative then or as the marriage approached. They tried to be accepting of their new son-in-law. Once she got over the fact that there was no ring yet, Trudy started to accept Jeff's quirkiness. Jim remained a skeptic. Jeff and Ruthie pushed on, were married at a Lutheran church in Wonewoc, and had the reception at the local American Legion Hall.

Pictures of the wedding show their wedding party in 1970s suits and dresses, the men with long mutton chops, and the women with the flowing locks of the time. Louis, whom Jeff had forgiven and actually thanked for backing out on the lease because it allowed him to court Ruthie much more privately, gave a rousing toast to the bride and groom at the reception.

For the honeymoon, they went fishing on the Missouri-Arkansas border at Table Rock Lake. They were both into nature and the outdoors, so it was an easy decision, if not a conventional one, for a honeymoon. The resort at which they stayed was appropriately named "Fitz's Fishin' Fun."

Thanks to Jeff's dad's remarkable kindness and Ruthie's parents' frugality, they started their married life together with no student loans or nursing school debt. They were both employed and making substantial money for the first time in their lives and spent the first few years of marriage dining at Madison-area restaurants and accumulating some of the material things that all young adults craved in those days. They were a happily married, young couple for two years before they decided it was time to start a family. All the while, Jeff freely admitted he wanted to have a son.

"My dad always impressed on me that the FitzRandolph name was steeped in history and it was up to me to carry it on, as an only son. There was never any pressure. It was just mentioned at some point. For me, it was like, 'Geez, I want to have a son anyway, no big deal.'"

But there was another, deeper and more personal reason, too. Being raised a Seventh-Day Baptist, Jeff had strict rules to follow from sunset on Friday through sunset on Saturday and spent the time focusing on choir, church, community lunch, youth groups, and Bible study. The Sabbath was devoted to church and family time.

"I was a decent athlete. I got to play football and basketball for the junior varsity teams in high school my freshman and sophomore years, when games were played during the week after school. These were things I liked to do. I got a taste for it, but I knew that when I made the varsity team it would be over because I couldn't play on Friday night. So, I became the sports writer for the high school paper. I watched the guys that I grew up with develop into really good athletes. We were very competitive in our conference and in the state of Wisconsin, but I couldn't ever be there because I was in church. That was always a bit of a problem for me because I was never able to pursue my own athletic dreams. I always wanted my children to have a better opportunity athletically than I had."

They set their sights on trying to have their firstborn be a boy. Ruthie found a study suggesting that you could control which sex your child would be. Jeff explained it this way:

"The studies indicated that you had to try to reduce the acidity in the woman's uterus during ovulation because there were significantly fewer Y chromosomes, which are the boys, than the X chromosomes, which are the girls. The study told us if you reduced the acidity and increased the alkalinity you killed some of the X chromosomes, which sounds cruel, but you gave the Y chromosomes a much better chance. On top of that they said if you monitored the temperature of the woman and found out when she was ovulating at the earliest stage of her cycle, the Y chromosomes had a better chance of swimming further up the stream to get home first."

Armed with all of this knowledge, Ruthie took her temperature daily for about three months.

"We got it down to where we knew exactly when she was going to ovulate," said Jeff. "In addition to that, when she started to realize she was close to ovulating she would enhance her alkalinity and reduce the acidity."

The couple went to a Beach Boys concert one night in mid-April of 1974. After dancing through "Good Vibrations" and "California Girls," this Wisconsin girl came home to find her temperature was perfect. An Olympic gold medalist was conceived.

"God smiled on us," smiled Ruthie. "It happened on our very first attempt."

"I told everybody I was sure it's going to be a boy because we took temperatures and we did the alkaline douches. Everyone looked at me like I had lost my mind." Jeff was swelling with pride as his wife's belly was bulging with the new baby.

They took Lamaze classes together, and Jeff learned to hold her shoulders up, comfort her, and help her with her breathing. Ruthie loved being pregnant.

"I felt good about myself. I was excited about the pregnancy. It was a very, very positive experience," Ruthie said.

In 1974, there was no such thing as an ultrasound, so they had no way of knowing the baby's sex. This was also when men were first allowed in the hospital's birthing suites. Before that, they were often confined to the waiting room, pacing like nervous ducks while doctors and nurses whisked in and out and the occasional wail from a woman's pain could be heard. This was new territory. Jeff was thrilled to see it all in person, and the FitzRandolphs could not wait to find out if they were right about a boy.

"I'm standing by Ruthie's head trying to comfort her, and the doctor is on the opposite end doing his business. After several grunts and groans, with my encouragement, Ruthie manages one final push. Suddenly, the doctor holds this baby up like a watermelon. I swear to God, the first thing I saw between the baby's legs were these little boy things hanging out. I let out a yell before he even said 'It's a boy.' I knew it, and we were both thrilled. We had our son."

Casey J. FitzRandolph had entered the world. Jeff had known what he wanted to name his boy, and Ruthie loved the name. Ruthie decided the first time she held him that he looked like a Casey, too.

"It wasn't a real popular name at the time, but in Milton, where I grew up, there was a little shoe store, and the owner was Casey Hutter. I bought a lot of shoes from the guy growing up. I just thought he was a cool guy, and I loved the name Casey. We didn't know any children named Casey, so we agreed to go with it."

The FitzRandolphs wouldn't find out until years later that Casey means "brave." They had a perfect, beautiful, healthy baby boy. There was only one problem.

"He was not a good baby," Ruthie lamented.

Casey turned out to be fussy and high maintenance, crying all the time. They paced their screaming bundle around their small duplex when he woke up at two in the morning every day. Ruthie decided to stay home with her baby, a decision they both supported. She nursed Casey for two years because it was the only peace and quiet she could get.

"Until my nipples were so sore," she remembered with a laugh. "Casey didn't like to let go."

Jeff decided to leave his marketing job at the credit union, although he liked it, to take a higher-paying position as a print salesman for Litho Productions. It was a gamble because his salary would be earned as a commission on his sales volume, and he had no existing ties to any businesses in the Madison area. But the upside was that if he succeeded, Ruthie would be able to remain a stay-at-home mom. He felt he had to take that chance and believed in his heart that he could make it work. The family-first philosophy reflected lessons his own father had taught him. Ruthie stayed home for thirty-two years.

"Strength of family came from both sides—Ruthie's and mine. Our parents were very devoted parents with strong family values. We were both very lucky to come from loving families."

And the new job just happened to turn into a perfect fit. The company flourished, Jeff was successful, and the owners, the Steil family, would later play a key role in building one of America's Olympians.

"It was the greatest professional decision of my life. I owe Bob Steil a deep debt of gratitude for taking a chance on me."

"Bob Steil and Litho Productions allowed my family to travel and do what we did. Every weekend for six months of the year, we'd be in the van traveling somewhere in the United States to skate. We went from New York to California with additional stops in Michigan, Illinois, Missouri, Indiana, Minnesota, and Iowa during the skating season. Ruthie and I were able to participate in our children's athletic endeavors and share in their successes and heartbreaks. Bob was a great boss, and he was good to me. He understood how important it was to me, and he made it all possible. He, like so many others, had an indirect influence on Casey. He allowed it to happen because he employed me and trusted me."

When Casey was still a toddler, Jeff had a new job, and the family moved to their first house in Verona. They didn't even put blinds up right away because they were only the third house built in the new subdivision, East View Heights.

The story of Jessi's conception is much different than that of Casey. There was no plotting behind it. It just happened.

"After Ruthie stopped nursing Casey and her nipples healed, she was more accepting of my sexual advances. We messed around a couple of times, thoroughly enjoying every minute of it, and all of a sudden, wow,

Ruthie was pregnant again. We had planned on having another child, but we wanted to wait a little bit. Jessi was unplanned, but the beauty of it was, it worked out perfectly. She was a girl, and we wanted to have one of each. And in retrospect the timing couldn't have worked out better. She wasn't that much younger than Casey, and we could do the same activities as a family unit," Jeff remembered.

Jessilyn Kae FitzRandolph was added to the clan in May of 1977 when Casey was not yet three. It was another fantastic pregnancy for Ruthie. Jessi weighed just over six pounds.

"She came out quickly, and we were lucky to make it to the hospital in time. While waiting for the doctor to arrive, the resident kept encouraging Ruthie to relax, telling her to try not to push to slow the process down. She did so valiantly for some time and then couldn't wait any longer. The doctor never got there until after Jessi was born. I just remember how happy we were that we had a girl and she was healthy."

They picked the name Jessilyn because they liked the nickname Jessi but thought the formal name Jessica sounded too harsh. The name Jessica was also gaining in popularity, and they wanted something unique for this special little baby girl.

"So we thought, how could we get Jessi with something softer? We came up with Jessilyn, which is soft but gave us the nickname Jessi for our daughter."

Jessi was a content and happy baby, the opposite of what they had experienced with Casey. She went with the flow on everything. She slept and nursed and nuzzled with her mother.

"It was perfect, absolutely perfect," said Ruthie with a smile. "She was the best little baby a mother could ask for. She slept through the night almost immediately, rarely cried, and was on a very regular schedule."

They had everything they had ever dreamed of in life so far. As they looked down at their two tiny offspring, how could they have known what the future would hold? How could anyone ever venture a guess? Life just seems to unfold, with many of us walking somewhere in the middle. Jeff and Ruthie FitzRandolph were destined to experience emotions that register among the highest and lowest a parent can endure.

CHAPTER THREE

The Early Years

1979

E very kid deserves to start life like the FitzRandolph children, with not only loving parents and a stellar school system but a comfortable house in a growing subdivision in Verona. They even had a wooded area to explore merely yards behind their property that included a creek to dip your toes in. The neighborhood was a web of parents who all knew you and looked out for your well-being.

"We would run through the backyard to a friend's house, go to the park, ride bikes, and play a little baseball," recalls Jessi. "I had a great childhood."

"It was kind of perfect," adds Casey. "There was nothing about life that wasn't good. We would build tree forts, shoot our slingshots in the woods, take off on bikes, and just ride forever. We would disappear all day at the park playing baseball."

The area was a collection of newly constructed homes in a suburb west of Madison. Verona was the fastest-growing city in Dane County in the mid-seventies, and East View Heights was home to many of the young professionals who worked for the state of Wisconsin, Cuna Mutual Insurance, and Nicolet Instruments. It was safe and idyllic.

Jessi played Barbies and Cabbage Patch Kids with her neighborhood girlfriends but preferred mixing it up with the boys. "I wasn't afraid to get dirty. I wanted to hang out with my brother and his friends, which I'm sure they just *loved*."

But honestly, it never bothered Casey much. She was always there to be the extra outfielder or hide-and-seek player they needed. The only problem was that they sometimes got too wild.

"I was chasing my sister around the house, and she dove headfirst into the couch and split her head open. That was her first trip to the ER," laughed Casey. "And she started kindergarten the next week." Casey would have a couple of visits himself over the next two years, first for stitches in his forehead from a biking accident and second for a headfirst fall from the top of his bunk bed.

And there were other mishaps. Casey was less than ten when he shot a friend with a pellet gun. Steve, a neighbor who was a couple of years older, had goaded him into the BB gun fight. When Steve snuck towards him Casey popped a pellet his way, forgetting that the gun had been pumped ten times, ready to kill a squirrel. Instead, the pellet penetrated Steve's skin and lodged next to a rib..

This happened on the morning of the huge neighborhood garage sale, when all of the East View moms gathered the stuff their sons and daughters had outgrown and set it up on their front lawns and driveways. Dad might even occasionally contribute an old set of golf clubs or a worn out fishing rod and reel to the sale. An ambulance ride to the ER was not what Ruthie or Steve's mom, Arlene, had planned for that day, so the sale went on and at a later visit, doctors decided not to remove it so to this day a pellet from one of America's Olympians is a battle scar that Steve carries proudly

The seasons in Wisconsin change rapidly and severely. Summer was for the big garage sale, trips to the cabin up north, and running through the sprinkler on ninety-degree days. Then came fall and Halloween.

"In second grade, Mom made me up like I was like a vampire. I remember the white makeup on my face and the blood dripping down my chin. The teachers would make a pretty big deal out of it at school. Mom was a room mother and she made a punch with dry ice and peeled grapes that you had to feel," remembered Jessi.

When Thanksgiving rolled around, they went up to Ruthie's parents' family farm for deer hunting and a huge feast. Even Grandma Trudy would grab a gun and head for the hills.

"Jessi and I would stay at the farmhouse and watch *Charlie and the Chocolate Factory* at least a dozen times in one weekend. We would go crazy with anticipation waiting to hear a gunshot or for somebody to come to the farmhouse in their blaze orange, just to hear their stories," reminisced Casey.

The weather would inevitably turn frigid, as it always does in Wisconsin, and thoughts progressed to Christmas and winter sports.

"Every year for Christmas when we were young, we would go up to the cabin on Big Siss," said Jessi. "We would string together popcorn and cranberries to make a Christmas tree garland in the van on the way up to the lake. As soon as we arrived and unpacked, we'd climb back in the van and head down a deserted gravel road to look for our Christmas tree. When we spotted one we liked growing beside the road, Dad would climb out and cut it and load it in the van. Most years we would shovel an oval on the lake so Casey and I could skate, but I remember one year when there was no snow and we skated around the entire lake for hours.

"But the best part about going up there was the snowmobiling. We borrowed our neighbors' sleds for a while, and it was so much fun. Then one year our parents surprised us and bought snowmobiles. Christmas morning, Casey and I looked out the window in the front of the cabin. There were two brand-new Yamaha, fire-engine red snowmobiles sitting there. We lost it, we were so excited."

The family also threw memorable birthday parties.

"We would invite friends over and have sleepovers. We did silly stuff like Garbage Pail Kids and Betty Boop. I remember wearing silly hats, blowing out candles, eating lots of birthday cake, and then trying to stay up all night."

It was, as you can tell, a very pleasant life. Yet nothing is ever perfect. Sibling rivalry crept in. One particular birthday incident still stands out in Jessi's mind.

"My parents got me this brand new stereo for my bedroom. It was the coolest thing, like the latest and greatest stereo, and I was so excited. Next thing I know, Casey is whining to Mom and Dad about the stereo I got. So they went out and bought him the same one the day after my birthday, and I was like, 'Are you kidding me?' I was so mad."

Casey and Jessi got along pretty well overall, although like any family there were the "If you don't stop fighting right now I'm stopping this van" moments. And the fact that this family spent so much time together in their van compounded the problem. In fact, one time, Jeff was pulled over by a police officer because he was swerving. He wasn't drunk, just trying to get the kids to stop fighting.

"I tried my best to get Casey into trouble whenever I could, and I was a little manipulator. I would do stuff to make him mad. Then he would want to hit me, and I would start crying, 'Casey hit me.' Now I see my niece and nephew do that and I laugh. I was probably kind of a little brat, but darn it, sometimes it worked," said Jessi.

They were a normal American family with the usual doses of love, bickering, rivalry, and traditions. They lived in a great neighborhood, and their children seemed well adjusted. The only thing that set them apart was that they had two exceptional little skaters.

CHAPTER FOUR

On the Ice

1980

I t was obvious from the time the kids could walk that the couple had a pair of talented athletes on their hands. Who knows why genes mix the way they do to create Olympic-caliber athletes? Jeff and Ruthie both had been decent at sports and liked them, but they were far from serious athletes.

Because of his family's religious beliefs, Jeff had not been given the same athletic opportunities as other kids. He had been relegated to participating in intramural sports through college, and then he took up slow-pitch softball when he moved to Madison. It was a way to get some exercise and socialize with the boys, by sharing a few beers after the weekly games. In the 1980s, he joined a health club where cardiovascular workouts were always part of his routine, but weight lifting was what he enjoyed the most. He fancied himself a body builder of sorts, although at five foot six and 145 pounds, he certainly didn't strike fear into the hearts of many serious competitors.

"I would be the first to admit that missing high school athletics drove me to ultimately live vicariously through my children's athletic endeavors. It wasn't necessarily a conscious effort on my part but rather a release of frustrations that had built up through the years," Jeff confided. "Was it the wrong way to approach their athletic endeavors? I honestly don't know, and I won't pass judgment. Each reacted in a different way. Casey didn't always agree with me, but he seemed to build off the constant reinforcement and prodding. I may have driven Jessi from speedskating. She just didn't respond to my intense style with her athletics."

Ruthie's athletic involvement in high school and college was even more limited. In the 1960s, fewer than five percent of women in the United States competed in athletic events. Ruthie's school, Wonewoc High School, offered no sports for female competitors and made no bones about it. Ruthie couldn't complain too much. Her dad was the high school principal.

"If we were lucky, we got to play volleyball and dodgeball in gym class," Ruthie recalled. "I thought I was fortunate to be a member of the band." She graduated in 1968, four years before Title IX would be signed into law by President Richard Nixon. While Title IX is widely known for creating equality for female athletes at the high school and collegiate level, it is also responsible for developing equality for women within educational and professional settings. Ruthie could have no way of knowing that because of Title IX, her daughter would be granted an opportunity to do so many things that were off limits to her in her childhood.

But as far as creating an Olympic athlete and another who could have been? The FitzRandolphs were just lucky.

"I guess Ruthie and I were just the perfect blend of physical body types. I'm not going to lie and say that marrying a woman who was at least my height wasn't important to me—it was. Geez, I'm a short guy, and I can remember being teased as a kid because of my height. There is no way I would wish that on my son. So, one of my criteria when I got in a serious relationship was that my mate be at least five foot six. Don't ask me what I would have done had I fallen in love with a woman four feet, ten inches tall. Fortunately it was never an issue." Ruthie is exactly Jeff's requirement: five feet, six inches.

"Casey has long legs in general and is very long from knee to ankle. This extra length in his calves would give him a strong advantage as a skater. He was able to generate a longer stroke or push than most athletes because of this length, and the longer his skate contacted the ice the faster he went. I believe the longer than normal calves come from Ruthie's family." Jeff smiled as he stated the obvious.

Jessi had a shorter, more compact body type than Ruthie, and her petite build was definitely a FitzRandolph family trait. Both Casey and

Jessi were blessed with the fast-twitch muscles that are so common in athletes with quick reaction times and high top speeds. That they would eventually pick speedskating and soccer as their primary sporting interests was no accident. They had bodies that were perfectly tuned for both sports, including the explosiveness needed for a speedskating start and the quick reaction necessary to control a bouncing soccer ball.

Casey continued to be a very fussy baby. He would wake up screaming most nights and had to be walked or rocked back to sleep. Ruthie spent many nights getting up with him at two in the morning only to fall back in bed as Jeff was waking up to his day. Casey would also practice standing while in his mother's lap.

"Up and down, up and down, up and down," Ruthie said. "Maybe that's how he got to be such a good speedskater. He was doing squats when he was less than a year old."

Casey pulled himself up in the playpen when he was six months. He walked at seven months and three weeks. Jessi would also take her first steps before her eighth month.

Casey would eventually grow into a rambunctious, yet extremely coordinated preschooler. Jessi, always more mellow than her brother, was nevertheless still full of energy that needed to be released. Ruthie needed to find an outlet, a place for them to burn energy so they didn't drive her crazy.

Casey was barely four and Jessi two when Ruthie took them to a local rink, the Madison Ice Arena, and signed them up for private skating lessons. It was something to do, just a way to get out of the house a few times during the week. In a northern climate like Wisconsin, ice rinks were plentiful both indoors and out.

Some kids can barely stand up on ice, some don't like the cold, and others don't have the patience to wait for the skates to be laced up every time. Casey and Jessi put on their skates happily and immediately started zooming around. They were absolute naturals. Within a few months, the brother and sister even starred as munchkins in *The Wizard of Ice,* a parody put on by the students of the skating school for their parents at the end of the skating session.

"Jessi was amazing on skates for being so young," Ruthie recalled.

The proud parents sat in the audience to watch their munchkins as they chased Dorothy, The Lion, The Tin Man, and The Scarecrow down the yellow brick road, which was actually the blue line in the hockey rink. They would later find out Jessi almost didn't make it on the ice at all.

"Her teacher, Patty, told us after the show that she had to wake her up just as the show was starting. She was sound asleep. She was taking her little afternoon nap," said Ruthie. Jessi was, after all, just two.

The FitzRandolph kids were so good on frozen water that it didn't take long for Ruthie and Jeff to decide to get Casey on a local hockey team. He joined Madison's West Side Flyers, even though he often complained about the equipment, gloves, and helmets hockey players had to be wrapped in before every game. There were bigger problems, though. He didn't like to sweat and wasn't a fan of the contact.

"He was always the first one to the puck, but he would get mad when all the other little boys caught up and climbed on top of him," said Ruthie. "He would try to do a little stick handling and skating, but bodies were falling all around him and over him."

"The problem we had was that he never got to show his talent or ability, and it got to be frustrating for him," said Jeff.

He and Ruthie tried to brainstorm what to do. They had the vision that a future Wisconsin Badger hockey player was in their hands, and they didn't want to waste his obvious talent.

"So we went to the board of directors of the West Side Flyers, a local hockey club, and said 'We know this kid is young, but you can see he can skate. We'd like to ask you to put him on the team with the six- and seven-year-olds so he can learn other hockey skills.'"

"We had a written statement from Mike Dibble, a goalie for the UW hockey team in the late sixties. He was coaching in Sun Prairie and had seen Casey skate. He wrote a wonderful and passionate letter explaining that he felt the older team would be a better fit for Casey's talents. We were pretty confident and made a pretty good presentation at this board meeting. When we finished, they asked us to step out while they discussed our situation. They called us back in five minutes later and said 'The only person we have ever made an exception for in this program was Rob Andringa, who later became a Badger hockey captain.' They refused to move Casey up. We were crushed."

They would find out later that Dr. Conrad Andringa, who was both Casey's and Jessi's pediatrician and Rob's father, was a member of that board but absent from the meeting that evening. Had he been there and spoken on their behalf, they may never have dropped hockey.

But fate was soon to intervene. Casey's hockey days were numbered. Amazingly, it was four-year-old Casey himself who had the epiphany just one month later.

"He actually heard an ad on the radio for an all-city speedskating meet that was going to be held at the Vilas Park lagoon." Ruthie commented.

Perhaps it was the name Vilas Park that registered in the four-year-old's brain. That is also where the zoo is located, and Ruthie had taken the kids there numerous times to admire the elephants and giraffes. The kids would also play on the brightly colored slide that was in the shape of a shoe from the nursery rhyme "The Old Woman Who Lived in a Shoe."

"He told us he wanted to go and he wanted to compete. We kept blowing him off, like, 'Oh, come on, Casey, let's just go to the hockey rink,'" said Jeff, who still had dreams of his son playing hockey. "But we finally agreed. I actually remember the day, January 15, 1980. It was clear and cold, about twenty above zero, a calm, sunny, beautiful day. We asked if we could sign him up. They asked how old he was. He was six days short of being five, so we lied and said he was five."

Bunk and Elayne Riley of the Madison Speedskating Club were organizing the event. They told the FitzRandolphs that no one that young was signed up.

"So once again, we asked if he could compete with the six- and seven-year olds. This time it paid off with better results."

Bunk was a soft-spoken guy with a big heart, and he agreed to skate Casey with the older group. There were three races.

"He went out and won all three races against the six- and seven-year olds!" Jeff remembers. "And not by a small margin."

An Olympian was born. The coach of the club, Bob Corby, who had been the coach of the US Olympic speedskating team four years before, came up to Jeff and Ruthie after the meet had concluded.

"He told us, 'You guys have the next Eric Heiden here.'"

The Rileys confirmed his praise.

While they accepted the compliment gladly, Jeff and Ruthie didn't know who Eric Heiden was. Heiden was still one month away from winning five gold medals in the Lake Placid Olympics. He was a local kid, but Jeff and Ruthie were not clued into the speedskating world, and Heiden had not yet exploded on the national scene. So the FitzRandolphs decided to tune in to the 1980 Olympics and see who this Heiden character was. They gathered the kids around the TV.

Casey was glued to the television for all five of Eric's races. Eric won all of them, earning five gold medals. That feat will never be duplicated again, because today's speedskating athletes specialize in one or two distances.

"I actually do remember watching those Olympics in our kitchen on this six-inch screen with a little radio on it. The darn thing was three times longer than it was wide," said Casey.

The experience was one of Casey's earliest lasting memories.

"That was it for Casey. It was like, 'Man, Eric's from Madison. I can do this,'" said Jeff. "That got us into speedskating and out of hockey. We dropped hockey like a hot potato. I'm not going to lie and say we didn't watch the Miracle on Ice. We did, and we cheered. But I can honestly say that next to Heiden's performances, to us it was a bit anticlimactic. After all, we were now speedskating parents."

Two years later, Casey was getting so good he would be interviewed by a local TV station. Asked what his skating dream was, he calmly looked into the camera and replied, "I want to go to the Olympics and do what Eric did: win five gold medals."

After Heiden's amazing and awe-inspiring Olympics, the FitzRandolphs looked for more competition for their little five-year-old. The only one left in the season was the Wisconsin State Indoor Championship at State Fair Park hockey rink in Milwaukee. Although the organizers thought he was too young again and discouraged them, the FitzRandolphs wanted to give him a shot. The beginnings of the fortitude that would later steer them through the maze of cancer treatments were starting to show as they stood up for themselves and refused to be rebuffed.

"Let's just go and see what he's up against," they thought.

Children under five are referred to as "Tiny Tots" in speedskating jargon. They first skate half a lap, then a full lap, and then a half a lap again. Most of the kids have to be helped across the line by the referees because they fall down so much.

The organizers relented.

Casey was allowed to skate, and he won all three races just like that, seemingly in an instant replay of the all-city meet. The FitzRandolph family was vindicated. Casey came home with a little, wooden, handmade trophy shaped like the state of Wisconsin. Over thirty years later, he still has it.

"It's now in two pieces," he laughed. "The Wisconsin part came unglued and un-nailed from the little platform it sits on. But even when pieced together, it's only pushing four inches tall."

Yet that first trophy meant the world to Casey. To this day when he speaks to CEOs of corporations, other professional groups, and elementary school or high school assemblies, he displays two things: his gold medal and that rickety little wooden Wisconsin trophy.

"From then on his love of speedskating just took off. He never looked back. And while there were some speed bumps along the way, it was mostly clear sailing for Casey. I hate to say it, but the kid was born under a lucky star," Jeff confided. "And to his credit, he never learned how to lose and just accept it. If there was a setback, he'd figure out why, go back to training to correct the problem, and then go back to winning."

Jessi, meanwhile, was a tomboy who followed her brother's lead and started competing and winning speedskating races. She was blowing away the female fields, but she also liked gymnastics. The FitzRandolphs look back and wonder if they should have encouraged her more towards the balance beam and uneven bars.

"If we'd had a ton of money and been smart we probably would have put her in gymnastics and her own career," said Ruthie. "But we also liked to have the family together."

And, as any parent can attest to, it was easier to have two kids in the same sport, especially one that required driving back and forth ninety miles to Milwaukee every Monday through Thursday six months of the year.

Ruthie was such a devoted mom that she still wanted Casey and Jessi to have home-cooked meals. So she prepared dinners and baked while they were at school and then brought the warm, healthy food in the van for the trip to the skating oval. Fast food was a once-a-week treat, generally Rocky Rococo's for pizza after practice. Once in a great while they would eat at Taco Bell (a company that would later sponsor Casey during his Olympic run). Casey and Jessi loved the very filling tacos. Ruthie would later admit that she stopped there only after a particularly stressful day hoping they would be so content that they would fall asleep on the way home from Milwaukee. If she was lucky, she might get a peaceful one-and-a-half-hour ride back to Verona.

Speedskating became the family sport, really the family passion, as they shuttled back and forth in the family van. Jeff swears that from 1981 to 1992, when customized vans were all the rage, the FitzRandolph family kept Suburban Vans of Verona in business. They were putting over sixty thousand miles a year on their van during the prime skating years, traveling four times a week to Milwaukee for practice and to competitions that took them from Massachusetts to California and just about every major city in between during peak season, October through March. Every two years, a newly customized, finely tuned machine would show up in the family driveway. They simply couldn't risk breaking down on the road and missing a training session or competition.

"It was a huge commitment for both my parents, but it was my mom's life," said Casey. "Her day started with getting us kids up for school. We were always overtired because we had been up late the night before coming back from Milwaukee, so we usually were running late and would miss the bus. She'd end up taking us to school, stopping on the way home to gas up the van because it needed gas every day. When she got back home she'd start cooking. Then she'd unpack the cooler and skate bags from the night before and spend three or four hours sharpening skates and drying the equipment out.

"The skates had to be sharpened every day to perfection because otherwise we'd be upset. We could feel the difference. We could detect even the tiniest burr on the edge of our blades, and it would affect our practices. Speedskaters sharpen their own skates, but she did it for me for years. I was even hassled about it (as an adult) when she was still checking my skates. No one ever did it better than her. After the skates were perfect, she'd repack everything, pick us up early from school at two thirty, and make the drive to the Olympic Oval. We'd skate from five to seven and then come back home and fall into bed."

Homework? They did it in the van every day.

"I don't remember doing homework anywhere else," Casey laughed.

It was quite a life and quite a commitment for all involved. But as the kids started to become teenagers, a change was coming for the FitzRandolphs. Their two children, with two unique and different personalities, were about to take different paths.

CHAPTER FIVE

Jessi's Change of Heart

1991

There's an important thing to understand about speedskating. It is made up of two distinct disciplines: long or short track. Casey pursued the long track, or metric, style of speedskating. For this race, two competitors race around a 400-meter track at the same time, trying to beat not only each other but the clock as well. Thirty-two skaters are divided into sixteen pairs for each of the five different distances. After all sixteen pairs have skated, the individual with the fastest time is declared the winner of the distance. The thirty-two competitors are always the best in the world at the distance being skated. The distances are 500m, 1,000m, 1,500m, 5,000m, and 10,000m for the men; women replace the 10,000m with a 3,000m. Casey usually competed at 500m and 1,000m and occasionally at 1,500m.

Over the course of three Olympics starting in 2002, Apolo Ohno made short track speedskating famous. In this discipline, a 111-meter track is set up inside of a hockey rink. The walls are padded for protection against falls. Most events pit five skaters on the ice at the same time and reduce the competitors through a series of quarter and semifinals until only four or five remain for the final race. There's a lot more jostling for positions, painful falls, and non-stop action because the first to cross the finish line is declared the winner. Is it any wonder that short track is where tomboy Jessi excelled in elementary and early middle school? She learned to be fast and aggressive, largely due to her brother and his friends. When they were younger, before any of them specialized in either discipline, they were just skating for fun, trying to beat each other to the finish line.

"All of the great females in speedskating trained with the men on their teams," explained Jeff. "Bonnie Blair trained with Dan Jansen and Nick Thometz, and you'll see that in other countries, as well. That made them better. Jessi skated every day against Casey and some of the other older kids on the team. When she chased the boys, she was at her best, and she was just amazing. There's a lot to be said for that. In some sports, it can really be a benefit for a woman to chase her male teammates."

Jessi's top year came at age thirteen, when she made the national short track team. This was a huge deal. Put in perspective, it meant she was one of the top five female skaters in the country and part of America's hope for a future Olympics. At first, Jessi was thrilled with the notoriety and all of the attention that went along with being the youngest member of the team. But as she learned more about the commitment that would be required of her moving forward, she started to second-guess her latest success. She loved the thrill of racing, but for her it was a pure and simple act. Older national team members made skating their lives and were on an emotional roller coaster from week to week and from competition to competition. At age thirteen, she was just having fun. Quite frankly, she was not emotionally equipped to deal with the pressure her early success had created.

Then came the ultimate blow for a young teenage girl. If she wanted to continue to develop as a speedskater, she would have to move away from home, her parents, her friends, and everything she knew. The national team trained in Marquette, Michigan.

"The next step for her was to move to Marquette and go to high school there. She didn't want to do it," said Jeff. "We couldn't force her to, because we'd told her all along it was up to her. Her performances started to fall off when she realized what her decision was going to be."

It was a difficult thing for Jeff and Ruthie to watch their insanely talented daughter tailing off, but they also completely understood Jessi's choice.

"We could see it. We knew what was happening. She's a thirteen-year-old girl. She doesn't want to leave home and go to Marquette, Michigan, with people she really didn't know. Well, she knew a few, but they were all older and from Minnesota and New York. There was no one close to her age in Marquette."

To make matters worse, Marquette seemed like the edge of the universe. Marquette is located in the upper peninsula of Michigan with a population of 21,000 and the highest average snowfall of any city in the continental United States. The winters are brutal and the summers one month long. What thirteen-year-old would want to move to Marquette?

Casey did not have this same heart-wrenching choice to make. As a long tracker he could train in Milwaukee, with a good home-cooked meal fueling his practice, the thought of another meal waiting for him on the drive back home, and his own bed to look forward to every night. If Jessi wanted to be a serious short track skater, she would have to leave this behind.

The truth of the matter was that by then, Jessi had determined that her soul was not in skating anyway. Even if the national short track headquarters were located in her kitchen, it's doubtful she would have stayed with it. She was changing and growing.

She stayed at home and attended Verona Area High School. While she continued to train with the local skating club, and sometimes with Casey in Milwaukee, her heart wasn't in it.

"I wanted to hang out with my friends and do what high schoolers do. I liked skating until it got to where it had to be my career, where I would have had to train every day, multiple times a day. When I realized I couldn't have much of a life outside of skating if I wanted to make it to the next level, that's when I started to not like it very much."

Still, she was torn. "I kind of went back and forth for a little while. I would take a couple meets off and then go back and skate again. I'd still do well and enjoy it. But I finally decided I didn't want to do that full-time."

Jessi stuck it out longer than she wanted to, just trying to figure out a way to break it to her mom and dad. She didn't realize that they already knew what was coming.

"A lot of it was more fear of telling my parents that I didn't want to do it. They always said it was our decision, but I felt some pressure to keep going, and I didn't have the desire for that. I knew they would be disappointed. They wanted me to be successful."

At sixteen, when she felt like she was truly missing out on too much with friends, she dropped speedskating altogether. Her brother had mixed feelings as he watched his best training partner step off the track.

"She shied away from the pressure and expectations and work. Part of me thought she was nuts. I looked at her, and at age thirteen she was ranked fifth in the country. Part of me was thinking, 'Are you crazy? I know I'm going to win a gold medal, and you're better than me!'"

But another half of him could vividly see her soul was not into it. "Those last couple of years I remember kind of feeling sorry for her because I knew she was going through the motions and wasn't having fun out there. It was obvious she was doing it for Mom and Dad."

In the meantime, Jessi started to move on to a more mainstream high school sport: soccer. To no one's surprise she was an instant star, making varsity her freshman year at Verona Area High School. The coaches saw her speed and ability right away. She was put in as a center-midfielder, a tough position where the most athletic person is often placed. That player needs to be able to move up or down the field for offense or defense. She then later moved to forward, the top scoring position. It was instant love. Jessi thrived in her new sport. She also relished the closeness she felt being part of a team instead of a solitary skater.

"We were a good group, and we were best friends, too. It was me and the girls—we did everything together, and we remain friends to this day."

The Verona Wildcats made it to the state soccer finals both her junior and senior year. Jessi's parents were in the stands to cheer her on at every game, home and away, as she kicked her way through high school. Casey played some soccer too, but he was still mainly focused on skating. Although Jessi had turned away from the sport, she wasn't going to shun her brother or his continued love of speedskating. She attended his meets when she could, lending her support when soccer wasn't consuming her.

"I went to, not a ton of his races, but any in the Milwaukee area. Mom and I even went to a World Cup event in Germany while I was still in high school. That was when I knew I'd made the right decision. It was great being able to party with Casey's competitors in Inzell without having to worry about competing myself. I saw a completely different side of speedskating. It was the bonus of being the little sister."

Back home, she was offered a soccer scholarship to the University of Wisconsin-Parkside and jumped at it. But college turned out not to be what Jessi was expecting or wanting.

"I was just not into school. I only went for a year. The experience was actually a good thing because it made me realize that that really wasn't what I wanted to do."

She dropped out of Parkside and took a year off, trying to figure out her next step. She didn't know what she wanted to be yet. There was not one career that called out to her, and she didn't want to feel pressured to march down the traditional four-year track most kids follow. She still loved soccer, and Edgewood College, a small private school in Madison, offered her another chance to play after her one-year hiatus. This time she lasted only a semester.

"Again, I wasn't into school. I think I needed a little more time off. I probably should have taken a few years off after Parkside. If I had to do it over, I would probably have taken more time off before Edgewood."

Interestingly enough, her one semester at Edgewood playing soccer would create one of the family's more intense parental dilemmas. The one season Jessi played for Edgewood College, she earned all-conference honors. It just so happened that the awards banquet fell on a Saturday evening in January, the same weekend Casey was skating an important World Cup competition in Roseville, Minnesota. He was struggling with a new style of skate, and Ruthie and Jeff both felt compelled to support him at his competition. Yet they wanted to recognize Jessi's accomplishment on the soccer field as well.

As luck would have it, Jeff mentioned his problem of having to be in two places at one time to a good friend and valued client, Stan Reed. Stan was the owner of Reed/Sendecke & Associates, a very successful design firm. Stan quickly suggested that he would be happy to dispatch their company plane to Roseville Saturday afternoon at the completion of the day's skating events to fly Ruthie and Jeff back to Madison to attend Jessi's banquet. After the ceremony, the jet would return them to Roseville before midnight so they could watch the final day of Casey's competition on Sunday as well.

"The whole experience was a little surreal. We jumped on a private jet, with no security and no long lines. We were eating hors d'oeuvres and sipping a good cabernet on the flight to Madison as we chatted with the pilot. A car was waiting at the airport to whisk us to Jessi's banquet and later that evening back to the airport, where our own private jet on loan was waiting to fly us back to Minneapolis. We felt like the king and queen for a day. I will always remember Stan's generosity," Jeff recalled.

Casey was doing a lot of national and international competitions by this time. Despite her successful college soccer season, Jessi realized college was just not for her. She was what she called a "very average" student in high school, and her coursework just wasn't clicking. She took two years off this time, working for a landscaping firm until she finally figured out her calling.

"I hated history, and I wasn't good at science. Math was okay, and English was one of my favorites. But my senior year [of high school] I took one semester of art, and I loved it."

She was, like her maternal grandmother, an artist at heart. Jessi enrolled at Madison Area Technical College. Eight years after high school, she graduated with an Associate of Arts degree in Graphic Design. She was on her way, finally steering toward a future that was right for her. It was like the old board game "Life." Her little car kept getting sent backward or landing on the spaces where you had to spin again. But now she could see the finish line. The little pink plastic car was rising over the green hills on the game board and emerging unscathed on the other side. She may not have filled the car with a stick-figure blue spouse, but she was happy. She was living in the Madison area, making money, working in a job she loved, partying with her friends at night, and just being her own unique Jessi, having a great time as an adult. Sadly, she had only seven years of enjoying her newfound life before discovering that lump in her breast.

CHAPTER SIX

The Smell of Success

1982

S mell is one of our most powerful senses. Coffee grounds, lemons, roses—you can probably conjure up those scents in your head immediately. For Casey, there is a smell associated with his early speedskating days, and it's not what you would expect: monkey poop.

After hearing the ad on the radio for the all-city speedskating meet as a four-year-old, Casey spent countless winter days circling the ice at the Vilas Park Lagoon, adjacent to the zoo, where the monkeys swung by their tails in an outside enclosure just to his west.

"Gasping for air with the smell of the monkey cages—that is one of my earliest memories of long track speedskating." He and his fellow skaters also had to be careful to step over the cracks in the not-so- professionally-groomed ice. There was no Zamboni to clear the way at the lagoon, and the ice surface was a victim of the elements for most of the season. But he liked the sport right away because he knew he was good at it and got a lot of praise. He could also enjoy being on the ice without the hockey equipment that had bothered him.

Picture this: young Casey would put on all of his gear, head to toe, at home and then travel to the hockey rink, because it was easier than transporting the full uniform and getting dressed there. You can imagine how that might feel on a hot summer day when your mom has you out on the front lawn waiting for her to emerge from the house and you're chasing your little sister around to kill time.

"I was thinking 'This is miserable—I'm hot and sweaty and itchy.' The irony is, I went from sweaty, itchy pads to freezing my-you-know-what off in a Lycra skin suit with no socks, let alone long johns or jerseys."

From very early on Casey had what he calls "naïve confidence" in his speedskating abilities.

"I had a belief that I was going to be the best in the world at this. From day one after the All-City meet it was like, 'Wow, that went well. I'm going to go to the Olympics and win gold medals. I mean, I'm the best in Madison, Wisconsin, out of what, five kids? So what could possibly get in my way?'"

He nearly stepped in his own way. Believe it or not, there were times when Casey considered leaving the sport, just as his sister had. He, too, was a kid with fluctuations in his heart. And he had to skate over those cracks in the ice in more ways than one.

"I did waver. That's probably the case with anybody that starts an endeavor at four or five and does it to fruition. It's a minor miracle if you make it through with all of the variables and circumstances. There were a lot of bumps in the road. The big thing with my folks was, I vividly remember them telling Jessi and me, 'We are never going to make you do this, but we do believe in commitment. So if you decide you're going to skate for the year, you're going to skate for the year. Then if you want out, we can reassess.' That was the message, and it was true. That having been said, they were not only our biggest fans and advocates but also our biggest investors. And because they were so invested, they did not like the idea of us pulling the plug.

"I don't ever remember a year where I said 'I want to be done,' but some years I felt like 'I don't know, but man, I've come this far and put this much in. I don't know if I should pull the plug now.' There was a lot of stress and a lot of expectations from my parents. A lot of people talk about how having fun is paramount. They think that the minute a kid is not having fun, they shouldn't be forced to or maybe even encouraged to do something. Our household mentality, particularly my dad's, was different. That mentality was, there's something to be said for having to work hard and not throwing in the towel if you're not having fun … and winning is important."

"I was wearing a T-shirt that said 'Winning is Everything' at a very young age. Winning and being good were important in our household. Was it to a fault? I don't know, because, by God, I learned a work ethic, and that's something too many Americans haven't learned from their parents. Part of me says I'm not going to put that pressure on my kids and I want them to go through life laughing, but where is that fine line?"

For several years, Casey had to compete against a behemoth of a kid from Minneapolis named Heath Haster. Heath was six feet tall at the age of thirteen, a foot taller than Casey and weighing perhaps twice as much. Casey had no chance of beating him. Casey knew it, and his parents knew it. Being defeated by Heath Haster became the only acceptable loss. But Jeff tried a motivational trick even then. Before the national championships one year, he gave Casey a framed photo of Heath and Casey skating side by side with Casey slightly in the lead. A sticky note attached to the bottom read, "Here's to shocking the speedskating world this weekend."

It took Casey years to beat Heath, but he didn't lose very often otherwise. He was born with a speedskater's body and a natural gift for the sport. And he himself was a perfectionist. Maybe that's one reason losing was a tough pill for him to swallow.

"In second grade my mom asked to speak with my teacher to tell her she was really concerned about me. Mom was concerned that I was not happy with a grade of ninety-nine percent," Casey recalled.

Ruthie was actually concerned he might not live to see his eighteenth birthday in this imperfect world. She remembered the incident well.

"I said 'You did awesome on that test,' and he said 'No, I got one wrong, and Nathan didn't get any wrong.' Casey was so hard on himself."

Ruthie was so worried about her type-A child that she told the teacher she actually hoped Casey would get a B once in a while.

"The teacher just chuckled and said, 'Wow, that's one I've never heard before.'"

Ruthie and the teacher worked to reassure Casey that it was okay to make a mistake. But as Casey moved into his middle school years, he felt there was pressure coming from his parents to perform well on the ice.

"The most stressful years in my speedskating career were ages ten to fourteen. By and large, the expectation was I would win. Second place was the first loser, to put it bluntly; second place was failure. It was not a very relaxing position to be in as a twelve-year-old boy in an individual sport that is as black and white, as exposing, as you're ever going to get. You're expected to win and win and win. Mom and Dad weren't exactly like 'Oh well, off weekend. So and so's good too.' Not that Dad would chew me out, but he was very intense, very intense. There were times Mom said, 'Jeff, go take a walk.' When I got second or third, I felt Dad's stress and tension and sometimes hurt. He said 'You didn't apply yourself.' Maybe he's right, but show me a kid that performed their A game every time through life and I'll show you a robot, not a human being. There was a lot of stress. I don't want to hide that. It's an important part of our story. His expectations never wavered as my competition got more and more global; I felt like the level of competition was not an excuse in his mind. Never mind that I was competing against guys that could squat more, jump higher, or run faster. I should still be able to skate faster.

"There came a point in time when I literally had a discussion with him and said, 'Dad, it doesn't matter how badly you want me to win a gold medal. You can't will it to happen. It's not going to come from how badly you want it or how much pressure you put on me or anything you could ever say to me. It has to come from in here [points to his chest]. And it doesn't even matter how badly I want to win a gold medal for you. It's not going to happen if it doesn't come from my heart.' So that was a hard conversation to have, and there were years where it probably wasn't in my heart. That's one of the biggest questions and double-edged swords that I've faced. How do you balance expectations of performance, work ethic, and passion with joy, relaxation, having fun, and enjoying your life? There were a lot of times and years where, yeah, I got enjoyment out of it. But there were also a lot of years when I did it simply because it was what I did. It's what Casey does and does well, and he's on a track to do very well. He's put this much in, and why would I stop now? It wasn't that there was nothing I'd rather be doing in life."

When Casey was twelve, he contracted a viral infection early in the season that zapped his energy and stamina. He couldn't train properly, and pretty soon Brian Kretchmann, a good skater from Milwaukee, started beating him regularly. It got into his head. He was a couple of months away from skating for the national championship for his age level, and he felt psyched out. He couldn't beat Brian even though his viral infection was gone and his health had returned. His parents asked him what he thought about seeing a psychologist. Showing remarkable poise for his age, he agreed.

"Dr. Shaw specialized in hypnosis. We worked on deep relaxation, breathing, and visualization. He took me on hot air balloon rides. We would do liftoff and landing, and that started and ended our relaxation sessions. It changed my mentality, and it changed my results. I went on to win the indoor and outdoor national championships that year, so it righted the ship. That was the point in my career I was probably closest to falling off the bandwagon."

Jeff recalls the experience this way. "Casey was recovering from his illness and losing to Brian every weekend. You could watch him skate and see it had gotten in his head. He would skate a smart race and wait for the right opportunity to pass. As soon as he did, Brian would pass him right back, and Casey would fold. It was heartbreaking to watch. At a competition at the Olympic Rink in Milwaukee, I was taking a bathroom break. I was standing at the urinal wondering what the hell to do, and the father of an older skater and a fan of Casey wandered up to the urinal next to me. The first words out of his mouth were, 'You need to take him to a hypnotist.' I'm sure I looked at him dumbfounded, but he continued, 'Same thing happened to Tim, so we took him to a hypnotist and the guy turned him around.' So I walked out of the bathroom and told Ruthie, 'Casey's going to see a hypnotist.' Not wanting to leave any stone unturned, he saw Dr. Shaw the following week. That year, he went on to win both the national indoor and outdoor championships in his age division and the North American outdoor championship against the Canadians as well. He was virtually unbeatable. I still thank Tim Quinn every time I see him today!"

Later in his career, Casey would work with another psychologist, Dr. Tyre, who helped him visualize himself as the fastest land animal in the world, a cheetah. This technique helped carry him from his early twenties through three Olympics. "I'm a huge believer in the whole world of mental preparation."

He had been on a strenuous speedskating routine since his early teens, and all his work was about to propel him to five national sprint titles, numerous World Cup medals, two top-three finishes in World Sprint Championships, and three Olympic appearances.

As for his dad, Casey understandably has very tangled emotions about Jeff's intensity. On the one hand, it's questionable whether Casey would have been a gold medalist, or an Olympian at all, without it. On the other, it was sometimes hard to carry the hopes and dreams of his father on his back.

"I always wished I'd taken my Grandpa Fitz out for a cup of coffee and asked questions about my dad's life. Was he really not allowed to play any organized sports while growing up? Not pulling any punches, I would tell you that he very much lived his athletic career vicariously through Jess and me."

That's a familiar theme with many parents and children, in sports and often in other areas of life. "I told him at one point, 'You need to do a better job of masking your intensity because I don't want to feel that. How many times have you put on a pair of speed skates in your life? Never? So how much do you really know? And it doesn't matter if your answers and advice are right; they're not going to be perceived or taken very well at this point. You need to chill.'"

But if you look at the total picture, Casey was extraordinarily lucky as an athlete. He had the means, the talent, the voracious support of his parents, and, usually, the desire. This would eventually make the right combination to propel him into the upper echelons of the first sport he had fallen in love with. However, he still lacked one thing.

Like Jessi, Casey played some soccer. Whereas Jessi thrived on the camaraderie of the sport, Casey would get frustrated if someone else made a mistake on the field. He was wired for an individual pursuit. He also didn't expect to have one of his most valuable moments handed to him from a relative stranger while running down the soccer field.

"It was the most vivid lesson I ever learned in my life in athletics. I was in seventh or eighth grade, and a couple of us Verona kids had joined a pretty competitive team from a neighboring community. We were at a tournament in Indiana, and I was the left outside halfback. I was loosely contesting the ball along the sideline. The other kid won the ball, again, and I heard one of the parents say with disgust, 'Would you just win one of these, Casey?' He didn't mean for me to hear it. He was disgusted and he said something to another parent that a kid should never hear, but I heard it. And I'll never forget it. I was so embarrassed and humiliated by it that a light bulb went off in my head. 'What a horrible feeling, I don't ever want this to happen again.' From that point on, I became team captain in high school. I was the leading goal scorer, arguably the best player on the team. It was monumental in my sports career because I needed some aggression. I needed to feel like I deserved to win just as much as the other guy."

His newfound aggression served him well as he climbed the speedskating and sports ladder. He even joined the high school football team as the kicker when the coach had no one else and went looking for someone with a good leg from the soccer team. Casey might have wanted to tackle an opposing player every now and again, but he couldn't risk injury playing other positions. Plus, technically, he wasn't supposed to compete in both football and soccer in the same season, so he never got to actually practice with the football team. He would have to go out during study hall with a couple of buddies, the center and the holder on the football team. He'd boot a few field goal attempts and kick offs until the bell rang for the next class and then show up on Friday nights for the games.

Soccer and speedskating all week, football Friday nights—are you wondering how he fit grades into all of this? From homework in the van to juggling three sports, he made it work. In fact, years later at a speaking engagement at a Department of Public Instruction convention, he said this:

"My grades were better, because of everything I was doing, than they would have been had I only been focused on school. My day was about as scheduled and organized and productive as a kid's can be. There's probably a reason certain countries are as successful in some regards as they are with the structure they have. I know there's a lot of creativity that comes out of America, but you look at our overall test scores and think, how can they possibly be so bad? And I think a lot of it has to do with the fact that many kids have no structure. Mom and Dad are busy, so the kids can just play video games or watch TV to kill time."

When he was ready to apply to colleges, there was only one requirement: It had to be in Milwaukee. He needed to be near the Pettit Center, the ice oval he had been driving to for years. He looked at Marquette, the University of Wisconsin–Milwaukee, and Carroll College, a small school in the suburb of Waukesha. Carroll appealed to him because of its more intimate size. As a bonus, Casey's uncle Brian Bliese was an assistant coach for the football team and invited him to be their kicker. And Carroll was just in the process of working out a system with US Speedskating to help student athletes, like Casey, who were training at the Pettit. He was one of the first to use the program, which granted him flexibility to miss classes for training. In return, Casey would help by making speeches to prospective incoming students. It would be his first practical experience with public speaking and would open doors to more lucrative speaking engagements for larger, professional organizations after winning his gold.

But that first fall semester just about killed him. He was skating like mad, playing football (and now required to attend practice), adjusting to college life, and trying to make it home for his favorite pastime, bow hunting. He managed All-Conference honors on the football field, but he nearly failed calculus until he got a tutor (he reasoned he was not trying to be a mathematician anyway). He was so tired he felt his skating was suffering as well. It was 1993, and his goal was to make the 1994 Olympics in Lillehammer, Norway. He was aiming at this more for the experience than anything else. He had always eyed the 1998 winter games in Nagano, Japan, as his big medal shot. Most speedskaters who medaled did so in their second winter games, and he figured it would be nice to have one Olympics under his belt before 1998. He was confident he would do well in Nagano, and when his dad suggested he have a license plate made up that said "Gold 98," he agreed.

"It was my dad's suggestion, but I was fine with it. It was my goal, and I was comfortable telling everybody that."

He also had a brief fantasy about becoming the kicker for the Green Bay Packers. But he knew his true talent was at the rink, and so he geared up for the 1994 Olympic trials.

"After sleeping for what seemed like two weeks straight following the end of the school semester, I skated the two fastest races of my life and barely missed the team by eight hundredths of a second in the 500-meter event. I hoped they would still take me as an alternate."

The team consisted of aging veterans with little chance of medaling other than Dan Jansen, and he thought US Speedskating might just want to add him to the mix to give him the experience. It didn't happen.

But at nineteen years old, he still had a chance to make some noise at the Junior World Championships held in Berlin, Germany, a month before the Olympics were to begin. He looked at it as a consolation prize for not making the Olympics, but it was still a very worthy goal. The speedskating venue was in old East Berlin—the wall dividing East and West had fallen two years earlier—and was connected with a sports training center where the East Germans had trained and were rumored, but never proven, to have experimented with steroids for years.

The US team got there nine days early to adjust to the time zone and have lots of time to prepare. Finally, race day arrived. Casey was in the last pair for the 500-meter race.

"I had skated the fastest 500 of all the competitors in a practice race a week earlier, and I told myself 'Don't screw up, FitzRandolph. You're going to be the junior world champ at 500 meters, and the world will finally start to take notice.' The gun went off. I was paired against a German skater. I'm telling myself to be careful—no slips, no falls. So I skate a very safe race. I cross the finish line ahead of my pair and look up at the scoreboard at the end of this antiquated, cold, steel arena and see 'C. FitzRandolph, USA, 6.' That one hurt because I had failed to take a risk. I had a fear of failure, and I went out and skated not to lose instead of to win. So lose is exactly what I did. It was another valuable lesson. I learned that there is a fine line between first and sixth place, and if you go through the motions without being aggressive, there's a big difference in terms of the end result."

The family was devastated. Jeff, Ruthie, and Jessi had flown to Berlin to watch Casey compete and were staying in the old training facility attached to the skating rink. It was their first experience with international competitions and accommodations, and to say they were "stark" would be putting it mildly. They were shocked upon arrival to learn the room in which they would stay barely had space for their three single beds. There were no closets, so they piled their clothes onto their beds during the day and onto the floor at night while they slept. The room itself wasn't as big as Jessi's bedroom at home. There was no need for a shower curtain: when you showered, the sink, toilet, and four walls of the room were part of the shower. Not only weren't they prepared for the experience, they didn't expect Casey to lose either. He'd been skating very well since the US trials. The highlight of the trip for the family turned out to be the day they rented a car, drove from East to West Berlin, and did some shopping. They did not leave Germany with the best of memories.

Now Casey had no choice other than to take the various lessons of his life and rededicate himself 100 percent toward the Nagano Olympics. "There was no such thing as an alcoholic beverage in my life. I gained strength by not doing what everyone else was doing. It gave me a psychological advantage. I was thinking, 'I have this dream, and it's not a pipe dream; it's a legitimate opportunity.' I was lucky to have a good group of friends. They had my back. Nobody ever peer-pressured me. What I was trying to accomplish and how I proceeded towards my goal was respected and totally cool with them."

He never finished his degree at Carroll College. The workload became too much. He was skating on a more full-time basis as 1998 approached. This time, he won the US trials and national championship and was on his way to his first Olympics. His parents threw a big going-away party at their house. Casey didn't know it, but it was at this party where he would meet Jenn Bocher, the woman he would fall in love with. She came to the party with a sorority sister of hers, Mandy Marcum, who had grown up in East View Heights and been a childhood friend of Casey's. He immediately thought the brown-haired, slender, bright-eyed friend of Mandy's was cute. Both Jenn and Casey were dating other people, but the attraction was immediate. He even cornered his mom in the computer room after the party and asked her what she thought of Jenn. Ruthie agreed that Jenn was pretty but reminded him he was dating another girl. A week later, Casey left for two months to prepare for his first Olympic games in Nagano, Japan.

"I would call Mandy, and I never called Mandy from overseas. I would talk a bit and then ask about Jenn. It was about as transparent as it gets. My girlfriend had made these nice little notes for me to open every day in Japan, and I'm opening them and thinking about this other girl. It was less than comfortable."

But while his love antennae were up, he had a bigger problem in Nagano. The clap skate had just been invented.

A traditional speedskate has a long blade that protrudes three inches in both the front and back of the boot and is attached at both toe and heel. Now imagine if the blade was only attached to the toe, so the back part of the blade would open and close like a director's clapboard on a movie set. This was the clap skate, and it revolutionized the speedskating world. The skate got its name because every time the hinged blade opened and closed, it made a clapping sound. This design allowed the blade to stay on the ice longer, giving the athlete more natural push out of their legs.

Digging a toe in the ice while skating and toppling over forward was one of the most common ways of falling during a race on traditional skates. When a skater would fall, his fellow competitors might comment, "He dug a toe." The clap skate made that statement obsolete, because you didn't have to lift your whole boot at the end of a stroke thanks to the blade's longer connection with the ice. This reduced the number of falls considerably.

"The Dutch invented and manufactured the clap skate, and their skaters got on them for a full season prior to the winter games in Nagano," Casey explained. As the Dutch athletes started shattering records, everyone wanted in on the action. But Casey was one of the world's most talented skaters, and the Dutch knew it. It was time for them to stonewall him, in Casey's opinion.

"The company in Holland that made them would not sell me a pair of their skates. 'Oh, sorry, we're out. Oh, sorry, we're out.' It was one frustrating fax to the owner of this company after another. It was ridiculous, a total debacle. I finally got clap skates less than two months before Nagano. We actually put the things together ourselves. US Speedskating was becoming equally frustrated because some of our athletes couldn't get skates, finally approached the Easton Sports for help. Easton was an Olympic sponsor and gladly took on the challenge of creating the blade and clap mechanism for us. So I took the newly created blade with a clap mechanism and attached it to the boot from my traditional skate after removing the old blade. Two months prior to the Olympics, we were sitting in Bonnie Blair's driveway drilling and screwing and gluing our hopes together. I was way behind the eight-ball."

This was supposed to be Casey's Olympics. He had already decided that it wasn't going to be a matter of if he would he medal in 1998 but rather how many and what color they would be. He was consistently in the top three in the 500m and had skated the fastest 1,000m in the world the year before the Olympics on traditional skates. As the season leading up to Nagano progressed and other skaters around the world started skating on the new skates, he was crossing the finish line outside the top twenty on his traditional skates.

"And there comes the psychological aspect, as well, and the panic. Oh my God, I have two months to get this figured out? I've spent my whole life preparing for this, and now this is going to happen? You've got to be kidding me," Casey lamented.

Every country was scrambling to find clap skates for their athletes, and some did a better job than others. To make matters worse, none of the countries that were successful were sharing any information about the skates with other countries. Blair who had recently retired, and many other former athletes from several countries, wanted to help the next generation. They filed formal protests against clap skates with the International Skating Union, speedskating's governing body. They pointed out that speedskating laws said you can't have a mechanical advantage. Even more importantly, they said, if the International Skating Union did approve the clap skates, they should wait until after the Olympics to do so to give everyone a fair chance to train on them for the next four years.

"But the ISU was run primarily by 'good old Dutch boys' whose country had the technology," according to Casey. His frustration would be shared by many in just a few short months.

The clap skate stayed in for the Nagano Games, and Casey, who had been looking forward to counting his medals, finished sixth in the 500m, seventh in the 1,000m, and thirty-first in the 1,500m. This was a colossal flop in the minds of the American public and media, who viewed Casey as a sure bet to be standing on the podium with a flag draped around his shoulders. That's not how Casey saw it.

"The reality of it was, it was a huge success coming from where I had been even a month prior. To get sixth and seventh, I had to skate above and beyond where I had any right being at that point in time. The most important thing I took out of the '98 Games was saying to myself, 'You saw Dan Jansen [when he fell in a race shortly after his sister passed away] and how hard it is when something gets in your head.' Forget about sixth and seventh compared to where you were a year ago, and recognize that you used all the energy surrounding the Olympics in a positive way. Consider this a huge success given where you were."

And good things started to happen the moment he got off the plane back in Madison, Wisconsin. "I found out Jenn and her boyfriend had broken up. I arrive at the airport, and I'm walking off the jetway. I see my sister and Mandy and Jenn standing there with "Go Casey Go" T-shirts, and I'm super excited to see all three of them, especially Jenn. Suddenly my girlfriend enters stage left, having driven over to be there for me, bless her heart, and she gives me a big hug and kiss."

Casey was greeted by a group of about fifty people, and many, including Jenn, were planning to go out that night to celebrate his return. Casey felt compelled to ask his girlfriend to join them, but inside he caught himself thinking, *please say no, please say no.*

Luckily for Casey and Jenn's future relationship, the girlfriend did decline the invitation. She had to return to Milwaukee, where she was also a speedskater, to prepare for a race the next morning. So Casey, Jenn, and some others went out in Madison. Casey had been waiting months to talk to Jenn again.

"I was far from a womanizer. As you can tell from what I've already said, I wasn't good in a relationship. I was easily intimidated by good-looking young women. I think the first words out of my mouth that night were, 'So, do you like to exercise or work out?' She answers, 'Yes, I love to run.' Then I ask her, 'What do you think about hunting and fishing?' You know, no beating around the bush. I cut right to the chase. She lied to me and gave me the answers I wanted to hear. In reality, her desire to hunt and fish with me is on par with my desire to get our hair and nails done together."

Casey knew he was on to something with Jenn, though, and invited her to go ice fishing with him and his friend Nate at the family cabin on Big Siss. The sorority girl somehow agreed to tag along in an activity she could have cared less about. She and Casey were really enjoying the northern Wisconsin experience and starting to have eyes for each other, but then Casey had to leave her and Nate while he drove to Minneapolis to support the girl he was supposedly still dating skate in her biggest race of the year in the Twin Cities. It was all too much. He knew where his attraction was and told his girlfriend shortly after the race that he wanted to just be friends. Casey and Jenn got serious quickly. But his skating was still not going as well as he'd hoped, even though he had convinced himself that his Nagano results were a success. He couldn't help but feel some bitterness and disappointment about the way it all unfolded.

"Nagano was a wonderful experience for my family, and in some weird way, I think they were pleasantly surprised by my sixth- and seventh-place finishes. But it should have been a better experience for me, for all of us.

"I came back from the Olympics and had two thoughts: one, a pity party for poor me, I got screwed by the clap skate, yada, yada, and two, the Canadians were second, third, fourth, and fifth. All four of their guys beat me in the 500, and it wasn't because they had traditionally been the powers in the world, so they must know something about this new clap skate. I thought if I was going to do this and do it right, that meant moving to Canada, if they'd let me, to train with people who have figured something out."

First, he got down on his knee to propose to Jenn. They had been dating for about fifteen months. For all of the sporting events Casey had been in, all of the times he had been nervous, this was a feeling like none other.

"A gigantic bullfrog jumped into my throat that almost prevented me from speaking."

After he finally got the "Jenn, will you marry me" out, family and friends erupted in cheer. Jenn cried. And then she said yes. He had proposed in front of the crowd gathered at his parents' home for a sendoff party for the two of them. He had made his decision. They were moving to Calgary to train with the Canadians, who were welcoming him and Jenn with open arms. It seemed the Canadians were looking for another training partner for their top two sprinters, Jeremy Wotherspoon and Mike Ireland. Casey was the perfect fit.

It was also at this time that Jenn's mother, Merody, was battling terminal brain cancer. She and her mom were very close, and that was another reason Casey wanted to propose before they left.

"The thought that some jock that Merody didn't even know very well was taking her daughter to another country without even the commitment of an engagement was probably a bit of a stretch, so Jenn and I thought we should do this before we leave. We wanted her to have some peace of mind."

Casey and Jenn took off for Canada the day after he proposed. She left her dream job as a kindergarten teacher in her hometown and went back to school in Canada to earn her master's degree in education. He had three years to prepare for the 2002 winter games. With the memory of Nagano still clear in his mind, he wasn't about to squander the next opportunity, even if it meant moving to another country to train. The Winter Olympics of 2002 were going to be held in his home country, in Salt Lake City, Utah.

The dream of competing in an Olympics in your home country is a reality that few Olympians get to experience. When you couple an athlete's brief window of opportunity with the facts that the Winter Games are only held once every four years and that there are dozens of countries lined up trying to host every Olympics, most athletes never get the chance to compete in front of a partisan crowd. The last Winter Olympics held in the United States was in Lake Placid in 1980. Ironically, that was the last time an American had won gold in the 500m Olympic speedskating event. And, more ironically, that American was Eric Heiden from Madison, Wisconsin.

He could have trained in Salt Lake City or Milwaukee. Yet, like his sister many years later, a guy who considered himself a proud American was leaving the United States to get what he felt he needed—in this case, the pursuit of his lifetime dream of winning gold.

CHAPTER SEVEN

Gooold!

2002

With a U-Haul full of clothes, furniture, skin suits, and skates, Casey and Jenn waved good-bye to everything they had known and crossed the US-Canadian border in July of 1999. They found an apartment near the University of Calgary, where the ice rink was located. In fact, they were close enough that they could bike through the clean streets of this beautiful Canadian city to the oval. Jenn landed a part-time job working at the front desk while Casey trained feverishly with his new teammates. The couple enjoyed what they saw as a slower-paced way of life in Canada. It amazed them that people obeyed the speed limit on the roads and frowned upon making work their priority.

"They take time out for friends and family. They just slow down and socialize and enjoy what they have," said Casey. "Coming from a guy who's fiscally very conservative and doesn't believe in high taxes, I will say that perhaps one apparent byproduct of higher taxes in Canada is people are less motivated to spend seventy or eighty hours a week working and more inclined to spend a little more time with loved ones. We were, dare I say, blessed to see the perks of it first-hand."

Casey and Jenn were accepted immediately by the Canucks. They felt as if they belonged and were asked to join in on every social and Sunday dinner the skating community had. It was the Canadian National Team and Casey.

Positive vibes were not, however, coming their way from Team USA. They believed that FitzRandolph, the best male sprinter in his home country, was turning his back on their program, essentially saying it wasn't good enough for him. They took it as a slap in the face, but Casey tried to reassure them this wasn't the case. He wasn't the only American skater living and training outside of the United States, and his decision to train outside of the United States was not US Speedskating's fault. It was simply he could train with the best in the world on the new clap skate in Canada.

"Would I rather train with two of the best guys in the world or numbers twenty-five and twenty-six? That might be insulting. I didn't mean it that way. When you make skating your life over two decades, compromise and cutting corners aren't very good options."

Casey felt vindicated when he started seeing results right away, and he relished the relaxed, fun attitude the Canadians brought to the ice. He and his new training partners would make bets to see who could skate 100 meters the fastest, often wagering fly fishing paraphernalia since that recreational activity was of mutual interest. Blasting music into the oval, they danced during down moments. More importantly, Casey's skate times were dropping, and he and Jenn felt very, very good about the move.

Then came an unexpected turn. Casey went home over Christmas in 1999 to skate in the US championships being held in Milwaukee, just six months after they had moved. Casey decided to spend part of Christmas Day ice fishing with a lifelong friend, Chad. They were driving to the day's fishing hotspot together, Casey at the wheel in Ruthie's Suzuki Sidekick, when the tires hit a slick spot of black ice and the car spun off the road into a drainage ditch. The seatbelt broke Casey's sternum in a diagonal pattern. He was lucky compared to his friend, who wasn't belted in and went face first through the windshield. Chad had to be flown by med-flight to the hospital. Thankfully, Chad's injuries were not life-threatening, although doctors used medical leeches—yes, leeches—to help debride the worst areas. The old-fashioned treatment, utilizing creatures that looked like the fishing bait the family used at Big Siss, allowed Mother Nature to help heal the wound. Four leeches were placed on Chad's nose, as he was having trouble generating new skin growth. Chad remained hospitalized for a month and had many cosmetic surgeries afterwards.

Casey felt some guilt, even though he had not been speeding or driving irresponsibly. He had to work through those emotions even as he nursed his own body. With the national championships one week away, he quickly resumed training after doctors told him a chest X-ray looked fine. But he knew something was wrong when he couldn't swing his arms in the violent way needed to start a speedskating race. He told the team doctor, and an MRI was ordered. The test painted a very different picture than the emergency room X-ray. His sternum was indeed broken. The fractured bone kept him out of serious competition for months and derailed his entire next year of skating as he worked his way back into world class shape. His injury affected him well into the 2000–2001 skating season.

The Olympics were approaching in the winter of 2002. As Casey rehabbed and regained full stamina, he and Jenn welcomed a long-term house guest. Jessi moved to Calgary to give skating one more try in her twenties. She had been out of the sport for almost a decade but had recently tried more skating in Milwaukee. After leaving college for good, she thought competitive skating might be worth another whirl while she attempted to put the puzzle pieces of her life into order. Back at home, in between skating sessions, she had worked for a landscaping company. Now she left the landscaping behind and thought Canada could be interesting. Jeff and Ruthie helped talk her into it. They had seen what a great experience Casey and Jenn were having with the Canadians and wanted Jessi to feel some of that, too.

Although she enjoyed the Canadian lifestyle as much as her brother and sister-in-law, Jessi spent only six months north of the border. Her heart still wasn't in it. She moved back to Madison and decided her speedskating career was truly over this time.

After Casey hugged his sister good-bye, he focused his intentions on Salt Lake City, the upcoming Olympic Winter Games in his own country. For the year leading up to the competition, he was training daily with Canadians Jeremy Wotherspoon and Mike Ireland. They were sweeping the podium. Casey estimates they won sixty-five out of roughly seventy-two medals given out from November through January in the World Cups and World Sprint Championships in the 500-meter and 1,000-meter events. The three became best friends and each other's best competition. They used this competition to push themselves to reach their potential.

In one of the last tune-up races before Salt Lake, Casey slipped coming out of the final turn and still finished with the best time of his life. His confidence soared. If he could make a mistake and still perform like this, the sky was the limit. He narrowed his eyes on not only winning gold but setting a new world record. The Olympics were going to be his playground, and he was ready to tackle the challenge. Yet, in his most private moments, he battled tiny demons of self-doubt. Casey knew that the Olympic stage often sent athletes one of two ways: you either elevated yourself to the top performance of your life, or you choked. Fear of failure lives somewhere in every athlete, and Casey had to work through the process. What if it didn't work out? How could he help to make sure it did? He continued to practice visualization and relaxation, and he also added Athletes in Action, a Christian organization, to his list of important commitments.

"That helped immensely. The catalyst for me was the recognition that, no matter how hard I trained, when the moment of truth came, there were going to be things out of my control. It would have been overwhelming to go to the Olympics and feel that my success or failure on the ice would dictate my life and who I am as a person. I was working hard to make something happen but also recognizing that it might not happen, and guess what? If it doesn't happen, the sun's still going to come up. Jenn's still going to love me, and life will go on. So I reached out to the Lord and acknowledged that my fate was ultimately in His hands."

By accepting this worst-case scenario, Casey was able to focus on the best. He viewed the buildup to The Games as a time for mental, as well as physical, preparation. He and his psychologist used all of the tools they had, including visualizing the perfect race over and over again, until Casey could play it like a movie in his head.

Finally, the 2002 Winter Olympics arrived. Jeff and Ruthie drove out to Salt Lake City feeling a tremendous amount of confidence in their son, boosted by the fact that their travels were going so well. Jeff had a bit of superstition and had come to believe that if their journey to a race was smooth, Casey would skate well. If they had problems in the air or on the ground, for some reason, things would "go to hell in a hand basket" for him. The good news was that the road trip from Wisconsin to Utah could not have not gone more smoothly.

The International Skating Union had selected Jeff to be a starter for the women's speedskating races, so he and Ruthie had their Olympic expenses—lodging, meals, and mileage—covered. They rolled westward with a trip-tik from AAA in their hands, charting their progress through each little town. Both had huge smiles on their faces. Every restaurant they stopped at was a good experience; every hotel they slept in left them feeling rested and ready to go the next day. They arrived at the Olympic Park with positive vibes warming their hearts and visions of gold medals dancing in their heads.

Jeff spent part of the next two weeks being a starter for the women's events. The International Skating Union rules prohibited him from starting Casey or any of his competitors, but he had worked hard to get his World Championship–level certification and was rewarded by his peers with the Olympic assignment. The process had begun when Casey was a kid. Parents were always asked to volunteer at weekend competitions, and Jeff helped out to give some of the other starters a break from the cold during the long days of outdoor competitions. He found he enjoyed starting the younger children. His reputation grew, and he eventually earned national and then international certifications. He had to take time off from work and pay part of his own way to Europe for training once a year, but he loved being a part of the fabric of speedskating. Before he knew it, he was starting World Cups. Most certified starters will get to work only one Olympics in their lifetime. So Salt Lake City was the culmination of years of hard work not only for Casey but also for Jeff.

Jeff was the guy with the gun. As the skaters prepared for their race, he would blow his whistle to call them to the prestart line. Once there, he would order them to "Go to the start," and they would advance to the starting line. On the next command of "Ready," the skaters would get in their final starting position. Finally, at the sound of the pistol shot, they would explode down the opening stretch. He started forty-eight pairs of female skaters during those 2002 Olympics. It helped to take his mind off the impending races that Casey would skate.

The 500 meters had once been just a single race. With the introduction of the clap skate, the participant who had to skate the inner track in the last corner was at a disadvantage. The speeds reached on these new skates made it nearly impossible to hold that final corner without slowing down or falling. In 1998, the Olympic committee tinkered with the 500-meter race to make it a two-day event. Each athlete would now compete in two races, and the total time would determine the winner. This allowed each competitor to skate the inner corner in one race and the outer corner in the other.

On Casey's first racing day, Jeff stepped away from his starter's duties and put his dad hat back on. The family settled in and watched from the stands in awe as Casey executed a flawless first race on the outer lane, so seamless his parents were almost dumbfounded.

"The fastest he had ever skated the first 100 meters was 9.6 seconds, and that's a good opening time. In his first race he's flying down the opening straightaway 15 yards in front of his competitor, who was a former world record holder himself. We looked up at the clock, and they showed the 100-meter split: 9.45. I looked at Ruthie, she looked at me, and I thought, 'Wow, this is too good to be true,'" marveled Jeff.

They were actually nervous that Casey might have too much speed going into the last corner. But except for one tiny bobble that didn't affect him much, he skated a nearly perfect race. After day one, the kid from Wisconsin was sitting two-tenths of a second in front of the rest of the field. That may seem like nothing to people outside of the sport, but in elite speedskating it's a lifetime, equating to about ten meters. Casey knew he was off to a great start, but his heart was also heavy. One of his training partners, biggest competitors and best friends Jeremy Wotherspoon, had fallen during his race. The easygoing Canadian, who had shared so many meals and laughs with Casey and Jenn, slipped and careened to the ice face first just thirty yards into his race, his Olympic medal dream squelched in a hail of ice chips.

Casey hadn't been able to see or talk to Jeremy after his race. First came a series of required post-race interviews, but he felt numb as he went through the motions with the reporters. What he really wanted to do was to find his friend. After finally wrapping up his last media responsibility, Casey bee-lined it to the Canadian locker room and encountered Wotherspoon, who was understandably overwhelmed with the reality of what had just happened.

"He was just sitting there, leaning forward, his head in his hands. I sat down next to him, wanting to say something, but no words came out. So we just sat there and cried together. Everyone else in the locker room quietly walked out."

Casey was sick for his confidante, but he had to stay mentally sharp himself—a very hard thing to do. US Speedskating had rented a house in the neighborhood adjacent to the Utah oval. The skaters were staying there, instead of the Olympic Village, so they could have home-cooked meals, avoid germs, and add to the "home ice" American advantage. Returning to the house, Casey chose to quarantine himself from the outside world, refusing to even talk to his family on the telephone. He wanted the evening to be the same as every other competition night, just him, his teammates and his routine. Jenn and the rest of the group were reveling in Casey's good start by taking in dinner and a party at the USA house.

"We figured in case we can't celebrate tomorrow, we might as well celebrate today," Jenn reflected. They ate and drank and laughed but were also nervous, with butterflies soaring through all of their stomachs. Most of the Fitz pack was staying at a house they had rented in Park City, while friends and supporters were scattered around Salt Lake City. Many had flown in, but Jessi took the Amtrak with her friend Becky Waugh, who was too afraid to fly after September 11. Uncles, aunts, friends, and former teachers were all there. Excitement, anticipation, and nerves ran through the gathering in equal doses.

"I don't know how to describe it. It was so exciting and such a high, but in the 500 anything can happen. There is no room for error," said Ruthie. But for now, there was nothing to do but to enjoy the moment and wait for the second race the next day.

The family was asked to do a live interview with a Madison television station that night, which Jessi remembered because she felt she came across as a jittery mess. "I was freaking out about Casey," recalled Jessi. "I'm sure I must have looked like a complete fool. I was nervous and almost panicky. You can't sit still, and you don't know what to do. So many emotions were going through us."

Back at the house rented for them by US Speedskating, Casey was glad to be sharing space with another American, fellow Wisconsin native Kip Carpenter, who sat in third place after day one. The two of them tried to joke and keep things light, although they recognized that each was on the verge of achieving a lifelong dream. The separation from family proved to be a good thing. Casey was able to talk himself down into a good sleep that night before race day dawned with an Olympic gold medal hanging in the balance.

The second leg of the 500 was set for early afternoon. Because this was the first Olympics after 9/11, security was virtually unparalleled. The rink was cordoned off in a one-mile radius, helicopters circled overhead, and police dogs sniffed every bag. Jeff drove a car designated for officials to the race, but it still took an hour and a half to get through the checkpoints that were manned by the National Guard. A routine part of the check included running a mirror on a long pole underneath each vehicle. The family left early to make sure they were in place, but they never felt unsafe and appreciated the work of the National Guard and the Secret Service on the behalf of everyone at The Games, even if it was a nuisance sometimes.

Inside, Jenn, Ruthie, Jeff, and Jessi had seats together in the stands. Their stomachs were tied up in knots. Other family and friends fanned out in little groups around the rink. A crowd of about seventy-five had come to cheer Casey, including his former high school principal, Kelly Meyer. He didn't want to disappoint. Even though he had an impressive lead over the field, it could all disappear in one slip.

During warm-up laps, with his favorite music in his ear, Casey made eye contact with his fiancée, sister, mother, and father. Jenn interpreted the look as "I got this. I'm not nervous. I'm at peace with this, and whatever is going to happen is going to happen." She exhaled, feeling that it was all going to be okay no matter the results. Casey remembers it this way:

"They were all looking a little pale and serious. I tried to get their attention and smile. It made sense that they would be white as ghosts because they had no control. I can understand. I remember watching Jessi race, and it was much harder being a spectator. But I felt so relaxed and confident it was almost surreal. I had put in twenty-three years of hard work and now it was time to enjoy the fruits of my labor. I felt as though I didn't need to make it happen....I just needed to let it happen.

Ruthie and Jeff couldn't help but reflect on all of the years they had put into his training, and both felt a mix of nostalgia and anxiety. Would it all be rewarded right here, right now, in front of millions of viewers spanning the entire circumference of the globe? Would he be able to hold onto the gold that was his to lose and fulfill a lifetime dream for all of them? Or would this turn into the most disastrous moment of their son's life?

Jenn had on her lucky cheetah gloves, a symbol of Casey's visualization of himself as a cheetah. The family was well armed with a collection of cowbells and horns, and many of them sported USA tattoos on their cheeks. Casey was grooving to the beat of Van Halen's "Right Here, Right Now" and Montell Jordan's "This Is How We Do It." He liked to listen to the songs in that order. Van Halen got him pumped up, and then "This is How We Do It" exuded a smooth confidence that put him in exactly the frame of mind he wanted when he heard the starter's commands. His musical mix had been made by the high school daughter of one of Jenn's Canadian friends. In the days before iPods exploded into our lives, she was one of the only people they knew who had the technical knowledge to create playlists and put them onto an MP3 player.

The Canadians were rooting for Casey and vice versa. Now the rink quieted as Casey and Kip, who were placed together in the final pair, stepped to the line. Jessi was in the stands desperate for her brother to do well. She thought about how long he had dreamed of this, and she felt no regrets about not being an athlete herself. She was purely nervous for him. Ruthie and Jessi had the same overriding emotion: They just wanted it to be over, no matter the outcome, so they could stop being so filled with anxiety.

None of the previous skaters had put up an especially fast time, and Casey knew going to the line that a solid race would win him a gold medal. But for just a moment, he reflected back to his 500m race at the Junior World Championships four years before, where he had taken no risks, skated not to lose and finished in sixth place. He did not want a repeat of that situation. Everything he had learned from that experience, from the clap skate fiasco, and from his broken sternum had been incorporated into his training regimen and his mental preparation for this race. Once again, the world was his for the taking, and he needed to seize the moment. But the race was not destined to go without a hitch from start to finish.

"The gun went off, and the first 300m went well. As Kip and I entered the final turn of the race, Kip went from the inner to outer lane," Casey explained. The skaters are required to switch lanes as they go so each skates an equal distance. "At the beginning of the corner, each lane is marked with a big orange construction cone to prohibit skaters from cutting the corner. At the Olympics, they have a ten-pound television camera mounted inside the cone to get shots of skaters coming down the backstretch. Kip misjudged his entry to the corner and leaned into the cone with his knee, and it scooted into my lane."

This came at the most crucial part of the race just as he entered the last inner turn at top speed. The cone spun in front of him and hit his right skate. Casey at first did not realize the cone had been pushed by Kip, so his first thought was, "How the hell did I misjudge that turn setup so badly?"

Technically, Carpenter had just interfered with FitzRandolph's race, which would have meant a referee consultation if Casey had fallen. That could have required Carpenter to be disqualified and Casey to do a reskate all on his own, a prospect that would have been a virtual death sentence for both of them.

"It's very difficult to prepare mentally again," Casey explained. "It's very difficult to be able to get your body to have the same physiological reaction, with fast-twitch fibers firing, etc., within the twenty-minute window they give you."

There was also the issue of the ice. They don't resurface during that twenty-minute timeframe so the ice sits, collecting a little layer of frost and making it slower. Casey had seen invariably poor performance times on reskates through the years.

It all happened so fast that Jenn and the family didn't even catch the cone with the naked eye; they just saw him stumble. It wasn't until the replay that they realized what had just occurred. Such an unexpected thing can throw an athlete completely off. A small slip in his 500m race during the 1994 Olympics in Lillehammer had cost Dan Jansen a medal. With the winning margin so small, any slip in this event usually spells doom for the athlete.

Casey felt his balance sway for just a moment, but the mental repetition of seeing himself skating the perfect race paid off in this most imperfect moment.

"I had thought about what to do if something goes wrong. Get back into your execution and visualization. You need to picture yourself skating perfectly about ten yards ahead so that your body can actually do it in the split second it takes you to get there. I thought, 'Oh boy that was bad,' but then I was able to think about how I wanted to look in ten yards. My body struggled through the first half of that corner a little bit, but my mind righted the ship."

"I was frozen in fear," said Ruthie. "That race wasn't a good race. I don't know how he stayed on his feet."

"I have never seen a person survive a slip of that magnitude in the 500 meters. It's amazing he stayed up," added Jeff. "He had just been hit on his skate boot by a ten-pound projectile while his right leg was fully extended. I'm sure that slip cost him at least half a second."

The race itself takes between 34 and 35 seconds. Casey needed a 34.82 to win the gold medal. He crossed in 34.80, a sixth-place finish in that second race. It was enough to give him the top spot overall, by only three hundredths of a second, over Japanese competitor Hiroyasu Shimizu. The five-meter edge Casey had enjoyed after day one was sliced to the equivalent of a skate blade. That's what he won by: a streak of metal, less than the blink of an eye. If you superimposed both Casey and Shimizu coming across the line at the same time, you'd have a hard time knowing who was first without the benefit of slow-motion replay. That's how close it was. Carpenter kept his hold on third place. No disqualification or reskate was necessary. His first race was an Olympic record, but the hurtling cone had cost Casey a shot at the world record. That mattered little. Jenn knew right away he had won when the 34.80 flashed across the jumbo scoreboard. She started screaming, "He did it, he did it!"

The family went into an other-worldly place of elation. "We flipped out—Jessi, me, and Jenn. Jeff was frozen for a while, staring at the clock. He didn't move at all. Then he cried. We were all screaming and hugging," recalled Ruthie.

"There were hugs and tears and smiles of pure joy," said Jeff.

Casey himself was so in the zone that he had no clue that he had just taken gold. In an amazing twist of fate, he was about to find out from his childhood idol, Eric Heiden. A movie script would have written it this way, but real life? It was a most unexpected moment right after he crossed the line. Heiden was US Speedskating's team orthopedist and one of the first people Casey saw standing at center ice.

"I crossed the finish line, and because that race hadn't gone as well, I didn't know where I sat overall. The crowd went crazy. I was paired with Kip, who was also in medal contention. I knew something good had happened, but what did that mean? Did it mean we flip-flopped, so he won gold and I won bronze? I didn't know. Of course, the finish line of the 500 is at the end of the straightaway, and the scoreboard is on the middle of the backstretch. You have to turn your body to see it, which isn't easy when you're going so fast. On the scoreboard there are all kinds of splits—your 500 meter, your lap split, your 100 meter opener, and then total times or plus and minus. It's too many damn numbers! You can't really focus on it because you're still going 40 mph. I'm thinking, 'What happened?' Finally, I caught eyes with Heiden on the inside of the track. I did one of these 'What happened?' gestures, and he gave me a big thumbs-up and a big smile. He was walking toward me fast. I said 'Me?' and he said 'Yeah,' and that's when I knew I'd won gold. That was memorable. It wasn't by design; it wasn't like I was looking for Eric Heiden. It was … fate."

Jenn was desperate to get to the ice and hug her fiancé. A cameraman from NBC saw the family jumping up and down and Jenn starting to scurry toward the stairs. He corralled all of them, and they followed him to ice level. There was only one problem. A huge wooden wall had been erected around the oval to prevent people from doing exactly what the FitzRandolphs were trying to accomplish: rush the ice. The wall was so high, Jenn could barely see over it on her tiptoes. The love of her life was barricaded from her at the highest moment of their partnership.

Just at that moment—one of the most exhilarating and now frustrating occasions she had ever dealt with—an dear friend stepped into the picture to help out. It was Wotherspoon, who was still dealing with the crushing disappointment of his own Olympic disaster. In a poignant moment, he came down the hallway right over to Jenn.

"Hey, congratulations!" he smiled.

"Thanks, Jer! I can't see!" She was still hopping up and down, trying to get a view over the wall.

The six foot, two inch Wotherspoon did not hesitate.

"Come here."

He hoisted her up onto his shoulders, both literally and figuratively. She pulled her camera out and started capturing the dramatic minutes right after victory. The kindness shown by Wotherspoon moved both Casey and Jenn. The moment was so powerful for the FitzRandolphs that both Jenn and Casey teared up talking about it ten years later.

"He was like a brother to us," remembered Jenn. "He created a family atmosphere for us in Canada."

Jenn thanked Jeremy again and gave him a huge hug, her heart still breaking for him while also pining to spend this moment with her future husband.

She also knew some of the people hand timing the event. Although the rink used an official electronic clock, each skater was also assigned three hand timers as backup. One of them was a familiar face, a woman they knew from Canada named April. April was able to get Jenn even closer. She pulled her onto the timer's bleachers next to the ice and Casey. When he saw Jenn there, he skated right over. She leaned down, and they shared a heartfelt kiss to celebrate the culmination of years of sacrifice, tears stinging both of their eyes.

Jeff had raced to the ice right after the victory as well, video camera in hand, telling a security guard on the way, "That's my son! He just won gold!"

In his other hand was an American flag, and Jeff wanted to give it to Casey. He couldn't get to Casey, but he did see Nick Thometz, Bonnie Blair's old training partner and a former coach of Casey's, who was now director of the oval in Salt Lake City. Jeff handed Thometz the flag and said, "Please give this to Casey."

Now, Casey took a victory lap waving the flag beside him to honor his country as opposed to draping it over his shoulders, which he considered a somewhat selfish gesture. Jeff was still videotaping, as close as he could get to the ice.

"Way to go, Case!" he screamed, pride swelling up in his throat as he watched his son go by. He could barely get the words out, he was so wracked with emotion. Jeff moved close enough to shake Casey's hand, a poignant moment as the fingers of father and son reached out to touch each other over that tall security wall. The family was overwhelmed with happiness, but it didn't all hit Casey right away.

"It was fairly surreal. I thought 'All right, I won. I performed. I handled the glitch.' It wasn't until the medals ceremony that the full spectrum of emotions hit me."

First, he had more interviews with NBC. Casey tried to put on a brave face, but he was still despondent that neither Jeremy Wotherspoon nor their other training partner, Mike Ireland, had medaled after the trio had owned the podium for months. Jeremy was standing just off to the side during the press conference as Casey was being peppered with "Aren't you thrilled?" and "What does it feel like?" questions by the reporters.

"If you look at me, I don't look like someone who just won a gold medal. I look more like I'm about to cry, for two reasons. Not only was it truly humbling, but I also knew what Jeremy and Mike were feeling. If they taught me anything, it was that it's not about winning a gold medal and beating people. It's about seeing how good you can be and trying to reach your own full potential."

Casey had done just that, and despite his nauseated feeling about the way things had turned out for his friends, he had to allow himself time to celebrate.

The family pulled a few strings and got approval for Jenn to stay with Casey at the Olympic Oval during the interviews following his race. It wasn't until Casey was done with all of his media obligations and mandatory IOC drug testing that Jeff, Ruthie, and Jessi were able to actually hug him. Hours passed, and the three of them retreated to the AT&T House with family and friends to celebrate and wait. AT&T was an Olympic sponsor, and the AT&T House was the home away from home for many athletes' families. There were large screen TVs piping in footage of competitions from the ski hills, ice rinks, and bobsled track. They served three meals a day, had a wall lined up with computers for personal use, and offered an open bar starting at four in the afternoon. The people from AT&T knew how to make Olympians and their family members comfortable, but this night the FitzRandolph family was emotionally charged.

Finally, Casey called to say he was done and on his way. When he arrived at the AT&T house with Jenn and an entourage of television cameras behind him, his proud parents muscled through the crowd to touch him. That first embrace was filled with over twenty years of blood, sweat, and tears. Jeff wrapped his arms around his gold-medal-winning son and broke up all over again.

"I couldn't talk. There were so many emotions going through my mind, it was all sort of a blur. I'd start to talk about something, and my mind would skip ahead to another thought. I couldn't speak in complete sentences. I did know one thing unequivocally, though. The color of the medal was gold, and it would soon be hanging around my son's neck."

One of the television crews on hand was from WTMJ in Milwaukee, a station that had followed Casey's rise from the time he was in high school. In fact, the FitzRandolphs videotaped their travels at all three Olympics for viewers back in Wisconsin to see through snippets shown on WTMJ. The station sent its main anchor, Mike Jacobs, to Salt Lake City. He wound up getting very close to the family, doing several stories on Casey and joining in on a couple of family celebrations. Casey trusted him and felt such a kinship that he later invited Jacobs to his wedding.

Now, it was time for the medals ceremony for that day's winners. Everyone made the ten-minute walk to the Medals Plaza and prepared for another surge of elation. The plaza, which would hold ten thousand people, was in downtown Salt Lake City and was packed. In addition to the presentation of the medals, hit bands performed nightly. Casey, silver medalist Hiroyasu Shimizu, and Carpenter all waited in the green room behind the stage as other medal ceremonies took place. The 500-meter speedskating race was considered America's highlight of the day, as Casey had won the only US gold in that twenty-four-hour window. In an effort to build up the emotions of the mostly American crowd, the presentation of the gold medal to Casey and the bronze medal to Kip would happen last.

Finally, they were brought on stage to the cheers of thousands who had paid ten dollars each to watch the ceremony and listen to the music. The noise was deafening. Jenn and Casey's families were in the stands bundled against the Utah cold and screaming until they were hoarse. It was so loud you couldn't hear the person next to you. It was a magical moment at the medal's plaza: Casey FitzRandolph was about to be presented the first gold medal won by an American speedskating athlete at the 2002 Salt Lake City Winter Olympic Games, and first in the 500 since his childhood idol Eric Heiden in 1980.

At the Olympics only the national anthem of the gold medalist is played. When the first notes of the "Star Spangled Banner" rang out, Casey was finally flooded with feelings of all sorts.

"I remember getting sentimental and then excited and then relieved. That may have actually been my strongest feeling: relief. I was relieved that it was over but also relieved I had accomplished something I always felt I could but never knew for sure I would. Then I was thankful and proud of two things—not so much the gold medal itself as what I had gone through to win the gold medal. And, I was also very proud to be an American. It was five months after September 11, and I felt very patriotic."

There was another sentiment that came into his body next, and it was an unexpected one—depression.

"I remember thinking, 'I just found this pot of gold at the end of the rainbow. Now what do I do?' Or to put it another way, 'I just climbed the highest mountain peak, and it meant everything to me. Now what?' Nothing I could do the next day, the next year, or very possibly the rest of my time on this planet would ever match this."

In the stands, Jessi had her eye on her sibling the whole time. "I was waiting to see if he was going to cry. He was singing the national anthem and, on the Jumbotron, I could see small teardrops start to form in the corner of each eye. I was just watching him, because at that moment it was all about him. It really wasn't that strange because yes, he won a gold medal, but he's still my brother. I knew he'd be the same person."

Casey may have felt a wide range of emotions, but his highest day was far from over. A flurry of activity followed the medals ceremony, including seeing United States Olympic Committee sponsors and celebrating with friends and family at both the USA House and AT&T House. He made an appearance on NBC's late-night coverage, being interviewed by Jim Nantz. Just hours later as morning broke, running on adrenaline and no sleep, he was also featured live on *The Today Show* and several radio broadcasts. Jay Leno's people called. They wanted him to fly to Los Angeles. Casey still had another race coming up; he was set to compete in the 1,000 meters three days later. That wasn't quite good enough for Leno. They needed the gold medalist right after his win. Casey declined in the interest of prepping for the 1,000-meter race and never got to Leno's show. However, David Letterman's representatives also rang him up and offered to wait until after the 1,000. Casey and Jenn made plans to fly to New York the day following the race. He wound up finishing a disappointing sixth, hitting the wall the last 400 meters after establishing a world record 600 meter split time. In retrospect, he wonders if he would have been better served limiting the post-race commotion even further. Although he turned down Leno and delayed Letterman, it was still less than ideal to exchange a night of sleep for the various events and interviews he did do with only three more nights to go before his final race.

The FitzRandolph family received an honor themselves. They were the silver medalists in the Campbell's Soup "Souper Parents" promotion. Each Olympic sport was invited to nominate their most supportive parents for the contest. Campbell's would select three medal winners from the nominees to be recognized as the parents who had gone above and beyond in being a support system for their Olympian. The silver meant a great deal to Jeff and Ruthie, and it came with a $5,000 prize. Jeff would joke: "If the family only gets to win one gold and one silver, I'm very happy to settle for silver and let Casey have the gold."

Their Salt Lake experience was everything they could have ever dreamed of, even with Casey's sixth-place finish in the 1,000 meters. Casey and Jenn jetted off to New York and were whisked by limo to *Sports Illustrated*'s swimsuit edition unveiling party and then to the Letterman show. Several producers met the couple in the green room to explain the particulars of the show.

"They said 'Here are some things he might ask, but it's Dave so he could ask anything under the sun,'" said Casey, "They said it would be cold on the set. Dave likes it cold, and he doesn't want to sweat in his suit and tie." "I told them not to worry, you're talking to a guy who is used to skating around the ice in spandex."

Casey came to the show armed with gifts for Dave and musician Paul Schaffer, a native Canadian. He brought "Roots" jackets, the official look of the 2002 US Olympic team, and they all talked and joked easily about Casey's time in Canada and the Olympic drama. Sitting in the guest chair next to Dave's desk, his medal hanging proudly around his neck, Casey was able to ad lib some good quips. When Letterman asked about the Olympic committee changing the 500-meter to a two-day race, Casey said:

"I'll tell you what, it's not easy to sleep the night in between."

"Why do they do that?" asked Letterman. Without missing a beat, Casey smiled and answered, tongue in cheek, "So we don't sleep the night in between."

Letterman cracked up, his signature gap-toothed grin in full force. Later in the eight-minute conversation he inquired why Casey had chosen speedskating over any other sport he could have done, including soccer, baseball, wrestling, kickboxing, or polo.

"I almost went with polo," Casey deadpanned to more laughter from the audience.

Letterman pulled out a clap skate to show the audience. He offered a suggestion that you could use it to slice sandwiches and reinforced his point by demonstrating the clapping motion.

"Would you ever consider putting these on and going down the bobsled track?"

"That might be dangerous, but could be a lot of fun," was part of Casey's answer.

Letterman inquired if he had ever skated sick or with broken bones. Casey told the story about the broken sternum and trying to "suck it up" prior to being told it was in two pieces. The interview wrapped up with a handshake and Letterman telling Casey to say hello to everyone in Wisconsin. The music played, and the show went to commercial.

Although being interviewed by David Letterman on national television could be an intimidating experience for some, Casey found it came naturally. He had even done some pre-show visualization on the plane.

"I remember thinking how it might feel and vowing to not let anything distract me. I was doing a lot of interviews at the time, and the more you're doing, the better you are on your toes. Handling pressure, whether on the ice or on the air, is a lot more enjoyable when you are prepared."

Jenn stayed in the green room and watched the interview on TV. Casey's fifteen minutes of fame were in full bloom, and it was an exhilarating time for them. They wrapped up the movie star New York trip and returned to Wisconsin, where Casey received a standing ovation at a Milwaukee Bucks basketball game at halftime and was introduced at both Wisconsin Badger and Green Bay Packers football games. There were other perks as well: a backstage intimate conversation with James Taylor during a concert, dinner with Heidi Klum, hand shaking with presidents, and his very own Casey Fitz day in his hometown of Verona. The event started with a parade and was followed by a pep rally at the local high school, where he was awarded the key to the city. He ended up signing autographs for three hours after the event. He was invited to speak at schools. He walked into a grocery store in Madison, and the employees spontaneously erupted in applause.

He and Jenn also traveled the country a little more, making national appearances. "I was an A celebrity for about two weeks. We'd go to New York or Los Angeles and people would take us to *the* restaurant to meet the chef and be seen," he recollects, laughing.

Back in Wisconsin, fans would point at him in awe but were sometimes afraid to come up and talk. "It was like being in a fishbowl. It gave us a new appreciation for what real celebrities have to live with every single day. I can't say I'd want that life. It's a pretty heavy price to pay."

There was no depression during those few weeks of stardom, but he had many questions as the sizzle started to fade. Casey had to decide what to do next, and his first thought was an easy one: that he needed a break. After talking it over with Jenn, she agreed a year off would be a good thing. The couple moved everything back from Canada and settled in where their roots were: Wisconsin. Jenn got a job teaching in the classroom again. Casey did not have a day job but was busy with a full plate of speaking engagements. He mulled over his future and finally concluded that he wasn't finished yet. He wanted to go back and skate in one more Olympics. He would be thirty-one years old at the Torino, Italy, games. Part of him knew his chances of medaling again were slim, but another part refused to relent to that fear of failure.

In 2003, after one full year of being home in Wisconsin, Casey and Jenn packed up one more time and trucked back to Canada. It was not the same exciting and dramatic buildup he had prior to Salt Lake. He wanted another medal, but the truth was he wasn't quite able to get back to the level he had been at four years prior.

"I got back to being one of the best in the world. I won some World Cup medals, maybe even a gold, but I didn't have that extra 2 percent, that extra tenth of a second that I did in 2002," said Casey.

For the 2006 Olympics in Italy, he knew he needed to find that tenth of a second to move into medal contention in the 500m, and that meant trying just a little bit harder. He was hoping the excitement of the Olympics would help propel him. The gun went off for the first race.

"Fifty yards in, I had a significant slip. That was it—game over. The ice in Torino was not in my favor. Salt Lake had been very, very fast, and in Torino it was sticky and slower. I like to glide a little more when I set my skate down, not just chop, chop, chop, because my strokes are a little longer. Fifty yards in, it grabbed my outside edge, and I had to stand up to not fall over."

He was in nineteenth place after the first race and couldn't make it up. For the second race, Casey flew to the finish in the top five, but it wasn't enough. He wound up ninth overall.

"We were probably a little disappointed just for Casey," said Ruthie. Of course, the whole clan had made their way over to cheer him on in Italy.

"It had to be rough for him to handle, being the gold medalist. He seemed a little dejected for a while, but I wasn't disappointed. He had accomplished so much; another medal would have been icing on the cake."

The family put it in perspective. How many athletes got to compete in one Olympics, let alone three? It was a joy ride beyond compare for the entire group, and they returned to the United States feeling complete and still tingling with the thrill of it all. Photo albums filled up with pictures from Japan, the United States, and Italy. Friends and family could boast that they knew an Olympic gold medalist. Jessi and Ruthie found the transition away from the Olympics "a little boring" at first, as there were no more exotic trips to take and the spotlight was off the family. Jeff and Ruthie even drove to the Pettit Center in Milwaukee a few times to watch other skaters compete, but it wasn't the same. After decades of having their lives revolve around skates, ice, split times, and Olympics, it was time to move on. But Jeff would often find himself thinking about those Salt Lake Olympics at the most unexpected moments of the day, and he would tear up nearly every time. For years after the events in Salt Lake City, he watched a video he had made from clips of Casey's medal-winning races, interviews, and the medals ceremony so often the ladies in the house tried to confiscate it and hide it away.

"When he gets to a nursing home, we're just going to put that gold medal race on a loop," said Ruthie.

"Over and over and over and I'll be as tranquil as can be," added Jeff. "Growing up, I was a frustrated jock. My greatest athletic accomplishment was making the City of Milton Babe Ruth traveling baseball team when I was fourteen." His voice broke as he remembered. "Now your kid's the best in the world—I don't know how to explain it. It should happen to everybody. The world would be a peaceful place."

CHAPTER EIGHT

Conventional Wisdom be Damned

Summer 2010

Eight years had passed since Casey had won gold in Salt Lake City and four since Italy. The FitzRandolphs' lives had been charmed in a way hardly anyone could imagine, and they felt they were blessed. Everyone slowly found a new rhythm following the Olympics.

Things settled into a relatively stress-free routine until that day Jeff and Ruthie returned from the cabin to find their daughter waiting to talk to them in the kitchen—the afternoon when the world as they knew it was thrown into a blender while someone pushed the high-speed mix button. Now the FitzRandolphs would be tested in ways they never could have envisioned.

The first step after hearing the devastating breast cancer news was to meet with the surgeon and oncologist. Jessi and her mom went together. They wanted to find out how advanced the cancer was, and the oncologist had some great news for the vibrant thirty-three-year-old.

"I was Stage II, very curable. He gave me a 95 percent cure rate."

Stage II generally means the cancer is confined to the breast and perhaps some surrounding lymph nodes. Jessi felt relief flood through her. She was going to be okay. The surgeon recommended a mastectomy to remove the cancerous breast tissue, followed by chemotherapy and radiation. Jessi agreed. There is not a woman in the world who wants to lose her breast, but Jessi saw it as the most common-sense course of action and took it in stride.

"I was more comfortable getting everything out. I felt that the lump was pretty big, and if I just did the lumpectomy, it would leave me with a pretty deformed breast. I really didn't want that. At the time I'm thinking, 'I'm so young, and it's early stages.'"

It was only later that she would regret agreeing to have the breast removed. Later, they would all think it might have been an unnecessary, even harmful, step. But now she followed the doctor's advice and consented to have the surgery. Then she underwent the painful process of reconstructing it.

"During the original surgery, they put a tissue expander in to hold the shape of the breast. The metal device was hideous. It protruded out of my skin and was so uncomfortable. I was told I'd have that in for six months, and it ended up being a year and a half [because of what unfolded later in her health journey]. I couldn't sleep on my left side or stomach the entire time."

But she was willing to put up with the horrific process of a mastectomy because she thought she had overcome one of the major hurdles. Once the breast was gone, the cancer was gone.

Jessi was HER2 positive as well as estrogen and progesterone positive. In a healthy breast, the HER2 gene makes proteins that help normal cells grow. But in about 25 percent of breast cancers, the HER2 gene goes viral and starts producing too many cells. This protein overload makes the breast cells grow and divide uncontrollably. HER2-positive women have cancers that can be aggressive, more difficult to contain, and more likely to come back. But just two of Jessi's ten lymph nodes were positive. She started chemo just to make sure any surrounding tissue was cancer free.

Her oncologist never mentioned having a bone scan to prove the cancer hadn't spread to the bones, and the FitzRandolphs didn't think to ask for one. They put blind trust in him. Jessi did have a little back discomfort occasionally and mentioned it to him. He asked her if the pain moved around or if it was stagnant, and she said it seemed to move. He told her it was probably nothing.

She began treatments on the chemo drugs Cytoxan and Adriamycin in July of 2010. The week before, the family threw a "head shaving" party for Jessi, inviting family and friends. Everyone took a turn at removing a lock of Jessi's hair, and the mood was festive. Champagne was poured as Ruthie shaved a mohawk into her daughter's hair. Jessi, always keen on edgy fashion, liked the hairstyle so much that she put a halt to the shaving process and decided to keep the look rather than go completely bald.

In September, Jessi went to a bridal shower for her friend, Libby, who had been the first to know about the cancer. Driving to the shower, Jessi's neck was bothering her so badly she couldn't turn her head in either direction to change lanes. Her back pain had suddenly spiked to nearly unmanageable levels, too.

"I was Libby's maid of honor, and at the shower I had to lift gifts and move them. It was excruciating. Anything, any little movement, made me miserable. On a scale of one to ten, it was, oh, maybe a twelve."

She still thought she just had an achy back. She made an appointment with a chiropractor. That didn't bring any relief but fortunately did not further complicate her condition. A couple of rounds of physical therapy didn't help either. In October, she had a regular appointment with the oncologist, so she brought it up again. Jessi didn't know what was going on, but she was at a breaking point.

"I was in tears. I had been in constant pain for so long and I was very frustrated."

The warning sign finally flashed for the doctor. He ordered a bone scan. Jessi was back at the hospital, lying on a rock-hard table as the scanner slowly moved over her entire body from head to toe.

When it was done, she and her mom sat in the waiting room anticipating results that would either make things monumentally worse or send her on another path to find out why she was having pain. Ruthie played on her iPad. Jessi tried to nap. First, the radiologist came back and ordered more x-rays. There was another half an hour of waiting until those were in. After reviewing the scans, doctors said Jessi needed a bone biopsy. Ruthie, being a nurse, had a pretty good idea why.

They were forced to wait several more days, over a weekend, for the final determination after the biopsy. They tried to keep their hopes up, but it was difficult.

"It didn't sound very promising," said Jessi. "But we didn't know for sure, although we had a pretty good idea."

The oncologist finally called with the results Monday afternoon. Ruthie was in Jessi's bedroom, putting away clothes, when she answered the phone.

"He said he had some disappointing news to give me. Jessi had bone metastasis. She went from Stage II to Stage IV in the blink of an eye. After having a 95 percent chance of beating this and having no reason not to look forward to a whole long, healthy life, my world suddenly changed."

"They said, 'It's in your bones,' and I thought, 'Okay, what does that mean?'" said Jessi. "But I didn't ask, and nobody offered up any more information. More than anything, I guess I was just confused for a little while because nobody wanted to say anything. I just wanted to know my outlook. What does this mean? I want to know."

It was the worst possible scenario. The cancer had spread. There were four spots of cancer on her bones: two in her back, one in her right hip on the top of the femur, and one in a rib.

It wasn't until she went to see her oncologist two weeks later that Jessi pressed for information. It was her body and her life. The last thing she needed was someone pussyfooting around because they were afraid to hurt her feelings. She wasn't prepared for what she was about to hear.

Stage IV is usually terminal. He gave her a 50 percent chance of living five more years. Wait, what? At the age of thirty-three? She should have been given sixty more years to live, not five. Her emotions ran the gamut.

"Obviously, you're upset. You don't ever want to be told that. At the same time, I'm thinking, 'No. That's not how it's going to happen. There's no way I'm going to be dead at thirty-eight.' I thought if I kept telling myself that maybe it would come true. I didn't want to accept it, and I don't accept it. I'm just not ready to die yet. You have to try to stay as positive as you can even when it sucks. It's obviously hard some days, and it gets old. I'd give anything to have my old life back and feel normal again."

Jessi really didn't want to tell her friends of her new diagnosis. She felt as though she had enough to deal with without having to console and reassure them that she would beat this thing. Casey was another matter. He had to know. When Casey found out his sister had Stage IV breast cancer with bone metastasis, his heart went into this throat.

"You realize, holy shit, we've got a major battle on our hands. This is really not good. When you hear Stage IV you know you're in for a ride. I was really worried about it. It was an 'Oh my God' moment."

There are several types of chemotherapy used to treat breast cancer. After discovering the cancer had spread, the oncologist took her off the chemo medication she had been on and put her on Herceptin, a chemo drug developed specifically for HER2-positive patients. Jessi agreed, and after the first treatment and a dose of localized radiation, some of her back pain did start to go away.

Jessi was already living with her mom and dad, so staying with them for cancer treatments was a natural. But it wasn't easy to be an adult back at your childhood home.

"At my age, I shouldn't be living with my parents, but it is nice having them around. On days when I'm not feeling well, they can help me out. That's obviously nice. But other times it gets a little crowded. Outside of my bedroom, I don't feel like I have my own space. It seems like cancer is the only topic in the house at times, and that gets really old. You want to have those days where it's not even mentioned, and that never happens."

Yet Jessi also recognized how lucky she was to have two healthy parents there for her. If not for their incredible love and support, she says, "I would probably be dead by now."

Jeff knew being home was a mental tug-of-war on his daughter. He also deeply understood her personality, so he tried to do what he could to help without being in her face all the time.

"I'm there for her always. If she needs me for anything, I'm there in a minute. She doesn't like to be asked how she's feeling all the time, but it's absolutely brought us closer. She's a tough one. She has two personalities. She's very outgoing and sociable and fun-loving with her friends, but around the house she's very quiet and withdrawn. I have chosen not to push her. She's dealing with enough. I was thrilled she was willing to come back and live with us. It would have been ten-fold worse worrying about her from a distance."

It was during a third chemo session, about six weeks into treatment, that Jessi first felt serious doubts about what was entering her body.

"Each treatment got progressively worse. During the first one, I had only a short moment where I thought I was going to throw up. The second cycle was worse and the third almost unbearable. I felt really tired and sick to my stomach for three or four days after each."

"I'd look away as they put the IV in my arm to start the treatment. Then I'd sit back and watch the bright red substance be pumped into my system. They call it the 'Red Devil' because of its color and the nasty side effects that are associated with the drug. Just the thought of it still makes me sick today," she recalled two years later.

On some intuitive level she felt her body was telling her not to put the red liquid in anymore. The experience of chemo was so disarming that she had bad associations with it for years. She couldn't eat crushed ice because that's what they gave her during treatments to decrease the risk of mouth sores, a common side effect. She'd get ill if she even looked at the water bottles she took with her during the chemo treatments.

"If I had a fourth [cycle], I think it would have been too much for me, but luckily I didn't do that one."

Something about chemo did not feel right. She knew that all of the professionals, the people who did this for a living and who had studied at the finest medical schools in the United States, were telling her to fall in line with their other cancer patients. Hold out your hand, wait for your ration, feel awful for a while, and then hopefully get better. But to the FitzRandolphs, the system of getting sick to get better, of stripping your immune system to nothing while zapping both cancerous and healthy cells at the same time, just didn't make sense. She also didn't like the five years, 50 percent diagnosis she kept hearing.

"They gave me a timeline for how long I would live. But even if I did live only for five years, I wouldn't want to spend those five years on chemo the whole time. That's not desirable. We started doing a little research and read a lot of success stories of people who sought out alternative options."

In fact, it was Ruthie, the registered nurse who was used to dealing with elderly patients, who was staying up late every night, pillows propped behind her head, reading about different ways to attack aggressive breast cancer in young women. "I would go to bed and research the type of cancer that Jessi has, her life expectancy on chemo and radiation, and I'm thinking, 'Whoa, this is not good. There have to be other options.' So I started looking for those. I concluded that we were going down the wrong path with conventional treatments."

This mindset shift required a huge leap of faith and was a major departure from her normal character. Ruthie was used to following doctors' orders. That was a basic function of her job as a registered nurse.

"I don't usually swim against the current. I've never been one to question authority. I've never even been to a protest. It just isn't my nature."

But she knew the current prognosis for her only daughter was dismal. She was bolstered after learning about successes people were having with different forms of treatment and with enhancing their immune systems to their full potential. Ruthie told the family what she was discovering, and Jessi had no problem listening to her mother on this one.

"I trusted her opinion. She's not an oncology nurse, but she is very smart and thorough with her research. That gave me comfort."

Not that there weren't moments of conflicted feelings. Jessi was considering leaving everything American medicine recommended. She would be striking out on her own, like a hiker who veers from the trail and starts stomping through brush and knocking over tree branches with only a machete in hand.

After thinking it over though, Jessi agreed. "It scared me a little bit knowing I wasn't going to be doing the doctor-recommended protocol, except the Herceptin, which I did stay on."

She felt Herceptin was not a true chemo drug. It didn't target healthy cells or have nasty side effects. It was more of an HER2 blocker. Still, giving up everything else gave her pause.

"It made me feel like, 'Well, if this doesn't work, am I going to be worse off than before?' There's always a little hesitancy of exploring the unknown," Jessi explained.

Before they would take the plunge, the FitzRandolphs decided to seek a second opinion on their oncologist's diagnosis. A family friend, Steve Cohen, an attorney from Chicago, whose daughter Sabrina and son Aaron had been fierce competitors of the FitzRandolph children in the eighties, offered to help. Steve had a niece, Dr. Laura Esserman, who was a highly respected oncologist and professor of surgery and radiology at the Carol Franc Buck Breast Care Center at the University of California in San Francisco. Steve asked her if she would examine Jessi's medical records and offer an opinion on the diagnosis that had been handed down by Jessi's doctors. When Dr. Esserman agreed, Ruthie forwarded the records and booked a flight to San Francisco. Ruthie and Laura visited several times via cell phone prior to the trip, and the arrangements were made. After a thorough review of Jessi's records and a clinic visit, the center confirmed what Ruthie had suspected: The current treatment schedule was ineffective and should be discontinued.

Jessi and Ruthie spent a little time enjoying San Francisco after their consultations. They walked up and down the "crookedest street," jumped on the cable cars and toured the city, visited Ghirardelli's chocolate headquarters, took in Alcatraz by boat, traversed the Golden Gate bridge by bus, and visited Napa Valley, where some wine tasting was in order. They also got caught up in the sports storm of the Giants winning the World Series and wandered along the piers on the beach.

The Cohens would later lose their son, Aaron, to a tragic hit-and-run bicycling accident in Florida in February 2012. This created an even stronger bond between the two families. The FitzRandolphs felt deep gratitude to Steve Cohen and Dr. Esserman for the time and compassion they devoted to Jessi.

When mother and daughter returned to Wisconsin, Ruthie was empowered by the Center's findings and what she was reading. Fear was not in the equation for her.

"I wasn't scared at all. I had one mission, and that was for Jessi to survive this thing. What I had discovered gave me hope. It's so not in my nature at all, going against the grain, but my instincts told me to go this way. There is no doubt in my mind that alternative options would give Jessi the best chance of survival. With conventional treatment, I think we all knew what the outcome would be. Chemo makes you sick and has terrible side effects. It will really drag you down, and in the end you might live a few more months. I can't see that it's worth it."

Based on Ruthie's research, they decided to stop chemo after that third cycle so Jessi's immune system would not be totally compromised. "When we told [the oncologist] he seemed okay with it," remembered Jessi. "He was, like, 'Okay, that's fine.' He kept me on the Herceptin, which was good. That's what we wanted. He didn't necessarily agree, but at this point in time, he didn't try to fight me on it. He did tell us we were wasting our money exploring alternative protocols, though."

There are dozens of alternative treatment protocols available, covering everything from natural supplements (so named because they can't legally be called cancer drugs) to diet programs and medical devices. Hospitals and clinics around the world offered treatments not approved in the United States. Ruthie was driven to sort it all out and select the best alternative option for Jessi. Jessi followed Ruthie's lead.

"My mom was saying, 'I think this treatment could be really good,' reading different success stories. I didn't make any huge decisions. I let her tell me what she thought was best and went with that. I felt pretty comfortable with her research."

One of the first things they did was to meet with an energy healer named Andrei, who worked out of the Appleton, Wisconsin, area. He recommended she get started on the "Bob Beck protocol," an alternative approach designed by Robert C. Beck, Doctor of Science. The treatment is supposed to help the body heal itself.

The three-pronged approach utilizes a paddle which, when applied to the affected area, decreases pain; a magnetic pulsar, a small device worn on the wrist with a black strap (it resembles what a jogger with an iPod might wear) that sends magnetic electric impulses to the tumors in the hopes of zapping them; and a water ozonator, which allowed Jessi to add ozone to her drinking water because they were told cancer hates oxygen.

The family consulted world-renowned nutritionist Los Angeles's Dr. Marilyn Joyce, who helped Jessi figure out a way to detoxify her body and boost her immune system so she could kill cancer cells with her own natural defenses. She started juicing with organic vegetables, making fruit smoothies, and following the Budwig protocol by combining cottage cheese and flax oil. Ten hour-long telephone consultations with Dr. Joyce cost the family a thousand dollars, providing the first hint of how expensive it would be to fight this cancer on their own.

Jessi's daily food routine, as she described it, included "A high alkaline diet, mostly vegetables, the more raw vegetables the better, a moderate amount of fruit, very little meat, and everything has to be organic. You're supposed to do a lot of juicing." The combination of carrot, apple, beet, celery, broccoli, and red cabbage was one of her favorites.

Ruthie also read about whole-body hyperthermia, a treatment that raises the patient's body temperature above 105 degrees and then administers a lower dose of a chemo drug, Mitomycin. In theory, once you heat up your body, the cancerous cells absorb more of the drug. Limiting the chemo to target cancerous cells also spares the immune system. Furthermore, inducing a higher body temperature mimics a fever, a natural defense mechanism for human beings.

Ruthie's research had turned up only one place in America that offered hyperthermia at the time: the University of Texas Health Center in Houston. But in clinical studies, they didn't raise the body's temperature as high as another out of country option, Germany. The German treatments sounded more promising because they combined other alternative protocols with the hyperthermia, which the Texas facility did not. Ruthie was on board with what the German hospital seemed to be offering, but how do you choose a facility somewhere else in the world? She read fifteen or twenty books, consulted a website she trusted, www.cancertutor.com, and made what she calls a best guess: Fachklinik Herzog, a small hospital in the middle of Germany, an hour from Frankfurt.

The next few months would be a whirlwind for the FitzRandolphs. And Jeff, it turned out, had his own medical situation.

"I suffered a herniated disc in my back in early 2010, and when I still was having pain in October they looked at the x-rays again and said, 'We should have caught this the first time around. You've got two hips that are bone on bone.' So three months later I had bilateral hip replacement."

While he went in for surgery, Ruthie organized the first trip to Germany. She also decided to start Jessi's CarePages site, using a free web-based system for families in medical situations to update friends and relatives through blog-like posts. The first entry was actually constructed by Ruthie, ghostwriting for Jessi.

"I'm a terrible writer and I'm a private person, so those two things don't make for a good CarePages entry. I was fine as long as I didn't have to do the writing," Jessi explained. She would offer her input and approve the post but would not be the initial author.

Ruthie sat at her computer and tapped on the keys:

> *December 5, 2010*
>
> *Hi! Thanks for checking out my care page! As you may know, I have stage IV breast cancer. I was diagnosed this past July 5. I had a mastectomy with two out of ten nodes positive. I underwent three rounds of chemo with Cytoxan/ Adriamycin and during that time was found to have bone mets in four places. After having one round of IV Herceptin with a few pills of tamoxifen and a radiation therapy appointment, which I canceled, I have decided to discontinue all conventional treatment. I know my prognosis is not good with conventional treatment. With this in mind, my mom*

(an RN) and I have done a lot of reading about alternative treatments. I have a pretty good chance of a cure with alternative treatment, but unfortunately those treatments are not available in the United States.

We have narrowed the alternative hospitals down to three: One in Germany, one in Austria, and another in Tijuana, Mexico. My dad is having a fit about the possibility of us going to Tijuana with all the turmoil going on, so even though the climate is tempting, we will probably opt for another winter wonderland, especially since he is in the hospital right now with two new hips as of this past Friday and would have plenty of time to worry.

I am thirty-three years old, and I think I can beat this thing. If you have a loved one or friend fighting cancer, I will share some of the things I have learned in my next post. There is real hope, even with advanced disease.

Thank you for caring.

Jessi

While Jessi and Ruthie prepared to take off for Germany, Jessi had to start making lifestyle changes. She needed her body to be as clean and pure as could be, and that meant no more partying.

"It was hard to get used to. I used to like to go out. I probably did drink too much, and now I don't drink at all while I'm out with my friends. I miss the drinking, but I think I'd be afraid to drink anything in excess now. I still do enjoy a glass of wine once in a while," she said in 2012.

Jessi was ready to devote herself to trying anything to get more than fifty-fifty odds for five years. And she knew if she remained with the status quo, she would be ill nearly all the time just from the chemotherapy alone.

"I wouldn't have any hair. I probably would have gone through a few different chemo drugs by now because you get to a point where one stops working. Your body builds a resistance to one drug, so you move on to the next and the next, each one more toxic than the one before it. I believe I would be worse off, but who knows? Maybe I'd be one of the lucky ones and we'd find something that works. But the stakes are too high."

When she took it all into account and weighed the many pros and cons, she was ready to throw the cancer demons a curveball. It would lead her away from everything she knew in America to try something few people had heard of and even fewer had done.

"I wanted to give this alternative approach at least six months to a year to see what happened. If things got progressively worse in that time, I could fall back on traditional therapies. Knowing that was an option was somewhat comforting, but at the same time, if I have to go back to that it means alternative isn't working."

"There are a lot of success stories," explained Ruthie. "Our dentist told us about his friend, Ray, who had Stage IV throat cancer. He was chemoed out, radiated out, and told by his doctor that there was nothing else that could be done for him. On his deathbed, he went down to a clinic in Mexico for alternative treatments. Eighteen years later there is no evidence of any cancer."

Ruthie went into her computer room again to give friends and family an update just one week after the first:

December 12, 2010

Hi! Ruthie here. We have selected a small hospital in Germany, but after a few discharges failed to materialize, Jessi's admission has been pushed back, and she is now on a waiting list. If all goes well, we will be there by Christmas. It is difficult to wait.

Jessi has not had any conventional treatment for about six weeks, which is a little scary, especially since she has the most aggressive type of breast cancer. She does seem to be very stable with just her home therapies. She is currently using the Bob Beck protocol. Jessi also juices organic vegetables daily, has a miserable-tasting shake of cottage cheese and flax oil every morning, and follows an alkaline diet. She also does yoga and has been seeing an energy healer, Andrei, who has been a great source of inner strength.

As Jessi promised in her last post, there are two books that have been very helpful to us in our pursuit of alternative treatments. One is Cancer, Step outside the Box *by Ty*

Bollinger. The other is Bill Henderson's Cancer-Free, Your Guide to Gentle, Nontoxic Healing. Both are excellent resources for alternative treatments. Once we have our arrangements finalized, we will share with you exactly what Jessi's treatment will consist of as well as the hospital where it will take place.

Thank you for caring.
Ruthie

They knew none of this would be covered by insurance, and they didn't care. Jessi and Ruthie packed for Germany, where they would spend Christmas of 2010 and usher in 2011.

CHAPTER NINE

The German Connection

December 2010

The Delta Airbus 330-300 touched down at Frankfurt International Airport at exactly 12:07 p.m. on Thursday, December 23, 2010. A driver from the Fachklinik met Ruthie and Jessi in the baggage claim area. It only took about ten minutes on the autobahn for Ruthie and Jessi to remember that the word "Ausfahrt" wasn't some vulgar German slang term but instead translated to "Exit" in English. They passed a half dozen such signs before their driver took one and proceeded down narrow, winding two-lane highways for the last fifteen minutes of their trip to Bad Salzhausen, where Fachklinik, their home for the next three weeks, was located.

There are many towns in Germany with names beginning in "Bad"; they had passed a couple of them on the way to their destination. So once they were settled, one of the first questions they wanted answered was, "What does 'Bad' mean?" They were surprised by the answer, but as their stay wore on, it became quite clear why the town had been named Bad Salzhausen.

Simply put, "Bad" translates to "bath"—but a very special bath indeed. In the nineteenth century, "taking the waters" was a highly recognized medical treatment for European citizens. Small German towns sprung up around hot springs containing various mineral salts and became tourist attractions. The Germans bathed in the hot springs, drank the mineral water from natural springs, and built parks around strange-looking buildings that contained a wall of twigs and branches from trees nourished by the local springs. Water from a nearby creek would be raised using a series of water wheels to the top of the wall. The water would drain down the wall, and as it evaporated on its descent, it would shower those who sat on nearby benches with a fine mist of natural mineral salts. When breathed in, these salts were believed to relieve respiratory problems.

Vacationers with health problems came from far and near, hotels sprang up in the towns to accommodate guests, and the park became the focal point. The parks frequently contained not only the springs and "water wall" but also fountains, a theater, restaurants, and a band shell for daily concerts. Jeff and Jessi would experience one of those afternoon concerts on a beautiful spring day on a later visit.

During the week, you could throw a stone the length of the main street in Bad Salzhausen and touch no one, but on weekends the street was packed with cars, and the park came alive with visitors. Most were not there for the healing benefits of the springs. Instead, the park was still a source of relaxation and family time.

The hospital itself was tiny by American standards; it looked like a very large house or compact apartment complex, and the front was painted a salmon-pink color. Enter the main door and you would find a reception desk greeting you. The rest of the first floor consisted of administrative offices and treatment rooms. The hyperthermia area was located here. The second floor housed a dining room, kitchen, and smaller treatment rooms; the third floor contained the patient lounge with a huge aquarium, a small TV and computer room, a chapel, and half a dozen patient rooms. The fourth floor housed a half dozen patient rooms, and the floor's fitness center and massage area were always busy. Floor five was exclusively patients' rooms, which were typically twelve feet wide and eighteen feet long. The room included a closet, two single beds, a sink, and a small table. The sixteen-inch TV was mounted above the closet. A bathroom, large enough to only accommodate one person at a time, held a toilet and shower.

It was quite a difference from the modern, gleaming hospitals of America. Although the place was clean and the staff friendly, the FitzRandolphs' initial impression was that, although it resembled a house, it didn't feel very homey. The walls were mostly bare and the furniture basic. The television had just one English channel: CNN International. Jessi had never been interested in watching that much news before; now, it was the only option. From this tiny room, the FitzRandolphs would, on successive visits over the next year, observe as Arizona congresswoman Gabrielle Giffords and nineteen others were shot in Arizona and Osama bin Laden was killed in Pakistan. But at this point, they were just arriving. They unpacked, and Ruthie updated anxious family and friends across the Atlantic Ocean almost immediately:

December 23, 2010
12:52 p.m.

The patient rooms are simple, small and stark, but we expected that, having been to Germany in the past to watch Casey skate. After a brief cry, we pulled ourselves together and are now in good spirits. Fighting for your life far away from family and friends isn't the warm-cozy that Christmas was meant to be.

The hospital is full, even over the holidays. Most of the clients are from the United States with others from Australia, England, Japan, and the Middle East. Clearly, some people are here because they have exhausted all other options. Some are painfully thin. Others, like Jessi, appear perfectly healthy. We are surprised by the number of younger folks. There are quite a few families with young children, mostly tagging along. We did meet a man whose six-year-old child is being treated for a rare type of lymphoma that they have been battling since he was four.

Jessi already had a local hyperthermia treatment and an IV infusion of large doses of vitamins C and B to boost her immune system. Tomorrow is another full day. Everyone here has been very warm and welcoming.

Jessi and I do want to extend a huge thanks to Bowen Best, Libby and Rob Cichy, and Justin Dorow as well as Casey and Jenn Fitz for organizing a fundraiser to help cover Jessi's expenses.

A word of warning, if you plan to travel, be careful of airport security. Jeff had apparently used my carry-on bag prior to me for a hunting trip. After going through four airports, including an international checkpoint, I discovered a shotgun shell in the bottom of my bag when unpacking at the hospital. I could be sitting in jail …

Happy Holidays!

Thank you for caring,
Ruthie

The next night was December 24, and the hospital organized a van to take families to a church for Christmas Eve services. Jessi and Ruthie initially decided to try it, thinking they could use all of the spiritual support they could get. As they waited for the ride, it suddenly occurred to them that listening to a full service in German might not be as fulfilling as they had hoped. They couldn't speak or understand much of the language, so they changed their minds and went back up to the room. Plus, Jessi had a load of treatments scheduled in the coming days. They settled into the hospital and started meeting other patients, many of whom had success stories to tell.

"I figured that was going to be us too," Ruthie felt. Jessi started tests and treatments the next morning.

The park near the hospital was filled with tulips and a well that held the mineral water the hospital encouraged patients to drink daily. Jessi would draw the water with a dipper supplied at the well and fill her water bottle as often as possible. Doctors at the clinic believed it was the cleanest and most purifying water you could find and encouraged patients to use it as much as possible. The ingredients were listed on the wall of the gazebo that housed the well, but in German. Ruthie and Jessi had to put blind trust in the doctors on this matter, just as they would for many others things. They agreed to drink it when they could.

The nearest city was Nidda, approximately two miles away. Jessi and Ruthie would walk there and check out the few quaint shops when Jessi was feeling up to it.

Ruthie wrote another CarePages note a few days later:

December 26, 2010
2:28 p.m.

Hello again from Germany! We hope that you had a very Merry Christmas! Things are going well here. Jessi had ultrasounds of her liver, kidneys, pancreas, and nodes in her neck, underarm areas, groin, and chest, especially checking the nodes in the area of the bone mets in the upper leg. She also had a battery of labs and an EKG as well as pulmonary function studies. Everything was negative, except we do not have the lab results yet. I am particularly interested in learning the tumor marker numbers. She had that done in Madison, so we will be able to make a comparison. Jessi didn't have any of these things checked at home other than some blood tests.

Jessi has had local hyperthermia daily except today. Sunday is mostly a day of rest. She had magnetic treatment the other day. She has had infusions daily. Some of the nurses don't speak much English, and of course we speak no German, so at times we do not know what is being infused. She did have an infusion of Zometa, a bone-building medication that she received once at home. She also had foot reflexology done.

This next week, Jessi's treatments start at 7:30 a.m. No more slacking! My next task is to do laundry. I will actually put my dirty clothes and soap in the washer next time, not the dryer. ☺

I'll be back soon, now that our electronic devices are charged. That's another story.

Thank you for caring,
Ruthie

Ruthie and Jessi were getting used to the rhythms of their strange new home. They watched CNN nonstop and read a pile of books they had brought. There was only one problem with the reading material: Jeff had suggested that Jessi read a Stephen King novel to keep her mind occupied. Instead, it produced nightmares.

"Everyone was trapped in this dome, and they couldn't get out. There was no air coming in, so everyone was dying. Literally, maybe five people in this town survived," Jessi remembered. She did her best to forget Stephen King and instead played games on her iPod and checked Facebook. She kept tabs on friends who posted about work, their love lives, and the parties they were going to that weekend while she sat in a foreign hospital room awaiting her next treatment. Why was life so unfair? Jessi shook her head to clear out those thoughts and looked out the window at the landscape. She tried to gather all of her strength and focus it on getting better.

After a week, they were almost ready for the big blast of whole-body hyperthermia that Ruthie had first read about. On December 27, she posted some exciting news with the headline

"A Good Day!"

> *December 27, 2010*
> *2:04 p.m.*
> *Hi all—We had a great day today. Jessi started the day bright and early with local hyperthermia to the affected upper leg and magnetic therapy. The highlight of the day was, without a doubt, when Dr. Herzog came into our room for morning rounds. He said Jessi has a 70 percent chance of beating this thing. Jessi had the biggest grin on her face. Actually, she still does.*
>
> *Tomorrow is the big day: whole-body hyperthermia with chemo. They will heat Jessi's body temperature up to about 107 degrees F for a couple hours and give low-dose chemo during that time. The malignant cells are much more susceptible to the chemo than healthy cells when heated. This will only be done once during our twenty-four-day stay. The side effects are few and brief. They will sedate Jessi so she is not aware of what is going on. Her head will be outside of the heated field with ice packs. It is a very safe procedure, although it might sound unsettling. She is being prepped tonight with IV fluids, which will continue, I believe, through tomorrow. A patient generally loses eleven pounds of water weight with this procedure, so hydration is critical.*

And if that isn't enough good news, we were not only able to wash a load of laundry, using the washer for the dirty clothes, not the dryer, but we also successfully placed a phone call home to Jeff via a SIM card from a phone we had from the Olympics in Italy. See, it pays to be a bit of a packrat.

Thank you for your support and prayers. We LOVE getting your messages. You help keep us going.

Thanks for caring,
Ruthie

The hyperthermia day arrived, and it went as smoothly as they could have hoped. Jessi remembered nothing. Ruthie had a long wait and kept walking by the room Jessi was in, but she wasn't stressed.

"I never felt it was a terribly dangerous procedure. She's young and healthy, and I couldn't see any reason why she wouldn't come through it doing real well." Indeed, Jessi sailed through:

December 29, 2010
12:47 p.m.

Hello friends and family—Another good day here in Germany. Jessi has totally recovered from the rigors of yesterday's whole-body hyperthermia treatment. After an afternoon snooze, she hit the treadmill for thirty minutes. On rounds this morning, I inquired about Jessi's recent tumor markers (done here by a blood draw). Dr. Herzog showed me the results, which read negative, i.e., it is unlikely that there is any active cancer going on at this time. I must honestly say that this may have been due in part to her prior treatments, which include conventional chemo, as well as a host of homeopathic treatments that we did on our own (Bob Beck protocol, alkaline diet, juicing organic veggies several times a day, drinking a gallon of ozonated water per day, a yucky cottage cheese and flaxseed oil mixture, yoga, energy healing, etc.). Coming into this hospital for multiple alternative therapies, I am very hopeful that the remainder of those nasty little cancer cells will wilt and die, as Casey put it. Jessi did not have normal tumor markers at her last check at home approximately six or eight weeks ago, and her prognosis at that time was quite dismal. So something is definitely working, and we are more optimistic than ever.

Today Jessi received local hyperthermia to the breast, magnetic treatment, and an ozone infusion where they remove some of her blood, ozonate it, and then replace it. She also had a thymus injection (I have yet to research that) and an infusion for liver cleansing. They treat a patient from many different angles.

Jessi and I are so grateful for your support, love, messages, and prayers. God bless you.

Ruthie

The New Year approached, and Jessi and Ruthie rang in 2011 with a glass of champagne and a movie, *The Secret*. The documentary-style movie teaches the power of the mind: if you think it will happen, it will. If you visualize it over and over, you can make it a reality. Jessi and Ruthie focused their minds on good health and vitality as they snuggled together on the twin-sized bed on December 31, 2010.

There was something immediate to look forward to. Jessi's good friend from Madison, Justin Dorow, was coming over for a week to kick off 2011. Jessi was eagerly anticipating his visit and, as it turns out, she was feeling well enough to do a little sightseeing. A post from Ruthie and Jessi combined told of a funny incident:

January 9, 2011
2:03 p.m.
Tuesday we visited Giessen, a little town a half hour from here. We did a little shopping and had pizza at a local pub. It felt really good to get out. However, we did manage to get our rental car stuck in the parking ramp. How were we supposed to know that the ramp locked its doors at eight p.m., whether you have your car out or not? With a little help from the waiter at the pub and security, we were able to retrieve our car for a mere forty Euros. Needless to say, we learned our

lesson and were more astute with the parking. We also went to Frankfurt later in the week and did some sightseeing. It was great having Justin here. It really made my second week fly by.

Jessi and Ruthie

After Justin returned to America, the FitzRandolphs had a few more weeks to go. Ruthie logged on again to describe the German hospital in a little more detail:

January 11, 2011
11:39 a.m.

The doctors and nurses give one quick tap on our door and then enter before waiting for a response from inside that door. Surprise! They also don't believe in draping the patient for exams or treatments. It's kind of a let-it-all-hang-out type of thing. All doctors and nurses are dressed completely in white (my workplace, Stoughton Hospital, would appreciate that)—very professional.

The food has been interesting as well. Some dishes are recognizable and others not. We have had wild boar, duck, lots of salmon, watercress salad, and radish salad, to name a few. The turkey for lunch today was not recognizable, but the veggie lasagna was divine. We have figured out what cheese comes from cows and what comes from goats. We both have come to love the fruit, especially what we think is dragon fruit. Inside of the red peeling is what looks like a mass of poppy seeds in some white substance—very yummy. There's also a fruit that we call porcupine balls (don't ask) that is spiny on the outside and with the texture of an eyeball with a pit on the inside. It's very good but tricky to eat.

We had a great day today. Jessi's treatments were done by early afternoon, so we walked to Nidda, the closest town, about a forty-minute walk each way. It reminded us both of the Crookedest Street that we walked in San Francisco. It is very steep and windy/curvy on one side of the hill. We were thankful that the last leg coming home was downhill. So we

*are both contently exhausted and entertaining ourselves on
our computers.*

Ruthie

Jessi and Ruthie would spend twenty-four days in the German hospital, with Jessi drinking the well water and getting treatments almost daily. In mid-January, her stay was finally over, and Ruthie and Jessi returned home feeling exhilarated. Ruthie couldn't contain their excitement about meeting so many people who seemed to be turning cancer on its head:

> *January 22, 2011*
> *10:35 a.m.*
> *The evening prior to our departure from Germany for visit number one, we were joined at our dinner table by a lovely couple from Toronto. This gentleman, a multimillionaire, has pancreatic cancer with metastases to the liver as well as golf ball–sized lesions in his lungs. His MD in Toronto told him there was nothing more they could do. So they pursued a second opinion at Mayo Clinic, which was the same as the first: "Go home and have your pain controlled." After that was a visit to a well-known hospital in Mexico. While they were pleased with that stay, it was not what they were looking for. The next stop was "our hospital" in Germany. He has been treated there now for about six months. He no longer has liver or lung lesions and works out in the gym. One would never know he had been knocking on death's door.*

Back at home, Jessi went in for a follow-up test to see if any of her treatments were making a difference. It seemed they were. They were all cautiously ecstatic. Ruthie's update:

> *Jessi's femur x-ray Thursday showed a "halo" around the lesion, which indicates a healing process. While I would have preferred complete obliteration, that is not a reasonable expectation at this point. Jessi did see her conventional oncologist Thursday and will continue on Herceptin, a treatment that*

both [German and American] oncologists endorse. Our hope is
that with both conventional and alternative treatments, Jessi
will have a remission that lasts into old age.

Jessi would be home less than a week. There had been a misunderstanding with the German hospital; something they said was "lost in translation." The FitzRandolphs thought she would only need to be there for that one long visit, when in reality the doctors had told her she would need to return for five more visits of ten days each. It was decided this time that Jeff would go with her, and he put his first post on CarePages on January 23, the morning of their departure:

January 23, 2011
11:20 a.m.
    I overslept today and as a result have been racing around
the house trying to remember all of the things I need for this
trip. That's right, I'm packing this morning for our 1:50 p.m.
departure today—no need to plan too far ahead. You always
forget something regardless of how well you plan.
    Jessi seems in great spirits this morning. I know it's with
mixed emotions that she will board the plane today. It's hard
for me to imagine what goes through her mind at times like
this. All I know is that since she returned from the first trip
to Germany she is a totally different person. She seems much
more at ease with herself, who she is, and what she is facing.
She is much more open to discussions about most any subject,
and I've really enjoyed visiting with her since she got home.
I see her self-confidence growing every day. My conversations
with her lead me to believe that she has a quiet confidence
that the alternative treatments we have sought out will help
her put this cancer in remission at the very least.
    I am very excited about joining her on this trip. I see a
little sadness in Ruthie's eyes this morning as she busies herself
helping us pack. She has mentioned to me more than once that
she wishes she was joining us. The stark reality of the situation
is that without her income we simply would fall deeper in debt.

This is our second visit and will last ten days. After this treatment session, there are four more remaining. Time will tell if just maybe the three of us will be able to travel together for one of the sessions. For now, we know that alternating the visits is the best alternative.

Once we get settled at the hospital in Germany, we'll send along another post. In the meantime ... Go Pack!

And as always, thanks for your support and continued prayers. We feel the strength you are generating.

Best,
Jeff

This was all happening as the football team the FitzRandolphs adored, the Green Bay Packers, were making a push in the playoffs for the 2011 Super Bowl. The NFC Championship game against the Chicago Bears took place while they were traveling. The winner would advance to the Super Bowl in Dallas. Jeff's update from January 24:

January 24, 2011
1:40 p.m.
We made it safe and sound and without any hassles ... well, almost. The driver from the clinic was an hour late in picking us up, but we were so darn happy about the Packers we really didn't mind waiting.

We actually arrived in Detroit in time to see the last four minutes of the first half. Then we found a little sports bar in the airport and were able to watch the entire second half ... wow! The Pack is Super Bowl bound! Thank goodness we return home in time to see it.

Our room is nice ... and cozy. You know how you shared a bedroom with your brother or sister when you were young, and because of the space available between the two beds you had to take turns getting up? Tonight might just be our first pillow fight.

They don't waste any time over here. We arrived at Fachklinik around 11:30 a.m. (4:30 a.m. our time) and were registered immediately. Jessi was then visited by Dr. Herzog at 11:45. We then grabbed a bite to eat, and she was off to therapy for a local hyperthermia to her hip plus an oxygen treatment, followed by an IV full of vitamins. Tomorrow she will receive the full-body hyperthermia treatment.

While she was being treated, I walked to the little store down the road, hoping to buy a USA Today and read about the game. There it was: Monday's paper. I picked it up, and the lead story on the front page (not just sports) was about the Packers-Bears rivalry. Then printed in parentheses under the headline was, "This article was written prior to game time." Oh well, I'm hoping to pick up a Tuesday paper tomorrow and get all the details.

We just finished dinner, a virtual potpourri of exotic dishes that neither Jessi nor I had ever seen or tasted before. Every meal is an adventure over here. I'm penning this epistle at 7:24 p.m., and it's not going to be very long before we have lights out tonight. Tonight we will pray for sweet dreams and a sunny day for tomorrow to keep our spirits sky high.

Stay tuned for more from Germany in the days ahead. No one is quite sure where this little father/daughter adventure will lead us. One thing is for sure: you can count on a few surprises as the week progresses.

God Bless,

Jeff

As Jessi continued her daily treatments, some taking up large chunks of time, Jeff began exploring the hospital and learning more about the success rate of their patients. He also had moments of intense emotion towards his daughter, both of which were reflected in his next post on January 26.

January 26, 2011
11:43 a.m.
The two wall charts I studied in the hall next to our room yesterday seem to confirm [that these treatments work]. From test studies performed in 2004 for both breast and prostate

cancer patients, the results are rather exceptional. While the treatments for each kind of cancer vary slightly and the control groups used for each were considerably older than Jessi, the results in the majority of the test groups showed reduced or eliminated tumors, a reduction in pain, and increased mobility. The illustration of before and after bone scans on the breast cancer study shows nearly an identical tumor (first scan) to Jessi's on the hip of a patient that completely disappears (second scan) after six months of treatment. Obviously, that is the very reason we have come to this clinic.

5:35 p.m.

Jessi is resting comfortably beside me in bed as I write this. She is very groggy but coherent. It's a scene that no one but family will ever see. As peaceful as she looks, there's a hurt in my heart that she has to go through this. I think as a parent you always ask yourself, "Why not me?" And I know both Ruthie and I would gladly trade places with her right now. At a time like this it takes all the courage a father can muster to convince himself that she is going to beat this thing.

We continue to need your support. Please say a prayer for Jessi this evening before you go to bed. I know God is listening and through his power will channel the strength from those prayers directly to Jessi as she sleeps tonight.

Today I've met two people, a woman from Australia and a gentleman from Zimbabwe. The patient from Zimbabwe was very open and candid about his treatments, which he says have been very successful. I didn't get many details, but the gleam in his eyes and smile on his face spoke volumes. I know with your blessing that Jessi will wake tomorrow morning with a gleam in her eyes and a smile on her face.

God bless you all,

Jeff

Jeff had several meaningful moments with Jessi, including the day they walked to Nidda, despite Jeff's recent hip surgery:

> *January 27, 2011*
> *5:04 p.m.*
>
> *Okay, my tail is dragging. We just got back from Nidda. We're on the third floor here, and the cafeteria is on second floor. I usually take the stairs because it's good for my hips, but tonight I'm using the elevator. Next time we go to Nidda, we're going to have the driver take us.*
>
> *As exhausted as I am, the trip was worth every huff and puff. Jessi opened up like she rarely does with me. We actually had several great exchanges that shall remain our secret, but the smile I got was worth every ounce of energy I expended on the trip.*
>
> *Please keep the prayers coming. You all obviously outdid yourselves last evening because today was a great day here in Germany.*
>
> *Auvetasain (how close am I?),*
> *Jeff*

Jessi also felt the kinship with her father, something she had never experienced in this way before.

"I maybe let my guard down a little bit more in Germany," she admitted. "I definitely got closer with my dad. It's hard not to, though, when you're spending that much time with someone."

Jessi received treatments every day, sometimes local hyperthermia and, once during each visit, whole-body hyperthemia. She was infused with vitamins and immune-boosting supplements. She received massages. The buffet-style meals were hearty. Each meal consisted of three courses and was prepared with natural ingredients. Most patients had already tried other chemotherapy and radiation, and their bodies were run down with the usual weight loss and fatigue that accompanies those treatments. The building of body fat was seen as a way to improve the immune system and build back some strength and stamina as well as allow the patients to tolerate the somewhat vigorous treatment program selected for them at Fachklinik.

When she wasn't in treatment, there was plenty of time for togetherness. Jeff and Jessi continued to meet other patients. Meanwhile, back home, a huge snowstorm had paralyzed the Midwest. Jeff wrote about all of it:

> *February 1, 2011*
> *12:16 p.m.*
>   *Is it the end of the world back in Wisconsin? When CNN spends nearly as much time on the winter storm that is sweeping through thirty states in the United States as they do on Egypt, I must admit they got my attention.*
>   *It was a great day here in Bad Salzhausen. Jessi had the busiest day she's had since her WBH [whole body hyperthermia] last week. She started today with a local hyperthermia on her hip with low-dose chemo and then was off to a magnetic treatment, followed by two IVs of who knows what. I'm betting they were vitamins and something else that showed up on the bill I received from the pharmacy today. Holy cow, I didn't know you could put that many medicinal fluids in a person in ten days.*
>   *Then came the best surprise of the day. She was off for a half-hour foot massage, and the masseuse (who just happens to be a twenty-three-year-old guy, 5'8" blond, with great hands) just happened to have an hour instead of half an hour. Hmmm, far be it for Jessi to not take advantage of that.*
>   *This afternoon we made our daily trek to the park for a drink of our favorite water. I wish I could say we wore lightweight jackets and basked in the warmth of the sun, but that would be a lie. Today I finally got Jessi to admit that the weather is considerably colder in Germany in late January than it is in late December, which is probably why Ruthie let me make this trip.*
>   *We have dinner at six p.m. this evening. We are usually the first in the dining room. I guess most Europeans and people from Australia, Zimbabwe, Canada, and Japan dine later than we do. I will remain at the dinner table for some time this evening saying good-bye to many people who have in their own way become very good friends in a very short period of time.*

Charlie, Arthur and Sue, Gary, Dina, and many others have touched my heart while we have been here. Each suffers in their own private little hell, and yet if you spend time with them you meet a person capable of looking death in the eye and saying, "Nope, not me buddy. It's not my time yet. Don't waste your time around here. Please look elsewhere. I have a lot of living to do yet."

For all the illness that is housed within the walls of Fachklinik, you would be hard pressed to find a more positive community of people. The people come and go, some staying ten days, some remaining three weeks, and others never knowing if they will go home but always believing. They tell their stories, which beg for understanding and support, and then they listen as you tell your story. They are an incredibly strong bunch, brought together by chance and research. All are here because they were offered no hope at home.

They are not willing to settle for the prognosis that conventional doctors and wisdom regarding cancer treatment offered. They are survivors who will stop at nothing. As much as most believe in a greater power, it is simply not their time to be called. All believe that the treatments they receive here will prolong their lives, and for most it will.

Count Jessi among the survivors, and say a prayer for her tonight.

God bless you all.

Hope to see most or all of you in March.

Jeff

Jeff and Jessi had an inspiring time together and finally flew back home to Verona on February 4. Jessi felt compelled to write her first CarePages post in a while, again with a little help from her mom:

February 4, 2011
1:46 p.m.
Hello all! Well, we made it home and basically on time despite all the snow. We had a little delay getting out

of Detroit, but all around it was a very uneventful trip. We were, however, the first flight that was able to land in Madison on Wednesday. I'd like to think they opened up the airport just for us. ;)

Trip #2 went off without a hitch. Ten days felt like an absolute breeze compared to three weeks. Now I'm home for two weeks, then my mom and I go back again for another ten days. The timing works out perfectly, as we will get home two days before the first fundraiser at Scatz. The gang here at home has been hard at work, and I am so looking forward to an awesome evening!

I'm very excited to be home, though, and can't wait to spend some time with family and friends. We even get to celebrate Christmas, finally!

I can't even begin to say how grateful I am to everyone who has taken part in my journey. Your thoughts, prayers, strength, and encouragement get me through every day. I am so lucky to have such wonderful, caring people in my life.

Mom and Dad, thank you and I love you! I am truly blessed to have you as my parents.

One last thing: Go Pack!

Jessi

Two days later the Green Bay Packers played in Super Bowl XLV against the Pittsburgh Steelers. The *Wisconsin State Journal* featured not only pages and pages of game preview coverage but also a story on Jessi and the experimental treatments she was trying. The headline was "Verona Woman Experiments for Her Life." The FitzRandolphs wanted to share their story with the world. They had always had good fortune dealing with the media during Casey's skating days, and they were thrilled with the way David Wahlberg, the newspaper's medical writer, presented their family's story to his readers.

Later that evening, they were joined by Casey, Jenn, Sawyer, and Cassidy along with Jessi's Aunt Nancy and her friend Andy. They settled in to watch the Packers win the Super Bowl at home together. They cheered, high fived, and celebrated as a family. Late in the game, Aunt Nancy commented to all in attendance that she couldn't believe how laid back and calm Jeff was. His usual MO for athletic events was to get emotionally involved, very vocal, and pretty wound up. Little did anyone know that the thrill of his son's gold medal performance and the strain of his daughter's situation had rendered football a mere afterthought for him in the overall scheme of life. Oblivious to the change in her dad, Jessi thrived on the normalcy of it all and was thrilled just to be back in her own bed.

But within a few weeks Jessi was on her way back to Germany and the treatments, again with Ruthie, who wrote an update about the trip right away:

> *February 22, 2011*
> *9:45 a.m.*
> *Hi! We arrived at Fachklinik in Germany Sunday after being delayed in Detroit for a couple hours. We had been told there were no double rooms available at the hospital—it's a full house—but they agreed to put a cot in the room for me so we could stay together. This is what we did on our first trip too. Not a problem. When we arrived at our room, Jessi gasped and smiled as she entered ahead of me. I thought, great! They gave us a family suite! Wrong. The room we were about to share was seriously the size of our master bath at home, if that. And we had a perpetually flushing toilet.*
> *Our driver had indicated that he took some folks to the airport earlier in the day, so that evening I got on my computer and e-mailed the hospital (I didn't want to risk oversleeping and missing my window of opportunity) and asked about this potentially vacant room. We now have a very nice double room. I feel like I'm at the Ritz.*
> *We are on the fourth floor, so I'm working out the legs a little. There are elevators, but it would be shameful for able-bodied people like us to be seen using them. The elevators are very European, i.e., tiny. We were greeted within ten minutes of our arrival by a very cute young guy with two trays of food. The meat was excellent, although we didn't know what it was*

until we read "rabbit" on the menu later. My last bunny feast had to do with Casey as an eight-year-old and a slingshot …

Jessi started with tests and treatments shortly after we arrived. She is having her whole-body hyperthermia as I write. The line after WBH is always, "How hot did you get?" That is a common subject around the hospital. One of the docs stopped by last night and indicated he wanted to try to get Jessi's temp a little higher this time. She left the room at seven thirty this morning and has not yet returned, eight hours later. I'll keep you posted.

Thanks once again for your prayers and support, and thank you for caring.

Ruthie

Addendum: Jessi just got back after 8+ hours. Her temp got to 105.6. Her pulse ox is a little low, so she's on oxygen, I'm sure from the anesthesia they gave her. She is very groggy. She also continues to get fluids, as this procedure is quite dehydrating, as one can imagine. All is well.

Back in Wisconsin, Jeff and some of Jessi's closest friends were organizing two giant fundraisers to be held in early March when Jessi returned from her latest trip. The first "Fighting4Fitz" event was set for Scatz nightclub featuring three local bands and a silent auction. The evening would conclude with a performance by Piano Fondue, a local dueling piano group. The second fundraiser was set for Wildcat Lanes, where over a hundred teams of bowlers signed up to knock down some pins and raise money for Jessi's treatments in Germany. In addition to this support, Jeff was touched by the incredible outpouring of virtual love the family was feeling on CarePages. He posted about it while his wife and daughter were overseas:

February 23, 2011
3:37 p.m.
To date we've had over three hundred different people visit the site an amazing 3,019 times. Jessi has also received over three hundred messages from people showing support.

Some people have visited the site as many as fifty times. Truly amazing!

Last evening, we had our final committee meeting before the events, and to say that the support we have received from the entire Madison area and surrounding communities is mind-boggling is an understatement. It is hard to put into words what the support we are experiencing means to our family. I guess it's best said that your love, prayers, generosity, and support are priceless.

Hope to see you at one of our events.

Godspeed,

Jeff

The Fighting4Fitz fundraisers turned into a wholehearted, monumental success, raising more than $75,000. When setting the original goal, they had hoped for $20,000. The logistics were spearheaded mainly by Jessi's friend Bowen Best. Jessi and Ruthie combined to post about it:

March 20, 2011

1:05 p.m.

With close to 500 people at Scatz on Thursday and nearly 1,000 at Wildcat lanes, needless to say the support was overwhelming. I know everyone on the committee that worked so hard to put this together for me was amazed at the turnout too. I will never be able to appropriately thank all of you who participated in my events, but I promise you that as soon as I beat this cancer, I'll start trying.

We raised considerably more money than we anticipated we would, in fact we blew away our original guesstimate that we could raise $20,000. None of this would have been possible without some great friends stepping forward with the idea and Bowen taking charge of the planning. I think I'll be buying Bowen Miller Lite for quite some time, but not out of the proceeds, as promised, every penny we raised is going to pay for my medical expenses. We won't be able to cover them all, but I can tell from the looks of relief and lack *of tension around the house that my parents are very happy with the results.*

Jessi

After Jessi and Ruthie's latest joint trip, Jessi was due to go back for another round of 10 day treatments. This time, she decided to travel to Germany by herself. Although her parents were a little wary, she was confident she could handle it and she looked forward to being on her own. Mid-way through her stay she wrote her one and only update from that visit:

March 29, 2011
11:07 a.m.
   Spring is here in Bad Salzhausen. The weather is beautiful right now; it makes me want to stay a bit longer. Well, not really, but I sure hope to bring the warmth back with me.
   The last week has been uneventful. I had my WBH last Wednesday and will get my second round of chemo tomorrow during local hyperthermia. I had all of the routine tests again, and they came back same as always. My blood counts are a bit low, but that's to be expected with the chemo.
   The time here by myself has been nice. It feels a bit quiet at times, but the clinic is pretty busy, so there's always someone to talk to. Besides getting treatment I've spent a lot of time sitting on the patio soaking up the sun and reading or walking down to the springs to get my daily ration of lithium water. My freckles have made an early appearance this year. ;)
   Tomorrow is my last day, and then I leave for the airport around 6:45 Thursday morning. As nice as the weather is, I am ready to be home. I always look forward to getting back to a somewhat normal life. I think a trip to the Kalahari [waterpark in Wisconsin Dells] is in the near future for my mom and me, so I'm pretty excited about that! Not to

mention that after this trip I only have two more to go. Now that's something to celebrate!

Thanks for your continued support.

Jessi

That was the only post for the next six weeks, until April 26. Without her parents there, Jessi wasn't inclined to write much. When Jeff returned with her three weeks later for their fourth of six stays, he picked up the tale of their adventures in great detail:

April 26, 2011
5:43 a.m.

Shortly after we arrived, we put on our flip-flops and short-sleeved tees and walked through the park in town to our favorite "watering hole," the famous mineral water of Bad Salzhausen. It tastes just as awful as I remember it. But in an insane sort of way, I must admit that shortly after drinking a cup, I feel as though I have done something very healthy for myself.

I can only hope Jessi feels the same way. We have decided to visit our favorite watering hole at least twice a day during our visit this trip, just because it is so beautiful here.

I must admit, this part of the world presents quite a conundrum for a simple boy from Wisconsin, where each season is clearly defined and the plants that bloom from spring through summer seem to have a very definite pecking order. Here it is quite different. In our travels today, we were treated to equal doses of daffodils, tulips, dandelions, apple blossoms, ferns, and lilacs. The deciduous trees are in their June green splendor, and miniature daisies cover the ground like grass. Each flower is less than half an inch in diameter.

Just before dinner this evening, Jessi enjoyed a pilsner, and I sipped a glass of rogue [a red German wine] while basking in the sun at one of Bad Salzhausen's main street's outdoor bier gardens. The temperature flirted with seventy degrees, and a mild breeze generated sufficient velocity to make the flags across the street and leaves on the trees dance as though inspired by a higher power. Forgive me for waxing poetic, but one couldn't help but believe that new life was in the air and in the beautiful young lady keeping me company.

   It's great to be in Bad Salzhausen again with my daughter.

Jeff

On this trip, Jeff had opted to stay in a pension across the street from the hospital. While still in Wisconsin, Jessi mentioned she had really enjoyed her space and privacy on the last trip she had taken, alone. Reflecting on their last trip to Germany together, she noted that staying in the same small room as her father had made her feel claustrophobic. So they decided that Jessi would stay at Fachklinik and Jeff at Pension Wiesenau. Three days later, April 29, Jeff wrote:

A Light at the End of This Tunnel (Ramblings of a Sentimental Senior Citizen)

April 29, 2011
9:54 a.m.
   There are usually two of us eating breakfast [at the pension] at the same time every morning. We have our assigned tables, and the coffee is usually waiting for me precisely at eight a.m. (another reason it might not be real hot if I'm a couple of minutes late). I share the dining room with a lovely older German woman who sits directly across from me. She could be my mother. Her hair is thinning but looks as though she visited the beauty parlor before breakfast, and the rosy color of her cheeks speaks to her good health. Honestly, I look up and see my mom (God bless her soul, I hope this message reaches her in Heaven. It would bring a smile to her face). Our conversation consists of me saying, "Good morning," to which she replies, "Morgen." We then eat in total silence. I usually leave first, so I wish her a nice day, and she responds, "Danke" and then says something I don't understand which

I assume means, "you too." She could actually be telling me to take a hike, but I doubt it. Her smile is warm, friendly, and convincing, just like Mom's. Tomorrow at breakfast I expect her to remind me to clean off my plate before leaving the table. Then I'll really feel at home.

What does all of this have to do with "A light at the end of this tunnel," you ask? If you recall my first post of this trip, I spoke of the sensation of experiencing "new life" when Jessi and I arrived here. That feeling has remained throughout our visit and has been supplemented by another revelation. I can't put my finger when it happened exactly. Possibly it was even before we arrived, but it has been in the last two days that I really have noticed a very definite change in Jessi's outlook. Historically, the longer we stay in Germany, the quieter and more introspective she becomes. In my experience with Jessi, she has always arrived in Germany in good spirits, apparently reconciled what was about to happen to her. But after several days of intense treatments, she would become more withdrawn, and meaningful conversation became very strained. At this point in the trip, I would refrain from trying to engage her in meaningful conversations and resort to making small talk. Eventually she would tire of listening to my gibberish and finally tell me that she needed some time for herself. I was never really sure what she was thinking during that private time, but in retrospect I believe she used the time to process what has happened to her, figure out how to deal with the day-to-day trauma, and formulate a game plan to help her to keep moving forward. I'm pretty sure based on conversations we've had this trip that this was not always an easy proposition.

I remember as a young child when depression would rear its ugly head, there was one place that I could always find solace. I would wander down to the pond behind our family home to be by myself and to think. It wasn't much of a pond, really, more of a drainage area for city run-off, but my memories of ice skating there in the winter and fishing in the summer were always positive. I think that is why I would feel safe and secure by myself there when I needed to be alone. I would lie down on the west-facing hillside in the afternoon of a sunny day with the tall grasses brushing against my face. This place provided a real sense of peace and tranquility. It is there I would be able to process my current dilemma and find a ray of hope, a light at the end of the tunnel.

It occurs to me that Jessi has that same ability and that just maybe Bad Salzhausen is her Links Pond. Even after her WBH and a second straight day of multiple treatments, she remains upbeat and easy to talk to this trip. I can only speculate, but it seems to me that she has come to the conclusion that this part of her journey is coming to an end and that she is now able to see the positive results of her trips to Germany. Her mood suggests that she has put behind the self-doubt that one must surely feel when faced with such a dire prognosis. Hope seems to have replaced denial, confidence replaced contemplation, and the light at the end of this tunnel has replaced the nagging fear of having no more life on this earth.

I sense that she is looking forward to reaching the end of this tunnel and seeing what the bright new world waiting will hold for her. She certainly still has a challenging road ahead but seems prepared to face those challenges head on, whatever they might be. Lord knows we'll be there to support her.

Jessi is a Gemini, and Ruthie just sent this email last evening—coincidence? I think not! A message from a higher power? Hopefully!

Gemini
May 21–June 21
Your patience may be wearing a bit thin, but you must hang on a little longer before a difficult phase passes once and for all.

Godspeed,
Jeff

The treatments for Jessi continued at a steady rate, just as Jeff's posts remained entertaining and detailed. At the end of this trip, he spoke of Jessi's progress:

> *May 2, 2011*
> *10:56 a.m.*
>
> *It's a beautiful Monday in Bad Salzhausen, sunny with temperatures heading toward the mid-seventies. Jessi has a full day of treatments ahead, and we will do some laundry. Jessi's blood levels are elevated (a good thing) compared to when we left for Germany. She expects them to drop some when she gets her next chemo treatment just before we return home, but the fact that they remain elevated after her first treatment is cause for some celebration. When she arrived home after her last visit she was lethargic and very tired, but she remains vigorous and upbeat this trip.*
>
> *I attribute much of that to her state of mind. And it should be noted that you, as a reader and contributor to her Care Pages, play a part in her outlook. We have nearly four hundred different people who have visited her site, and the average number of visits per person is over twenty, with fifteen people visiting more than forty times each.*
>
> *But it is really your messages of love and support that have lifted her spirits. She has visited her own site over seventy times, and you have left her 421 messages to date. She has read every one of those, and several have brought tears of joy to her eyes. God bless you all for sharing in Jessi's recovery. Please feel free to add a comment after you read our latest post ... it's easy and greatly appreciated.*
>
> *Godspeed,*
> *Jeff*

It was during this stretch of trips to Germany that Jeff began re-evaluating his job in sales for the printing company. He had been working for forty-two years, but his focus was naturally moving completely toward his daughter. Back home again after this trip, he had lunch with his boss.

"He said, 'Are you motivated to sell anymore?' and I said, 'I can't honestly say I am,' so he said 'Maybe we should look into your retirement.' I thought that was a good idea. The cancer probably forced me to retire a year or two earlier than I would have otherwise, but at that point in time the most important thing for me, after getting my own self back in shape [after hip surgery], was to be supportive of Jessi and make sure she got what she needed."

Jeff retired. Ruthie continued working to bring in a steady income, and Jessi went back and forth to Germany. Things seemed to be going well for her; she experienced many fewer side effects than with conventional chemo. Her hair grew back, she remained upbeat, and the FitzRandolphs felt she was making slow, but steady progress. There were no problems on any of her visits—until the last one.

CHAPTER TEN

aHUS

Summer 2011

Jessi's final trip to Germany was planned for early June. She thought she could handle travel again just fine on her own. Her dad was going to join her halfway through the usual treatments, so she hopped on a plane to the familiar salmon-colored hospital in Bad Salzhausen. Yet almost as soon as the wheels touched German ground and she got settled into the tiny room, she realized something was very off.

"I noticed my ankles were really swollen, and I just felt kind of bloated. They put me on a saline drip, and I just kept getting bigger and bigger. I couldn't eliminate any fluids. They kept pumping it into me, and I finally told them, "You have to stop this.' It was all sitting right in my stomach area."

The doctors did agree to cease saline, but Jessi's condition continued to deteriorate. Soon she needed oxygen to breathe. Even resting suddenly became torturous.

"I didn't sleep much because I was afraid I wouldn't wake up. There were only two ways I could sleep. One, I was sitting on the edge of my bed. The nurse brought the table that was in my room up to it, put a pillow on the table, and I put my head on the pillow. In the other somewhat comfortable position, I would put my knees to my chest with a pillow in between. I couldn't lie down. I couldn't breathe if I was flat on my back. As soon as I would lie down all my oxygen was gone. I was really frightened; I didn't know what was going on, and the doctors weren't sure either."

There had been an outbreak of E. coli in Germany about a week before Jessi arrived. At first, the doctors thought she might have contracted it in the hospital, but she knew that wasn't the case. It didn't make sense. She had noticed the symptoms as soon as she landed, and she hadn't even eaten anything, so how could that be? The medical professionals were baffled and weren't certain how to proceed. Jessi called her parents back in Wisconsin and asked if Ruthie could come in place of Jeff. She wanted her mom. Jessi left a message on the home answering machine that set off alarms in Ruthie's head when she listened to it.

"She said 'Call me anytime, whenever you get home,'" remembered Ruthie. "'It doesn't matter what time of the day or night, just call me.' When I called it was five o'clock a.m. in Germany, and she sounded so weak and so frail. Jessi is a very, very brave person. She tends to under do it rather than overdo it. She said, 'I feel terrible.'"

Ruthie scrambled, threw clothes into a bag, and jumped on the next plane to Frankfurt, but the eight-hour flight was pure misery. Just before Ruthie left for the airport, Jessi's German doctors called and said, "I think Jessi has HUS. You'd better get over here right away." Ruthie did a quick google search of HUS while waiting to board the plane, and the information indicated that it was usually fatal. The flight seemed to last forever. She felt like she'd never get there, and there was no contact with Jessi during the travel time. Ruthie's mind raced with every possible scenario, but she also felt positive that at least she was on her way. After she touched down in Frankfurt, around midnight, a hospital van picked her up. She raced to her daughter's bedside to find her in respiratory distress. She could not get her breath and clearly had a lot of fluid in her system. Jessi's discomfort was only made worse by the fact that there was no air conditioning in the hospital, and it was a steamy hot summer night with no breeze from her room's open window. The window had no screen, and the only things coming in were some pretty healthy moths, drawn to the light in the room.

"I kept putting on the call light, but the nurse on duty said she didn't want to wake up the doctors. I said, 'She needs further care. Maybe we should transfer her to Frankfurt.'"

Ruthie was getting frantic. Finally a doctor came to their room. Ruthie repeated her concerns and again suggested a move to a bigger hospital in Frankfurt.

Jessi's German doctors quickly decided that she needed dialysis. This treatment was not offered at Fachklinik, and the doctors there were clearly outside their comfort zone. Despite their best efforts, they were told that due to the E. coli outbreak in Germany, all of the dialysis machines at the Frankfurt hospitals were already being used. They discovered that every hospital bed was full as well. So there was no choice for Jessi but to remain at Fachklinik for a few more days with her mom at her side. It was agony despite the hospital staff's best efforts to keep her comfortable.

"She never slept, so I wasn't about to sleep either," said Ruthie. "I was afraid if I fell asleep she wouldn't keep breathing. It was that bad. It was just horrible, awful."

Neither closed their eyes for more than a few seconds. Yet the trauma also brought the two of them closer together.

"Some of my most tender moments with her were when we were doing hospital time together, when she was able to let her guard down and allow herself to be vulnerable. She let me help with foot massages. I would rub her back or rub her head if she hurt. I have a lot of wonderful memories of going through the journey together," Ruthie remembered. "Even though it was a living hell."

Ruthie rushed to get them on a flight back to the United States as soon as the German doctors believed Jessi was strong enough to travel. The journey itself was difficult, starting with the booking process.

"I explained our situation to Delta airlines and asked them about upgrading Jessi because of her condition [the extra leg room in first class would be much more comfortable for her, as her feet would get swollen if they were on floor level too long]. They told me that would cost us $5,000 apiece. It was ridiculous. I told them she would probably need oxygen during the trip and asked if it would be available if needed. I was told yes, but they didn't say how much, and I didn't ask."

At the gate, mother and daughter informed the agent about Jessi's illness and inquired about an upgrade again, but they were denied. They boarded the plane when called and started the eight-hour flight back to the United States seated in coach. Just ten minutes into the journey, Ruthie looked at Jessi struggling and pushed the flight attendant button.

"I said, 'My daughter is having trouble breathing and needs oxygen.' Finally that got their attention."

The flight attendant who responded to her call went up to the cockpit. She came back just a few minutes later to tell them the captain wanted them in business class. Finally, they could move to a more spacious seat where Jessi could elevate her feet. She was given some oxygen from a portable canister using a nasal cannula, but she still couldn't find a comfortable position. Every time she would start to doze off, she suddenly felt like her heart was trying to jump out of her chest. She was awakened constantly by this startling sensation. It was during one of these moments that the flight attendants chose to tell mother and daughter that if Jessi needed a significant amount of oxygen, they would have to make an emergency landing because they didn't have enough on board.

Somehow, Jessi mustered the strength to make it through the flight without depleting the oxygen supply. They still had to transfer planes in Detroit for the rest of the trip back to Madison. She was quite sick, but she was back on American soil.

The family had no choice but to trust what they saw as one of the strengths in the US medical system: emergency care with no shortage of supplies. They were also leaving what they had come to believe was a weakness in the German hospital: an inability to deal with the unknown. It was a Western-alternative tango, and they felt as twisted as the pretzels Jessi never touched on the long plane ride home. But once again, her parents were advocating for Jessi, finding the best treatment routes no matter where in the world that took them.

As soon as they landed, Jeff picked up the exhausted duo and drove straight to the emergency room at St. Mary's Hospital. The doctors in Madison had a different diagnosis within an hour: congestive heart failure. The FitzRandolphs, by now quite skeptical of ER diagnoses, just looked at each other and shook their heads.

Then the endless parade of doctors, nurses, lab technicians, and specialists started. Jessi was poked, prodded, pricked, and stabbed from head to foot as they tried to figure out what was happening to her. She lost track of the tests that were being done but received some good news when the results of an echocardiogram showed that her heart was fine. She hadn't suffered congestive heart failure, as diagnosed in the ER.

The doctors put their heads together for a new theory, the same suggested by the German doctor when he called Ruthie across the ocean:

atypical HUS, hemolytic-uremic syndrome, a very rare complication that can arise from chemotherapy, genetics, cancer itself, or other unknown causes. AHUS is a disease in which your internal system is triggered by an infection, cold, or flu virus. That trigger sets off a chain of events that injure microscopic blood vessels. This causes the body to start shutting down, destroying red blood cells and platelets and causing your kidneys to go into a tailspin. Finally, the FitzRandolphs had a reasonable diagnosis, and doctors could start treating Jessi. She was immediately moved from the cardiac unit to 5 South West, a unit that was home to quite a number of oncology patients as well as the plasmapheresis and dialysis suites. After a little finagling, Ruthie managed to get the two of them into the largest room on the floor, one that would accommodate her inflatable bed and would later become known as "Jessi's Suite."

Jessi never blamed Germany for the aHUS, saying it never was proven that the aHUS was directly caused by chemo treatments received there. Her doctors in Germany were well aware that the chemo drug they were using, Mitomycin, could be known to cause aHUS and were always careful to keep her dosage within the established safe range for the drug when used with hyperthermia. In fact, she reasons, it might have been worse had she been treated in America because she likely would have gotten the chemo at a much higher dose. She thinks she was just one of the unlucky ones to contract the rare condition.

The team of doctors watching over Jessi were never able to get a consensus of just exactly what caused her aHUS. The chemo-induced theory gained the most traction because some oncologists on the team were hell-bent on blaming German doctors for shoddy patient care. Many of the other doctors were not so convinced and said so in private conversations with Ruthie and Jeff. They all agreed that Jessi's kidneys were in free fall, her platelet count was life threatening, and plasmapheresis was the best treatment they were aware of. Though they didn't admit it, Jeff felt the body language of the doctors suggested that they were flirting with unchartered waters, recommending a treatment protocol they hope would work for Jessi. One thing they did admit: She was one of their first aHUS patients, if not the very first.

Every day she would spend roughly four to five hours in the plasmapheresis suite, hooked up to the machine that emptied her body of the previous day's plasma transfusion and replaced it with new plasma from hundreds of unknown donors. Despite their best efforts, her doctors were not able to find a cure for the disease, and Jessi's kidneys suffered considerable damage during her two-month hospital stay. The daily doses of plasma were credited for keeping her alive and her kidneys functioning.

"There were days I wanted to be dead; it was that bad. I mean, I never actually wanted to die," remembered Jessi. "I just felt like I wanted it all to be over, and if that meant I had to die it was like, okay. But I never truly believed I was going to die. There were a few days that I started getting a nasty headache as soon as I woke up, and I was in a great deal of pain. On days like that all I wanted to do was just sleep and have everybody leave me alone, but there were five doctors and nurses surrounding me, saying 'What's wrong?' and I'm thinking, 'Please, give me five minutes, go away.'"

"I don't want to sound like a hypocrite, because the doctors and staff at St. Mary's really did a wonderful job. They kept me alive, and I owe my life to them. But I'm a very private person, and all of the attention would get to me. Sometimes I just wanted my space all to myself."

She was miserable, carrying forty pounds of water weight around. She couldn't eat because she constantly felt full. Ruthie and Jeff took turns by her bedside. Ruthie requested family leave from her job at Stoughton Hospital for the first time to be with Jessi at all times. One night was over-the-top scary for Ruthie and Jessi, rivaling the panic and fear they felt in Germany at the height of the confusion.

"Her kidneys weren't getting rid of any of the fluid. She had so much water weight. She absolutely couldn't breathe. She was on oxygen, and I could hear the fluid in her lungs with every breath she took. I stayed up all night with her. I kept calling the nurse. The first thing she did was give her cough medicine. I said to Jessi, 'We have to stick it out twenty minutes before we can call her again.' She sat up in bed, and I rubbed her back. After twenty minutes I rang the bell and told the nurse, 'She's getting worse, not better.' Finally they put her on a respirator to breathe for her, so at least she didn't have to struggle for air. Dr. Edward Ahrens, one of the nephrologists, bless his heart, called his team in at five o'clock that morning. They put her on kidney dialysis, and forty pounds came off in three days."

"I was kind of like, why didn't we try this a month ago?" said Jessi as she looked back in frustration. "I finally felt normal again. I could breathe. The whole summer had been just miserable. I was constantly hooked up to something, having something taken out of my body and replaced with something else. I had to have help getting out of bed, and going to the bathroom was a real struggle."

A post from Jeff on July 25 summed up the zigzag of fears and hopes in all of them:

July 25, 2011
7:47 a.m.

A week ago today, as she lay sleeping in her hospital bed at St. Mary's Hospital, Jessi was drawn toward a bright light in her dreams. She told Ruthie and me afterward that the light was friendly, soothing, and made her feel good as it drew her closer. But something (or someone) told her to turn away and not proceed toward that light ... not just yet. Monday would be her worst day since she was diagnosed with cancer a little over a year ago. Between headaches, stomach aches, lethargy, hours of daily plasmapheresis treatments, and the promise of more prodding and probing to find a good vein, she wished she could just curl up and be left alone. She couldn't find the will or energy to get out of her hospital bed that day. She did manage to drink some ice water throughout the day, but nighttime couldn't come fast enough.

Tuesday brought more of the same, and Wednesday wasn't any better for Jessi. Ruthie, who has been living with her at St. Mary's, kept researching for answers to the multiple questions she had for Jessi's doctors. We have so many questions, so few answers, and so little progress. There are just more transfusions of blood and platelets put in through a new PICC line in Jessi's arm with a direct line to her heart. She receives blood one day and platelets the next, constantly rotating just to keep her counts above the dismal range. And of course those five-hour daily plasmapheresis treatments are put in through the port in her left chest that sports two lines. You see, when you get "pheresis," as they add the new plasma, they remove your old plasma, so there is one line for in and one line for out. This treatment is to keep her kidneys functioning and fight off the effects of the HUS. Did I mention that the blood transfusions take about four hours and the platelets about two every time they are needed? And don't let me forget the Lasix, prednisone, antibiotics, blood pressure meds, and whatever else they decide they need to use to keep her relatively stable, help her fight infection, let her remain moderately comfortable, and help her sleep at night.

Thursday dawned with a gray sky outside, some light rain, and an equally dismal outlook in hospital room 5642. Jessi awoke to another headache and stomach pains. After a brief look in the mirror, she realized that the prednisone she was taking was at least working one of its usual side effects: She had blown up like a balloon. After four hours of blood transfusions and five of pheresis, Ruthie and I were waiting in her room when she was wheeled in. As we stood on either side of her bed holding her hand in ours, she opened her eyes and said: "I am so tired of being in this hospital bed. I just want to feel normal again."

Ruthie and I looked at each other in that moment, and it was obvious that the thoughts running through both of our minds at that time were identical. We mouthed simultaneously: "That's our girl. Nice to see the fight is back"!

I'm not going to lie and say that it's been straight uphill since that moment, but I do truly believe that was the moment during which Jessi decided that she was going to beat this HUS. On Friday she awoke with no ill effects and relatively full of energy, Saturday brought more of the same, and Sunday she had that feisty attitude when she woke up as well. This morning she was hampered by a nasty headache but quickly fought that off with the help of medications and headed to pheresis with labs that continue to show signs that she may be stabilizing. Both weekend days, she was able to take significant walks around floor five of the hospital, something that was impossible earlier in the week.

We are not out of the woods yet. She still is at risk and could suffer another setback, but we have chosen to build on these latest developments, and each and every day we search for the good news that is to be found in the latest labs and Jessi's newfound attitude. We continue to take it a day at a time, and between the three of us we manage to find strength, comfort, and hope in each little ray of light that comes our way. I have no idea where Jessi finds the strength she has shown. She remains a rock and has shown no fear in dealing with her situation. She is by far the strongest of us. Ruthie has been the perfect cheerleader and mom, and she has forged respect from all of the attending doctors with her research, stick-to-it-iveness and knowledge of Jessi's various conditions. I am certainly the weak link but am able to handle the difficult variety of mundane tasks that I am called upon to perform. I'm actually getting quite proficient at doing laundry, washing dishes, and tending to our three pups.

Please continue to send messages to Jessi via CarePages and any other social media of your choice. We all cherish your comments and will readily admit that much of our strength has been gained by reading the loving wishes from our unbelievable support group. God bless you all.

Jeff

Ruthie inquired about donating a kidney to Jessi due to the significant damage Jessi's kidneys had taken. Both Ruthie and Jeff were willing to do it in heartbeat for their daughter. The nephrologist on duty said Jessi would have to be stable from the cancer for five years before a transplant would be an option. The attending oncologist added: "There's nobody in their right mind that would ever give her a kidney transplant." Jeff had to restrain Ruthie because he thought she was going to punch him.

Over the course of a two-month hospital stay, you work with a number of different doctors. Oncology and nephrology doctors at St. Mary's work in teams of five. These teams rotate through the hospital to allow doctors to also have office time with their own patients. This setup allows each doctor to have four weeks of personal office time and then one week serving as the doctor of record in the hospital. While in the hospital, they care for all patients needing their specialty. Consequently, there was an oncologist and nephrologist looking in on Jessi every day. While this system has some flaws, it also provides the patient with an incredibly broad wealth of knowledge. And, in the FitzRandolphs' case, this allowed Ruthie to be a very strong advocate for Jessi without alienating any certain doctor because of her persistence. Of course, all doctors are not created equal. Most seemed very open to Ruthie's ideas on Jessi's care, others humored her, and still others seemed to have a reason why nothing she would suggest could possibly be helpful.

Towards the end of Jessi's aHUS stay, before she started rallying, the doctors and a social worker called a family meeting with Jeff, Ruthie, Casey, and Jessi in her hospital room. It turned out to be one of the lowest points they would have to endure in the entire cancer journey. The oncologist informed the FitzRandolphs that they were just spinning their wheels, that Jessi wasn't getting any better.

"She was needing plasmapheresis daily, blood transfusions, two units every other day, and platelet infusions just to keep her alive," explained Ruthie. "The doctor, who we have referred to as the doctor with the bedside manner of a barracuda, basically said she was screwed. 'If the HUS doesn't get, you the cancer will. I recommend you go to hospice care where they can control your pain. It should be no more than a couple of months.'

"Jessi wasn't ready for that. Jeff and I weren't ready for that. Casey spoke up and said, 'With all due respect, we have a history in our family of doing some pretty amazing things. We know that amazing things can happen.'"

Casey was remembering his grandma, Ruthie's mom, who had been diagnosed with lymphoma years before. There was a point when they said she would die within a matter of days. Ruthie recalled the entire thing extremely well:

"I thought she would die, too, because she had a grayish appearance. I've seen quite a few terminally ill people, and my mom was definitely there. But my mom decided she wasn't ready to go yet. The next day I went in, and she was pink again. She said she felt great and her pain was gone. She went home and lived for another five years. Knowing that our family has a history of beating the odds, Casey spoke up again and said, 'Just because the odds are against us doesn't mean we're not going to beat this.' I will never forget this—the doctor pushed forward on his chair, looked at

Casey, and said, 'Are you questioning me?' Casey was very respectful as he leaned forward in his chair and said, 'I'm disagreeing with you.'"

"That doctor was an asshole," piped in Jessi as they recalled the event over a year later.

"There's no other way to put it," agreed Ruthie. "Jessi's friend Justin, who had visited us in Germany, worked in human resources. When we told him what happened, he took it upon himself to call HR at St. Mary's where the doctor was employed. We don't know if the two are connected, but a couple of months later, our dear doctor retired," said Ruthie.

The FitzRandolphs never went to hospice care, even though Jessi was still oxygen-dependent when she was discharged from the hospital. Her pulse-oximeter (a measure of oxygen saturation in the blood) would drop to fifty-five or sixty after just thirty seconds without the oxygen support. The ideal is a hundred. Ruthie had never seen anything like it in her years of nursing.

They took Jessi home and arranged for Home Health United to bring oxygen canisters and a hospital bed to be placed in the living room. After just a week at home, Jessi showed considerable improvement, and the second week she improved even more. Before they could believe it, she was feeling well enough to cancel both the oxygen and the bed.

Jessi remembers it this way: "I still don't know how I got better. Despite everything the doctors tried, nothing was working until finally they did the dialysis and took the weight off. I came home because they said there was nothing more they could do. I slept a lot, and eventually I got better."

"Miracles do happen, and that was probably one," smiled Ruthie. "Once you give up and agree that there's nothing else—well, put it this way. I remember when the kids were little, there was a speedskating saying: 'If you aim at nothing, you will hit it.'"

On August 15, Jeff had a remarkable post for loved ones, considering the state Jessi had been in just one month before and the "go to hospice" instructions from the doctor:

> *At the Lake*
> *August 15, 2011*
> *11:42 a.m.*
>
> *Jessi's at the lake. Yes, you read that right: not the "flippin" hospital, Big Siss!*

We (Ruthie, Jessi, and I) arrived late in the day Thursday, after Jessi's appointment with her oncologist (more on that later). We were joined by Jenn, Sawyer, and Cassidy on Friday afternoon, and Casey rolled in around noon on Sunday. We're returning home on Tuesday afternoon.

We have spent the weekend fishing, tubing, having a picnic lunch on the pontoon at Blueberry Point, swimming, watching Bean [Sawyer's nickname] catch bluegills in the net off the pier, visiting the Hayward bakery for the best bread in the whole world, eating (Jessi's appetite is coming back), and avoiding the candy store. We spent two hours on Blueberry yesterday.

Blueberry is a beautiful sand point on Big Sissabagama Lake that juts out under the water about fifty yards. It is thirty yards wide and is about two feet deep. It is an amazing sight because you can clearly see the beautiful sand right up to the edge of the drop-off, where the water immediately changes color to a deep, dark blue. The bottom plunges from two to thirty feet deep in the span of a four-foot vertical drop. There's room for about seven pontoon boats to anchor on the point while the occupants play in the water, tossing a Frisbee or football, throwing toys to their dogs, or just enjoying a carbonated beverage while making small talk. Jessi waded in the water playing with her pup Kirby for the better part of an hour and then enjoyed floating on her water lounger for another half an hour while tied up to the back end of the pontoon.

She has also caught the biggest fish of the trip, a plump two-pound bass. The fishing in general has been typical for August, very slow. The best action is right at the end of our pier, where the bass lay in wait under the pontoon boat and the bluegills chase anything thrown in the water at them. Tomorrow we will most likely enjoy bass, bluegill, eggs, and toast for breakfast. It doesn't get any better than that.

It wouldn't be a trip to the lake without a little excitement, and on Friday we had our fill for this trip. It was our first trip to the emergency room at the Hayward Hospital in many years. When Casey and Jessi were younger we'd average one trip every two years, but that was years ago. This visit started innocently enough. I was standing on the end of our pier casting for Muskies around four thirty on Friday afternoon, and our pup Kona decided he wanted to be a fish and get caught while the lure was floating in the water and I was clearing a backlash in my fishing reel. The lure he liked so much was a six-inch minnow imitation with three treble hooks, one on each end and one in the middle. He managed to get his lip hooked on the end hook. Thankfully, only one of the treble hooks was in his lip. After fishing him out of the water (I would have much rather been landing a Muskie), I tried unsuccessfully to remove the hook from his lip and in the process managed to get hooked myself. So now it's dog and man hooked together on opposite ends of the lure. Fortunately (for me but not for her) Ruthie was watching from the cabin and came to our rescue. After she tried to cut the hooks out of both dog and myself with two different pairs of totally worthless wire cutters, I suggested that Ruthie just jerk the hook out of my finger, as it was a somewhat superficial wound. She succeeded in freeing me and embedding the same hook in her thumb when Kona retreated in pain with the movement of the lure. Twenty dizzying minutes later, I was finally able to find a neighbor with a pair of wire cutters that did cut the barbs off the embedded hooks, both in Ruthie and Kona. This was after we had asked Jessi to call 911 and had an ambulance on the way ... from Hayward (twenty-five minutes away), of course.

Fortunately a first responder was working nearby and arrived about the same time as we were making our way from the pier to the cabin, with both combatants freed from each other but still sporting the tips of the hooks with barbs in their respective jaw and thumb. The paramedic was able to wrap Ruthie's thumb for the trip to the emergency room. Ruthie's explanation of the events to the nurse was quite comical. Two hours later, with the barb of the hook successfully removed from her thumb, we returned to the lake and our vacation. It wasn't funny at the time, but looking back, we all are able to have a pretty good laugh at our calamity. Ruthie seems to be healing nicely, and luckily it was her left thumb. Kona still sports a little hook in his lip that will be removed when we get home, but it hasn't affected his vacation at all.

Jessi's appointment with the oncologist went very well last Thursday. Her labs showed that her hemoglobin count remained stable at 9.8 and that her platelets (the big troublemaker) had actually increased from 10 when she was released from the hospital to 49 at the appointment (with no transfusions). Creatinine levels remain slightly elevated. Her energy level has gone through the roof in the little over a week that she has been home. She has not napped since we arrived here and is sleeping through the night, a miracle in and of itself considering the fact that there are four dogs, two grandchildren, and five adults packed into our modest little log cabin at the lake.

Please continue to pray for Jessi. We are starting to believe with guarded optimism that all of our prayers for a miracle may just have been answered. As we watch Jessi continue to improve with each and every day that passes, we are filled with gratitude for all of the support we have received.

God bless you,

Jeff

Everyone healed from the fishing lure accident, and Ruthie added an update on Jessi's continued remarkable progress just three days later. The headline screamed of their excitement:

OMG!
August 18, 2011
11:47 p.m.
This will be short and sweet. I returned to the job I love as an RN on geriatric psychiatry at Stoughton Hospital after being out on family leave for nearly two and a half months to support Jessi, so I must be judicious with my time.

After being sent home from the hospital less than two weeks ago and being told there is nothing more that can be done and to "sign on with hospice," Jessi continues to make a miraculous rebound! She had an appointment with her oncologist today and labs came back at—drum roll, please—platelets improved at 62 (up from 47 a week ago—they had been less than 10 just prior to discharge from the hospital), hemoglobin down just a tad but basically stable, and creatinine (kidney function) much improved at 2.6, down from 3.6 a week ago. This is nothing short of amazing. This is with no transfusions or plasmapheresis, only some oral meds, which are being gradually decreased. We will be forever grateful to the folks at St. Mary's Hospital in Madison, WI, for maintaining Jessi's life while her body was fighting this very rare and lethal illness.

I came across one case in my endless hours of research when Jessi was an inpatient of a woman who survived chemo-induced HUS. Her journey was not unlike Jessi's. I took that story to heart because she not only survived the HUS, but her stage IV breast cancer never returned. That is our next hope, vision, and prayer.

We hope to get rid of the hospital bed, wheelchair, oxygen, etc. early next week. Jessi has returned to living once again and is cheering her former volleyball teammates on tonight—yes, a social outing, for the first time in I don't know how many months.

My family has always believed in miracles. We have seen them and experienced them. It's in the blood.

Life has no guarantees, but there is one thing that I am certain of. Without your messages, support, and most of all prayers, I would probably not be sending such a positive message tonight. Thank you from the bottom of my heart.

> With love and gratitude,
> Ruthie

Jessi had beaten atypical HUS, a rare and potentially life-threatening disease. It is believed that there have been a total of three to six hundred cases of aHUS diagnosed in the United States since the discovery of the disease. Record keeping is incomplete, and because it is not an infectious disease, it does not have to be reported. The survival rate for aHUS is dismal, but Jessi was still in an elite group of the very few who made it. She was still in a battle for her life against cancer, but she emerged victorious from this round in the ring. Maybe that good immune system Casey had noticed and raved about after her knee surgery really had worked. She was one of the lucky ones.

The aHUS hospital stay and treatments in America were covered by insurance. Had they not been, they would have wiped out the family's finances. As for the other costs, the FitzRandolphs would put close to $100,000 of their retirement money into Jessi's care in those first few years. The initial trip to Germany was over $25,000, and each subsequent ten-day trip cost approximately $12,000. They also used funds from Ruthie's parents. Jim and Trudy Whitinger, who had looked down from their porch at young Jeff in his bell-bottomed flag jeans so many years before, wound up playing a role in their granddaughter's care. When they passed away, they left Ruthie with a much-appreciated inheritance. That, and the money from the fundraiser, kept the family from falling into true financial trouble.

"Without the inheritance and proceeds from the fundraisers, we would be mortgaged to the max and have bankrupted our retirement accounts," said Jeff.

Jessi never had to worry about money. That was one thing she could remove from her mind. She knew she would always be well cared for. What she had to do was to get better from the aHUS tightrope she had walked. As all of the FitzRandolphs have repeated time and time again, Jessi's body seemed to heal itself, and all of her breathing problems disappeared.

Looking back, Ruthie reflects with a little anguish: "I'm really not sure she would have survived her hospital stay if she had not had somebody looking out for her, being an advocate, making sure that she could breathe."

That somebody was Ruthie. She rescued her daughter, and both she and Jeff nursed Jessi out of the throes of death.

It would remain to be seen how much damage had been done to her immune system while she battled to stay alive and beat the aHUS. Her cancer treatments had been discontinued. They would have most certainly killed her had she tried to fight cancer during her two-month battle with aHUS. But the daily transfusions, plasmapheresis, dialysis, and inability to follow a healthy diet had certainly all taken a toll on her body's balance. That immune system question would soon be addressed.

FitzRandolph Family Photo Essay

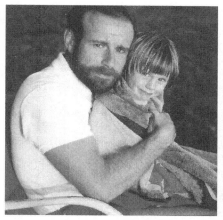

Dad and Jessi after she had just jumped in the pond at the Whitinger family farm to cool off on a hot summer day. The early years. Circa 1981

Jessi's annoying habit of always catching the biggest walleye during our family vacations on Big Sissabagama started at an early age. Circa 1985

Jessi sporting six stitches, compliments of a little roughhousing with brother Casey. Circa 1982

Verona soccer's leading scorer her Senior year. Circa 1995

A photo only the Verona Babes would pose for, trying to pull Becky's car from the ditch in our yard. Left to right: Erica, Becky, Michelle, Amy, Jessi Fitz, Jessica M., and Erin. Does something look amiss with this photo? Circa 2013

Jessi enjoying an evening out with her "best friend ever," Libby. Circa 2001

Jessi and friend Justin Dorrow enjoy a pilsner in a pub in the small town of Bad Salzhausen, Germany, during Justin's visit to be with Jessi during her whole-body hyperthermia treatments. Circa 2011

Jessi shows off her new kimono in the home of the Japanese family who took us in for the Olympics, the World Single Distance Championships, and the marriage of their youngest daughter, at which Jeff gave the bride away. We visited them three times, and they came to visit us twice including for Casey and Jenn's wedding. Circa 2005

Jessi and Ruthie on the front steps of the family home shortly after Jessi's first chemotherapy treatments. She retained her playful heart, beautiful smile, and undying spirit throughout her journey. Circa 2010

Casey and Jessi enjoying a beautiful afternoon on Big Siss, just waiting for Jessi to catch the biggest walleye yet again. Circa 2013

The family pauses for a formal portrait at our cabin on Big Sissabagama, Hayward, Wisconsin. Circa 2012

Jessi and Casey just prior to Casey and Jenn's wedding. C&N Photography circa 2002

The bridal party for Casey and Jenn's wedding, including Olympic teammates Jeremy Wotherspoon and Mike Ireland (Canadian training partners), Dave Cruikshank, and Marc Pelchat (US teammates). C&N Photography circa 2002

Dad, Mom, and Jessi dining out at Northwood's Steak House near Hayward, WI. Circa 2013

Jessi and Kirby share a kiss. Circa 2012

Jessi walks the runway in a local fashion show featuring breast cancer patients as models. The funds raised were donated to the Carbone Cancer at the University of Wisconsin for breast cancer research.

Casey and Sawyer prepare a pair of white pines as part of a planting of 6,000 trees on his farm Golden Moments near Hollandale, WI. Circa 2012

Once diagnosed with aHUS, Jessi could be found every day for eight weeks in the "dialysis suite," hooked up to the plasmapheresis machine that exchanged twenty units of plasma a day, the process taking four hours. Circa 2011

Casey's first 500m race in Salt Lake City was historic. He had the fastest 100-meter opener ever of 9.44 seconds and skated to a new Olympic record of 34.42 seconds. This record still stands after three more Winter Olympic games. Getty Images circa 2002

The medal ceremony was held in Olympic Square in Salt Lake City. Because Casey won the only US gold medal during that day's competition, the presentation of his gold medal was the final presentation of the evening's events. Ten thousand plus spectators paid to witness the presentation and then be entertained by the Canadian rock group Nickelback, whose lead singer sported a speedskating skin suit during their performance that rocked the world that evening. Getty Images circa 2002

Casey winning two golds, one silver, and one bronze at the Olympic Sport Festival (short track speedskating) in Minneapolis, MN. C&N Photography circa 1990

Jessi and Casey, national champions, short track speedskating. Circa 1991

At thirteen years old, Jessi became the youngest female to ever make the US National Short Track team, one of five women selected to represent the United States in world competitions during the 1990–1991 season. C&N Photography circa 1990

Jessi with Cassidy and Sawyer getting ready to open gifts, Christmas day. It would be Jessi's last Christmas. Circa 2013

CHAPTER ELEVEN

Mexico

Summer 2012

J essi went through the early part of winter, 2011 continuing to recover from aHUS and getting back on her feet. By January, she was almost her normal self. She was finally able to have the reconstructive breast surgery she so desperately wanted. It went remarkably well; in fact, she was released from the hospital that same day. Her mental outlook was bright, and she decided she had the energy to sign up for online fashion design classes at the Academy of Art University in San Francisco. The coursework in a field she was interested in invigorated her.

But on February 7, Ruthie posted a discouraging setback that took them all off guard:

> *February 7, 2012*
> *7:08 p.m.*
> *The bad news is, Jessi noticed some right hip pain last week, and we noticed that she had developed a limp. At her appointment yesterday, her oncologist did x-rays of the hip where she previously had a lesion. These revealed "significant progression" of the disease process in this area. They promptly sent her to radiation therapy, where she was seen today. There we were told that she has a 50 percent chance of a pathologic fracture and needs to undergo a hip pinning prior to radiation. The orthopedic surgery will be done this Thursday. After a week of recuperation, she will then start*

two weeks of radiation, which will be pinpointed to that lesion. At that point, we are considering going to Mexico for a two-week wellness clinic where they detox the body and work on boosting the immune system.

Jessi was pretty down yesterday but today has her fight back. She was told not to bear weight on the right leg, so she has been getting around on crutches. After the radiation therapy appointment, we took a little outing to the fabric store where she tried out the electric shopping cart that she could ride. Those things have one speed: Fast. I'll say no more ...

Once again, thank you for your support and prayers.

Ruthie

Four days later, it was Jeff's turn to add an update on the surgery to insert the rod in Jessi's leg. He had a lot of emotions running through his head, but the prevailing one was reflected in the headline he chose for the post:

There's NO Quit in This Girl ...
February 11, 2012
8:22 p.m.

I was sitting in Jessi's hospital room Friday afternoon, taking a break from chatting with her and from reading my book—another Stephen King thriller—and my mind started to wander.

I thought back to the day Ruthie and I arrived home from a week at our cabin at Big Siss in July of 2010. Jessi was sitting at our kitchen table waiting for us with news that would change our family's lives forever. She told us that she had breast cancer but that we shouldn't worry because she was going to be okay. She delivered the news with that reassuring Jessi Fitz smile that we all love her for. She was calm, cool, and collected and gave us the news very matter-offactly. I wish I could say we received it in the same manner.

Outwardly we both maintained our composure, but inwardly we were shaken.

Fast forward to Thursday of this week. As all of you who read her CarePages know, Jessi has beaten the odds several times since her original diagnosis and recently has partaken in some new endeavors. Learning to play the guitar, exercising, and going back to school for fashion design were at the top of her list. Then two weeks ago, I noticed a slight limp as she climbed the stairs at home. Over a week's time, the limp became much more noticeable, and Jessi seemed to be struggling a bit as she made her way around the house. She never complained once during that time, and that smile was ever present. After I mentioned it to her, she admitted to having "some" pain in her hip. Fortunately she had an appointment with her oncologist scheduled for Monday of this week.

On some level as a parent you never lose your optimism, so of course Ruthie and I wanted to believe that Jessi simply had developed a muscle strain resulting from her recently renewed exercise regimen on the treadmill. After all, the limp started about the same time. But realistically, after what we've been through, deep down, where part of you is already hurting, you know what the diagnosis will be even before it's delivered. This "dumbing down" of your senses doesn't make it any easier to accept the inevitable. When the x-rays showed that her bone mets had grown in size and were compromising the strength of her hip, we knew what was coming.

Pause to regain my composure …

So Jessi had surgery at St. Mary's on Thursday that placed a titanium rod down through her femur and then screwed two pins through the bone and into the metal rod. Her surgeon was kind enough to draw us a picture of the procedure while we were discussing it with him prior to the operation. We've posted it in the photo area of her CarePage and you are welcome to take a look. He's not a bad artist for a doc, but I'm sure glad the surgical procedure is a little more technologically advanced than his drawing.

The surgery went very well. With all Jessi has been through, you are never sure about the possible complications she is more susceptible to. There's potential for bleeding because of her low blood counts, the condition of her kidneys make it necessary for special saline solutions to be used to keep her hydrated during and after the surgery, and the potential for a reaction to the anesthesia is always a concern.

Jessi sailed through the operation. It was scheduled for two hours but lasted only one. Dr. Richard Glad, the orthopedic surgeon, said there was minimal bleeding and they used a spinal anesthetic to lessen the risk of complications. The first question she asked the doc after the surgery was, "Did you do something to my hip?" He smiled, and she smiled right back at him and then went back to sleep.

She was in quite a bit of pain Thursday evening immediately following the surgery, but as I sat there yesterday visiting with her she said that she had no pain when she was off her feet. She had just returned from PT, and they had put her through the paces, which she aced with flying colors. She did indicate that when putting pressure on her right side there was "some but not a lot" of pain. She delivered the news with that sweet, reassuring smile. How could you not believe her?

But I digress (I've always wanted to use that term in my writing; it strikes me as so absurd). Thursday, as my mind was wandering I realized there was an emotion Jessi had not experienced through her entire journey over the last two years. I recall her first surgery, when her breast and some lymph nodes were removed successfully, and then the discovery of the bone mets. I remember with joy the fundraising events held in March of last year and how her smile lit up the venues. I think of the trips to Bad Salzhausen for treatments which arrested the cancer and how on the last trip to Germany the bottom dropped out. That was followed by a harrowing two months in the hospital just trying to survive a "ghost" of a *disease that escaped definition and required superhuman efforts by all parties involved to simply keep Jessi alive. And when one of the oncologists told Jessi she had maybe two months to live, she gave him that smile and told him, "I'm not ready to die just yet." That was last July.*

Through it all, her smile remains unchanged and beautiful. I have not seen her shed a tear of fear or self-pity (if she has it has been in the privacy of her own bedroom) since she first told us about her cancer. She has defeated every roadblock this terrible disease has thrown at her, and I have every reason to believe she will do so this time as well. "Quit" is not in her vocabulary. She simply doesn't know the meaning of the word. It is an emotion which she is incapable of feeling or accepting. You can't be defeated if you won't quit. Jessi believes that, and I believe in her. Jessi's strength has buoyed our resolve, and the support network that you have built around our family has given us an unshakable faith that Jessi will win this battle and the next (if necessary) until the cancer demons decide to take their battle elsewhere and leave Jessi alone to live a long, productive life.

Ask me how I know this? Simple—I saw it in her smile today.

Jeff

PS: Jessi came home today, and the healing continues.

Jeff's optimism was rewarded with a relatively quiet few months. Surgery and radiation took away all signs of the limp, and Jessi resumed light exercise. But in April, another bone scan revealed a new lesion on her neck. The radiologist recommended surgery. However, after reviewing Jessi's scans, the surgeons came to the conclusion that surgery was too risky. They put her in a neck brace and recommended she have more radiation to treat the area. The oncologist wanted to put her on another chemo drug, along with Herceptin, but Ruthie was hesitant because the drug, Gemzar, had known complications that included HUS. They were not willing to risk Jessi suffering a relapse.

Ruthie started researching additional alternative methods, and immune boosting came even more sharply into focus. Up until this point, the FitzRandolphs had been doing many protocols, but the family wanted to put more emphasis on the immune system, the body's own ability to fight back. Ruthie discovered a clinic in Tijuana, Mexico, in her late-night research. People were raving about it.

"This clinic boasts that 'stars' looking for alternative cancer protocols seek out their services. Somebody with an endless amount of money, they normally don't get treated in America. That's interesting, isn't it?" said Ruthie.

The FitzRandolphs' dentist had a friend with cancer who also saw great success after going to the clinic. Jeff told loved ones about it in early June of 2012:

> *Roller Coaster Ride*
> *June 6, 2012*
> *7:01 a.m.*
>
> *It's been quite a stretch since we've contributed a new post to Jessi's CarePage, but as we embark on the next phase of our rollercoaster ride, it seems appropriate to bring everyone up to speed (no pun intended).*
>
> *I had to reread the last post to help me remember where we were in our journey. So let's pick up where we left off, because the reality of the matter is that Jessi's roller coaster ride is far from over. She has healed from the hip surgery performed in February and walks with no trace of a limp. She's not playing soccer yet, but she continues to exercise to help rebuild strength. Hopefully the localized radiation treatments applied to her leg have eliminated the lesion that had appeared there.*
>
> *After the surgery and treatments, her nephrologist (kidney doctor) decided that she should start on dialysis, but between the time the decision was made and her first appointment her kidney function improved considerably and he decided to wait. As of today, her kidney functions remain stable.*

In late April she had another bone scan, and this time they discovered a small lesion on her neck. She was immediately placed in a neck brace, and local radiation was started to treat the affected area. No surgeries were required with these treatments, and she has weathered yet another storm.

The reoccurrence of these spots on the bone is troubling and not the sign of healing we were hoping for, so her oncologist has decided to add Gemzar (a chemo drug) to her Hercepton treatments. Ruthie is not thrilled with this because one of the known complications from this drug is HUS. If you remember, Jessi's two-month battle last June and July was with HUS, and we will not allow any treatment that might cause the HUS to return. Subsequently Ruthie went on another search for alternatives to the chemo treatments.

So, at the end of the month Ruthie and Jessi will depart for the International Bio Care Hospital, where she will enter the Alivizatos treatment program. In a nutshell, this treatment process regenerates, enhances, and modulates the immune system so that the body can withstand abnormal influences (read, cancer) while also promoting mental health. The processes used may include nutritional medicine, detoxification therapy, comprehensive antioxidant therapies, live cell therapy, autologous stem cell therapy, Laetrile therapy, EDTA Chelation treatments, acupuncture and acupressure, bioelectrical repolarization, integrated standard treatments, specialized therapies, autologous dendritic cell vaccines, Chondroitin Sulfates, ultraviolet blood irradiation therapy, and advanced oxidative therapies(just to name a few). I couldn't begin to explain what these treatments do, but Jessi will be evaluated by a team of doctors upon arrival, and a program tailored directly to her needs will be established using some but not necessarily all of the processes available. Ruthie will be sending updates from IBC Hospital once they are settled and Jessi begins her treatment regimen.

Ruthie has done an incredible amount of research on the facility, which is located in Tijuana, Mexico, for obvious reasons. She has spoken directly with Dr. Rodriquez, the medical director and founder of the facility. The facility also comes highly recommended by numerous healthcare professionals with whom we've spoken in the United States. Jessi and Ruthie will fly directly to San Diego, CA, and be picked up by hospital staff for the twenty-minute ride to Tijuana. They will return home on July 24.

I cannot believe how naive I was when Jessi was first diagnosed and had the original surgery to remove the lump in her breast. I actually believed that there was a cure, that someday I'd be able to say with certainty that "Jessi is cured!" What a fool I was. All who have actually experienced the disease and their family members know that you live every day with the dreaded "C" word regardless of how long you have been in remission. It's always hanging out there, like this dreaded dark cloud, and in your weakest moments it can torment you if you let it. That's why your prayers and messages are so important to us. They truly do comfort us.

Please keep Jessi and Ruthie in your prayers during this trip. The strength you have provided us in numbers has helped us through the ups and downs of the seemingly never-ending roller coaster ride that is our lives.

God bless you all.

Jeff

PS: Through it all, Jessi is still smiling and fighting like a girl! She also just turned thirty-five two weeks ago.

Jessi was thirty-five years old and headed to another foreign country in search of a way to save her life. Mother and daughter packed for a different part of the world and left right after the Fourth of July.

Hola from Tijuana, Mexico
July 5, 2012
5:44 p.m.
Hola!

Even though we have not been in Tijuana very long, there is already so much to talk about. Our trip was comfortable and uneventful. We managed to get exit-row seats, so we had plenty of leg room. We breezed right through customs in a hospital van that picked us up from San Diego. We didn't even need identification.

The hospital isn't new and modern, but it is fairly nice, comfortable, and clean. Jessi and I share a large two-bed room with a bathroom and a small fridge at our request. We have a good-sized flat-screen TV with many US channels—in English. The staff has been wonderful, very eager to please, and all speak English. They strive to outdo the competition, as we do at Stoughton Hospital and Agrace HospiceCare, my workplaces. We have not ventured out of the hospital yet, as Jessi has been hooked up to an IV most of the day. Her fluids are run in very slowly and not with saline in order to be kind to her kidneys.

Speaking of, just prior to leaving home, Jessi got the labs back from her recent oncology appointment. We were ecstatic with her kidney function numbers. Her creatinine was 2.8, further improved from 3.8 on the last draw and 5 a couple months back. Her BUN was 62, down from close to 100 not long ago. Platelets were improved as well at 138. On this joyous note, we went to our cabin for a few days with the whole family, where Jessi thoroughly enjoyed herself, as did all of us. Once again, she outfished everyone.

Jessi had labs drawn here yesterday and again were improved! Creatinine is now 2.6, BUN 47, platelets normal at 154! Just last summer, Jessi's platelets were less than 10, indicating they were pretty much nonexistent. And that was with two platelet infusions every other day. We met with Jessi's doctor, Dr. Romero, this morning, and she agreed that *kidneys don't normally heal themselves. I sure would like to send this info to a doctor that Jessi had last summer who said there was no chance that Jessi would survive the atypical HUS and we should "just keep her comfortable."*

They are treading lightly with Jessi's treatment down here because of her extensive medical history and compromised, though improved, renal function. I had a ream of medical records faxed here from home and am so glad I did. She is receiving daily IVs with DMSO and laetrile as well as different vitamins. She will spend time in an oxygen chamber (malignant cells do not like oxygen). She will also have ozone therapy for the same reason. She is on an alkaline diet, as cancer thrives in an acid environment. There are some treatments that she is unable to get at this time so as not to disturb her healing kidneys. Hopefully she will be able to advance her treatment as she heals.

We have met some amazing people already, other patients. We had breakfast with Judy this morning. Judy is a lovely lady who was diagnosed with stage IV ovarian cancer spreading to the lymph nodes and her intestines. This is her twenty-sixth visit here, and there is no evidence of cancer at this time. She was diagnosed in 1990. As you probably know, ovarian cancer is among the worst. These results are simply amazing but not at all unusual with these alternative treatments. I hope and pray that someday (preferably in the very near future) we will have access to this type of treatment in the United States and that it will be covered by insurance.

I have so much to talk about, but this is a CarePage, not a CareBook, and I don't want to risk boring you with too many details at once. I will post again soon with more info about the treatments and other patients that we have met as well as the food (the food is a post in itself).

We aren't homesick yet—we've been kept busy, but we both so appreciate your messages. If you would, please pray for Jessi's health, that we soon have access to alternative medicine in the United States covered by insurance (this would take

a miracle), and please add Jen S. to your prayer list. She
is another cancer warrior (from Illinois) with this terrible
disease and is Jessi's age, far too young.
Thank you so much for caring.

Ruthie

Jessi's Mexico regimen would again include hyperthermia, although the treatment was handled differently than in Germany. "In Mexico, they did it by increasing the core temperature by continually flushing warm water through the colon, so I thought it was a better scientific approach because you could monitor it better," explained Ruthie.

They also gave Jessi infusions of DMSO, a commercial solvent derived from wood byproducts. It was actually sold in hardware stores decades ago.

"Alternative practitioners have found that it really targets cancer cells, but no one can get a patent on it because it's been on the market forever," explained Ruthie.

"Nobody here in the United States will pursue it as a cancer treatment. The FDA blackballed it, and the drug companies developed similar products with higher toxicity. None of them are as effective as DMSO," stated Jeff. "It's kind of weird because whenever one of his athletes would get a bad bruise, Lyle LeBombard, speedskating coach for Casey and Jessi for quite a few years, would say 'Just go home and put a little DMSO on it.' He carried a bottle with him, and Ruthie had a little supply he'd given her. It would make bruises go away just like that. At first I was skeptical because a bruise is internal, not on the surface of the skin, but it worked like a charm. So it doesn't surprise me if it's a miracle drug. Of course, it's no longer available in hardware stores because people found out it could be beneficial to cancer. It's only available online today."

On July 8, 2012, Ruthie had another update from south of the border:

Buenas Noches!
July 8, 2012
10:36 p.m.
We are doing well here in Tijuana, where the temperature
is comfortably in the seventies during the daytime. I never
thought I'd go to Mexico to escape the heat of the Midwest!

Jessi had hyperthermia Friday, and it was uneventful. They heat the body from the inside out here, different than how it was done in Germany. She was heated to 107 degrees for several hours and very slowly cooled down to normal. She was uncomfortable coming out of the sedation as she was still 104 degrees, but a little lorazepam effectively allowed her to sleep. She slept most of the day yesterday as well but was perkier today, so we took advantage of it.

Jessi had asked the staff to start her IV therapy early this morning, which allowed us time to walk to a nearby mall this afternoon and do a little shopping. It felt good to get off the hospital grounds. I snapped a photo of Jessi at the entryway of the hospital as we were leaving, which I have posted. We are tentatively planning a trip to the San Diego Zoo on Tuesday if I can work everything out. If you have any ideas of things to do/see in the Tijuana/San Diego area, we would love your suggestions. The drivers here at the hospital are very accommodating, and a change of scenery is a nice diversion.

The food has been interesting. Sometimes we do not know what we are ingesting. Our first meal after arrival started with a glass of tan-colored liquid, identified as "grape juice." By this, they mean taking red grapes and juicing them. It was very good! The entree was a stuffed tomato with something brown on top. At first I thought it was crumbled bacon, but that was wishful thinking. We were never sure just what it was stuffed with. Dessert consisted of what Jessi called birdseed held together by some unknown force. It looked like birdseed and tasted like what we would imagine birdseed would taste like, so we concluded that it was, indeed, birdseed. This treat brought back memories for Jessi of her high school days, when one of the "Verona Babes" discovered that puppy treats actually tasted like cookies. ☺

I am very excited to discover a CarePage visitor from our area who is extremely knowledgeable about alternative therapies. He did the research when his father had cancer and has generously been sharing his information with me.

It is hard to find people on this same page, I believe simply because alternative therapies are not endorsed by our health care system. Thank you, Greg!

Again, we thank you for your support and prayers. We love the messages! There are 475 kind souls following our journey on CarePages! That is one big warm fuzzy.

Wishing you the best,

Ruthie

Jeff stayed at the family cabin for the first week that Ruthie and Jessi were in Mexico. It was a very relaxing time spent with Casey, Jenn, and the grandchildren. When he returned home in mid-July, he felt rejuvenated, recharged, and ready to help Jessi in any way she needed when she returned home. He looked forward to the return of his wife and daughter. The house was empty without them there.

Treatment in Tijuana
July 17, 2012
12:03 p.m.

Hello again from Tijuana! Another week of treatment down. Neither Jessi nor I feels terribly bad about being here. The weather is so comfortable—we are happy to be escaping the heat of Wisconsin. What a bonus!

Jessi is still recovering from the hyperthermia ten days ago. She has had a heart irregularity for the last week. We aren't really sure what is causing it. It is gradually improving, and there has been no cardiac damage. Her energy is up and down. Some days she feels tired and needs more rest. Other days, like Sunday, she has a fair amount of pep. We have decided to forego the second hyperthermia at this time until Jessi is less fragile.

I have continued to study the many alternative cancer treatments and have discussed them with Jessi. Her goals are (1) to have no further progression of cancer for six months and after that, (2) that her immune system overtakes the malignant cells. Jessi does not plan on any more chemotherapy,

other than the Herceptin that she has been on from the start.
I honestly believe that with an unlimited amount of money
as well as time for extensive research, one can beat stage IV
cancer. This requires a huge commitment and resolve as well
from the patient.

The International BioCare Hospital will send Jessi home
with some immune-building medications and on an alkaline
diet, mostly consisting of vegetables and fruits. After further
research, Jessi has decided to add treatment with a Rife
machine to her home regimen. We are very excited about
this. So as to not mislead you, there is only one machine that
is recommended.

We met Barb here at the hospital, also from Wisconsin.
She is here for her every six-month booster. She has had breast
cancer which spread to the bone and lungs for three years. She
has been treated here for those three years and has no evidence
of active disease. She will continue her medications and strict
diet at home as well as a few other nonpharmacological
treatments of her choice.

On a lighter note, we finally made it to the San Diego
Zoo Sunday and had a wonderful time. It was a pictureperfect
day. I have posted a couple of our favorite pictures to check out.

As always, we are so grateful for your support, prayers
and messages. Wishing you the best.

Ruthie

Jessi and Ruthie returned from Mexico in late July armed with pills, vaccines, teas, smoothie mixtures, and a list of organic items she should eat. She kept up with the Bob Beck protocol, sending electrical impulses through her body, did coffee enemas, and started utilizing this latest treatment, a Rife machine. This is a $6,000 radio frequency device that followers believe kills cancer cells and leaves healthy cells alone. It looks a bit like something out of a 1940s war movie. You could imagine someone frantically typing a telegram on it. Jessi would lie down on the couch and place the light source facing the middle of her back. Then she would turn the dial to one of three appropriate frequencies for killing cancer cells and send radio waves through her body for thirty to sixty minutes, depending on the selected frequency.

A few weeks later, Ruthie wanted to go to the lake while Jessi preferred some time alone. Jeff talked about all of this in more detail:

> *An August Day at the Lake*
> *August 21, 2012*
> *7:49 p.m.*
>
> It's another beautiful day at Big Siss Lake as the summer of 2012 winds down. Sitting at the computer this morning as the mist rose off the water, it occurred to me that we have much to be thankful for. And having our daughter with us is among the blessings we count daily.
>
> She's not actually with us at the cabin these last few days; she's at home, enjoying some downtime from the parents with her dog, Kirby. I know she relishes the times she gets to have the entire house to herself without fear of bumping into either Mom or Dad as she goes about her daily regimen. A little decompression is good for all of us.
>
> And as I sit and look out over the lake, I can't help but feel how lucky we are that we still do get to bump into her almost daily. Jessi has come a long way since last August when her doctor recommended hospice. Jessi's intestinal fortitude and Ruthie's research and stick-to-it-iveness have a lot to do with that.
>
> Since her return from Mexico, Jessi has been on a very regimented protocol. She eats only organic foods, and the alkaline diet she is on requires juicing, tons of vegetables and fruit, very little meat and then only fish and chicken, and drinking enough water to sink the Titanic. Her favorite daily treat is the coffee enema that detoxifies her liver. She spends two hours daily using an electro-medicine protocol, which is a highly controversial form of alternative cancer care. In addition to that, she is currently borrowing a Rife machine until the unit we've recently purchased is delivered later this week. This very costly equipment uses different

radio frequencies to eliminate undesirable cells from one's body. Depending on the frequency she is using on any given day, the treatment takes from half an hour to two hours. Once a week she receives a vaccination from Ruthie derived from her own blood modified with other immune-building medicines.

The water she is currently drinking is pure spring water that I get from the Rock Springs area. There is a spring located just north of Rock Springs that is quite famous. Whenever I take our two seven-gallon water jugs to fill them, I'm always about fifth in line to use the spring that bubbles freely from a pipe in the ground nonstop.

Jessi will follow this daily regimen for six months before returning to Mexico in January. At that time, her doctor hopes to be able to step up her immune system treatments and incorporate the Alivizatos regimen to assist with her healing. Ruthie and I are currently arguing over who gets to make the next trip with Jessi, and I'm starting to sense that it's a losing battle on my part.

Maybe we'll just have to compromise and extend the Mexican stay by a week after she finishes her treatments so we all can enjoy some time to decompress together. There … argument solved. Now it's time to go fishing.

The Alivizatos treatment he referred to was developed in Greece; it included a very strict diet, low in protein and acid intake, with an IV infusion every day. The diet prohibits canned foods, white flour, refined sugars, smoked or fried meat, hot dogs, salted nuts, and alcohol, just to name a few. After the first six months of intense treatment, an occasional glass of wine may be added. The diet pushes raw, organic fruits and vegetables and whole grains. It was another successful alternative in the FitzRandolphs' eyes.

"The people who are on it have just done amazing," explained Ruthie. "They couldn't put Jessi on it [that summer of 2012] because they felt her kidneys might not be able to handle the waste."

The FitzRandolphs hoped and prayed for Jessi's kidneys to improve to the point where she might be able to start the Alivizatos protocol. They were scheduled to return to Mexico in six months for a re-evaluation. That would have been January 2013, but they never went back to Mexico because of events that happened over the following two years.

CHAPTER TWELVE

Battles Won and Lost

Fall 2012

A bout this time, the summer of 2012, the FitzRandolphs began tinkering with the idea of writing a book. They wanted to help people involved in cancer treatments, hoping they would see there are other ways to do things. And they were brave enough to open up about their own story even as they were in the middle of it, with an uncertain ending. Jessi insisted that it not be a "We've Found the Cure for Cancer!" book, because she wasn't sure they had. The family's goal instead was to offer a true representation of two parents, two children, and the choices they made in a lifetime of highs and lows.

Jessi was having a mixed fall. Sometimes she looked and felt almost normal and would go out to lunch with her friends, the Verona Babes. She continued the treatments from her Mexican visit, and she gave the outward appearance of a pretty, athletic thirty-something-year-old. Other days were not so good.

In September of 2012, Jessi was one of sixteen models invited to participate in a fashion show for local cancer survivors held in one of Madison's premiere hotels. She moved up and down the runway in outfits supplied by local retailers. The organizers, who were raising money for cancer research at the University of Wisconsin Carbone Cancer Center, had hoped for an audience of 120 people. Instead 300 attended, including a huge cheering section for Jessi that included Casey, Jenn, Jeff, Ruthie, the Verona Babes, and a large group of friends who had skipped a Green Bay

156

Packers–Chicago Bears game to cheer a true hero instead. Jessi strutted the aisle in boots up to her knees.

"I cried when Jessi walked down the runway and didn't stop until the show was over," said Jeff. "She was simply stunning."

She looked confident and smiled radiantly at the crowd, but inside she wasn't feeling well. After the show, the whole group took two pictures, one serious and one silly. In the picture, Jessi was in the middle of the group, smiling. Shortly after the picture taking, she told her parents she was exhausted and then threw up into a leftover plastic cup.

Jessi also admitted the event, although lovely in many ways, was hard on her psyche. The other models could smile with relief and call themselves survivors. Jessi was still in the thick of it and the only one trying alternative methods.

Her stomach continued to give her issues after the fashion show, and she wasn't sure why. Maybe it was a whole-body sweep she did with the Rife machine that could have been too much for her system to handle. Or perhaps it was the many vitamins from Mexico that her system had to get used to. She tried acupuncture without much success. Now, she was barely eating. Ruthie decided to get some lab work done to try and diagnose the problem. The oncology lab called with results that afternoon. Jessi's calcium levels were sky high. High counts are the result of calcium leaking from your bones into your bloodstream as bone mass deteriorates with the spread of cancer. The high calcium also causes vomiting and a general feeling of lethargy and despair. It can be controlled temporarily with IV medications. The doctors said she would need fluids and overnight observation. Jessi and Ruthie took off for the emergency room. Jessi had grown to despise hospitals, especially their sterile smell. Being placed in her usual hospital room, the one that would come to be called "Jessi's Suite," was the only consolation.

That month the *Wisconsin State Journal* newspaper did a follow-up story on Jessi's protocols, bringing readers up to speed on her Mexico treatments. But the FitzRandolphs were not happy. A conventional American doctor was quoted as saying: "People who are facing their death are prone to charlatans. They are preyed upon because of the hope they are offered." The doctor also admitted that some in the medical field can be offended when a patient seeks alternative care, especially in foreign countries. He offered reasons why he didn't think these types of treatments would work, including his opinion that drugs that were considered lower- quality were being dispensed in other countries.

Jeff and Ruthie responded with a letter to the editor that they repeated in a CarePages post:

> *September 17, 2012*
> *2:33 p.m.*
> *We find the article written in the Sunday, September 16* Wisconsin State Journal *very informational but somewhat misleading, apparently because of the space limitations in the newspaper. We particularly take objection to one comment made by a UW Health cancer specialist and one omission in the article.*
>
> *By using the term "prone to charlatans," Dr. Cleary casts aspersions on every alternative care provider in the world, even legitimate providers—and there are many. They practice outside the United States because of our powerful drug companies and their stranglehold on US doctors. [The doctor] even references the "lower quality of drugs" used on his patients outside the United States. in his comments. In many types of alternative cancer treatments, drugs are not the primary source of healing and are rarely used.*
>
> *The term "charlatan" might better be used in reference to the doctor at a local hospital who told Jessi and our family that after two months of failed treatment, they couldn't do anything more for her so she should go to hospice and prepare for death over the next two months. Jessi is vibrant and alive over a year later.*
>
> *The omission is also curious. There is mention in the article of the many of the kinds of treatments Jessi received while in Mexico but no mention of the purpose of those treatments. There is also no mention of the completely organic alkaline diet served in the hospital there. Legitimate doctors outside the United States believe in treating cancer by rebuilding a patient's immune system from the ground up as opposed to*

killing cells (good and bad) using chemotherapy and radiation. That is the reason for the variety of treatment options used, as along with proper diet, each serves an important function in the rebuilding and healing process. As the patient's immune system is rebuilding it is also eliminating the cancerous cells through the use of the person's own DNA and dendritic cells.

Once the immune system's strength is restored, the cancer survivor's own body works to prevent the development of new cancer cells. We are firm believers in building the body from within and opposed to destroying cancerous and good cells simultaneously using conventional treatment methods. This treatment philosophy gives the patient hope, and the life-saving results are well documented. The AMA turns its back on these successes.

Conventional treatments manage pain and offer the patient no hope during their "end of life care." And rarely are these patients ever informed by their doctors that alternative options exist. We sincerely believe that it is every doctor's moral obligation to provide their patients with information which may save their lives. If you would like to learn more about alternative cancer treatments, please visit www.cancertutor.com and draw your own conclusions.

Sincerely,
Jeff and Ruthie FitzRandolph

Meanwhile, things were getting worse, and at an alarming rate. In addition to nausea, Jessi felt an explosion of back pain and, most discouraging of all, a scan that showed new bone mets in her left shoulder, left hip, and left buttocks. She still had energy to babysit for Sawyer and Cassidy one night, coloring at the table and watching TV until bedtime, but many days she was very tired. Everyone worried for about a week until the old Jessi slowly started returning. When propped in a semi-sitting position on the couch, she felt mostly fine and had her usual humor and energy. It was getting up and moving around that caused her pain. She took conventional painkillers—oxycodone—but there was tension in the house. A stubborn clash of wills was brewing over whether or not she would use another alternative treatment, Cellect powder, in smoothies.

Her parents believed in it. They had read success stories about this powder chasing cancer out of the body. The Cellect powder protocol was developed by Fred Eichhorn, a biochemist and survivor of advanced pancreatic cancer. He created the proprietary powder to cure his own cancer. It's described as a very fast-acting, yet nontoxic nutritional supplement used to kill cancer cells in advanced stages of cancer. The FitzRandolphs had hoped Jessi could tolerate its foul taste, but it left her feeling bloated. It ruined even the best of fruit smoothies.

"It's been documented that people with lung cancer on the Cellect will cough up bits of tumor, clumps of cancer. I wish she would have been able to handle the Cellect, but if she can't tolerate it then she just can't," sighed Ruthie one fall Sunday.

Jessi just didn't like the side effects of Cellect, even if her parents believed in its benefits. She took only four scoops a day—the protocol called for up to twenty—but it wasn't going down well.

"I felt uncomfortable the entire time I was on it. My stomach constantly felt full and bloated, like something was pressing on my stomach, and I couldn't handle it."

Jessi had to make her own care decisions, and in the final analysis she decided to go off the Cellect. Jeff was more open to her stopping and trying something new; Ruthie was upset. Jessi dug her heels in. There were some hard moments.

"I would have just liked to see her stick with the Cellect a little longer. To me, it would be worth a shot. But Jessi is in the driver's seat, and I just have to remember that sometimes," said Ruthie.

"I don't want to feel like that constantly, and it was constant. It was like I had no relief. I think it probably is a good product, but I had a hard time feeling like that all the time. It reminded me of how I felt when I had aHUS," Jessi explained.

So she stopped. Jeff immediately began doing research on other treatments that perhaps wouldn't have the same uncomfortable side effects.

"Initially we wanted to do the Rife, Bob Beck, and Cellect, but when she couldn't take the Cellect, Jeff, with the benefit of his early retirement, had the time to do more research," explained Ruthie.

His next stop was Poly-MVA, a combination of vitamins, minerals, and amino acids. In a liquid form, it touts itself as promoting cellular production and overall health. The makers also say it has antioxidant properties that replace nutrients lost during therapies.

"You have to take it every six hours," said Ruthie. "If you wait longer than six hours it's like giving the cancer cells chicken noodle soup. You really have to do it every six hours."

So Jeff ordered his first batch, and Jessi ingested Poly-MVA around the clock, waking herself up at midnight and six in the morning to make sure she didn't miss a dose. It had to be refrigerated, so she slept with a small cooler next to her. The new liquid cost six hundred dollars for a three-week supply, but she felt relieved that she didn't experience any of the stomach problems she had with the Cellect—at least at first. Although Poly MVA didn't give her the bloated feeling, she did vomit frequently for about a week. In week two of the Poly treatments she was finally up to the recommended dosage. As hard as it was on her, her parents thought it actually could be a good sign. Jeff pointed out that what she threw up was reddish in color, a mucousy material.

"Our research tells us when cancer cells die off, they present themselves in a mucousy form. We're hopeful that that's what it is. It was kind of slimy and gooey, with small chunks of a fleshy substance in it. It's encouraging," said Ruthie.

Jessi wanted to match their enthusiasm but couldn't muster up that kind of optimism.

"It's kind of hard to be excited when you're throwing up. I don't get as excited as my parents probably do. It's hard for me to know what's going on or what's causing it."

Her appetite was so down she would just have a small piece of toast with some fruit or applesauce. Sleep for her was going well—that was the good news—but this was a difficult, arduous stretch for the whole family. Ruthie was working a ton, even picking up extra hours, to help pay for the treatments. Jeff was at home with Jessi.

"Last Thursday was probably one of my worst days," said Ruthie on that October 2012 Sunday. "I came home after a twelve-hour day and asked Jessi if she needed anything, and she said no. She's so low maintenance it's ridiculous. I said, 'Do you need help getting into your pajamas?' and she said, 'Well, I'm kind of in them.' In talking with her it came out that she hadn't showered or changed clothes in five days, which is so not like Jessi. That made me really sad. I have to give Jeff a little lesson on how to be perceptive and to clue in. I know he would help her, but Jessi has to bring it up."

Ruthie created a notebook filled with ideas for Jeff to keep better track of Jessi's comfort on the home front, things like "Ask her if she needs a bath" or "Fluff the pillows behind her." They bought essential oils to put in the Jacuzzi tub. The jets and warm water did seem to ease the pain a bit, and they vowed to get her into clean clothes every day; they also brought her toothbrush upstairs so she didn't have to go down to the bathroom. Ruthie assisted Jessi when she needed to wash her hair.

"She allows me to help her with those things, which is really nice because she's not the type that would normally accept help."

Ruthie was torn about work. She could see that it was good for her to go. She felt she sometimes gave too much advice when she was home for long stretches. A sense of routine was positive for all who were involved, but there was one thing that Ruthie had a very hard time with when she was gone.

"Nobody here at home is in touch with me. We have three land lines and Jeff has a cell phone, but he still can't pick up the damn phone. I don't know how difficult it can be to carry a cell phone, but apparently it's rocket science. That's something we're working on. There's a whole lot of me that wishes I could retire, but it's the money. I'd like to be here for Jessi."

While Ruthie continued to work, Jessi stayed home and tried to get comfortable despite constant pain. Often she was in that semiseated position on the couch with a heating pad at her back. She passed the time by reading and watching her favorite TV shows and any game involving the Packers.

Her days of socializing had gone down. Two of Jessi's friends, a young couple, had just purchased their first home and were having a housewarming party, and Jessi wanted to attend. She planned on it, but she was in so much pain and still vomiting that had to e-mail them and bow out at the last moment. She was touched when the doorbell rang later and it was the whole gang, coming to see her.

"That was really cool. It was nice to see them and hang out and chat with someone other than Mom and Dad," she said, smiling. The friends stayed for an hour, and Jessi had a gift for each of them. It was a giant-sized version of the classic children's book *The Little Engine That Could.*

"I wrote a little note in each one that said 'I love you,'" Jessi said. She signed her name under that inscription. Her friends told her they were going to cherish it so much they were not going to let their kids tear into the book. This one was for them, a symbol of everything she was going through.

Jessi's pain was consistently pretty bad, and elevated calcium levels landed her back in the emergency room. There, the doctor had a blunt and negative statement.

"The hospitalist came in at about seven thirty, and it was a bizarre little meeting," remembered Ruthie. "He kept saying 'I'm so sorry, I'm so sorry.' He treated her like she was dying. After he left we both were scratching our heads, and we said, does he know something we don't? Because Jessi really is not planning on checking out at this point. He kept saying 'This really sucks.' He ended up by saying a prayer, which I think was lovely, but he talked as though Jessi was very, very terminal and we didn't want to come to terms with the inevitable. We were like WTH—our jaws dropped.

"He's a nice guy, and I know he meant well. He was well aware of Jessi's alternative treatments and that she was going against the current. He basically pronounced Jessi terminal once again and said that with alternative methods nothing is proven and all these people want is money. I so disagree with that. There are so many living examples that it just baffled me that our doctors here think that nothing is proven. I think it's a lack of knowledge and exposure. If they knew some of the information that we know, I think they would go the same path if they had to search for a way to survive. I will not accept the fact that Jessi can't turn this thing around or that we can't help her turn this thing around. I know what her prognosis is in the conventional oncology world, and I'm just not willing to go there and sign that death sentence."

Ruthie felt the conventional world could not even answer some of her basic questions. She asked one of the doctors once what the goal is of conventional treatment.

"And he said, 'That's a very good question.' He couldn't answer what the goal was. To me that's not putting a lot of faith in the treatment. It makes you sick, it makes you throw up, it will drag you down, and in the end you die anyway … I can't see that it's worth it," Ruthie said.

But despite their belief in alternatives, there was one chemo drug they believed in: Herceptin, made especially for HER2-positive cancer patients. All of the doctors around the world had agreed that this was a good drug for Jessi to be on, in harmony with her other treatments. The FitzRandolphs felt the medication had been quite effective. So it was with shock that they ran into a roadblock with their oncologist, who had initially acted like he was okay with their treatment decisions. He suddenly seemed to have a change of heart.

"Jessi had a regular visit scheduled, and he actually sent her home with a handwritten note suggesting she take Herceptin and two newly approved chemo drugs, Taxotere and Pertuzumab. The note ended with this admonishment: 'Stop going to Mexico,'" Ruthie explained.

The warning labels on Taxotere and Pertuzumab were startling to say the least. Possible side effects common to both drugs included extreme weakness, nausea, cold and flu symptoms, hair loss, dry skin, swollen ankles, loss of appetite, anxiety, chest pain, rapid heart rate, bruising, unusual bleeding, shortness of breath, and on and on. The advantages, as the FitzRandolphs saw them, were reduced pain levels and an extension of life by three to six months.

Jeff, Ruthie, and Jessi were beside themselves. They decided to switch oncologists and set up an appointment with a new, perhaps more progressive oncologist. It took six weeks to get an appointment, even though Jessi was in dire need of seeing someone and her health was considered to be in crisis mode. Part of the problem was they were required to see a physician who was under their insurance plan, and thus their choices were limited. It was time for another CarePages update, this one frothing with Ruthie's frustration:

> *Progression of Disease*
> *October 29, 2012*
> *10:29 a.m.*
> *Good morning,*
>
> *Do you ever feel so overwhelmed you don't know where to begin? The house is a mess and I have 7,880 unread e-mail messages (this is not a typo), but instead of whittling away at*

my to-do list, I felt an urgent need to post an update. I think you will be shocked by what you read.

Jessi was doing quite well this past summer. She was getting Herceptin every three weeks. Look back at the family photo in front of our cabin.

We decided to be more proactive about Jessi's treatment regimen and chose a clinic in Mexico for further treatment. Please look back to the photo of Jessi in the blue dress with that million-dollar smile. We toured the San Diego Zoo by foot while we were there.

We arrived home. Things were looking good. Jessi was stable, and we had new hope. Jessi had a routine appointment with her conventional oncologist. She was upfront about having been to Mexico, and he told her she needed to take a chemo trio, which included Herceptin and two toxic chemo drugs. He wrote out "No more trips to Mexico" on a paper that he gave her. That would have been in direct conflict with our alternative treatments that work to boost the immune system. Plus, she wasn't too excited about losing her hair again.

It wasn't long before she had intractable nausea, vomiting, and pain. A younger, possibly more open-minded oncologist was recommended, and Jessi finally had her appointment this past Friday after an agonizing six-week wait to get in.

The "good girl" Ruthie was in attendance at the appointment, not the newer, more assertive version that I have become over the last two years. I was just happy to have an oncologist again. And he seemed like a nice guy.

Looking back, Jessi was doing well upon her return from Mexico. She was on a good protocol, and as most proponents of alternative therapy believe, one should tackle such a disease from multiple angles. But the progression with four new lesions had occurred just recently, since the Herceptin had been stopped.

Jessi has not been out socially since Passion for Fashion. She is in a lot of pain to the point where she was not able to keep an appointment for a pedicure yesterday. She had looked forward to a little pampering.

Breast cancer is "the darling" of cancers. We even have a month devoted to it, Pinktober, but trust me, there is nothing darling about breast cancer. It's a dreadful disease. With all the money donated for cancer research, it is a crime we have made such little progress, but that's another post.

Thanks for following our journey.

Ruthie

The FitzRandolphs simply could not understand why a doctor, sworn by the Hippocratic Oath to help you, would not do everything in his or her power to work with a patient, even if that person brought some new ideas to the table. Why wouldn't an oncologist be anxious to see if these things did work on cancer cells? Why would they be so stuck in their ways that they were practically blindfolded? Why not try methods other researchers and doctors worldwide were using?

Back at the house, Jessi was trying desperately to keep her spirits up.

"I'm just frustrated. It's no fun sitting here not being able to do things. There are days I get sad or down, but it usually doesn't last too long."

"I sure don't see those times," added Ruthie, who was perched on a chair a few feet away, always ready to get anything Jessi needed. "She's the strongest person I know, and we're going to keep fighting as long as Jessi is up to the battle."

"I'm a trooper," said Jessi.

Although her mother assisted her with baths, food, and general living, in the next breath Jessi admitted that it was hard for her to accept such assistance.

"Why is that hard for you?" asked Ruthie gently, leaning slightly towards Jessi. You could tell she was eager to hear the answer because her daughter hardly ever spoke of these types of inner thoughts. Jeff and Ruthie had been encouraging her to see a counselor, but Jessi had not done so.

Jessi, wearing a gray sweatshirt and jeans, her legs wrapped in a blanket and propped up on the other end of the couch, looked at her mother. The sun was dipping and the light in the living room fading as she spoke her honest, deepest emotions.

"I feel bad because I feel like there are so many other things you guys would rather be doing than taking care of your sick daughter."

Ruthie paused for a moment, taken aback, forming words in her head. She drew in a halting breath, her eyes filled with tears. Her voice broke as she spoke:

"Jessi, right now there is nothing I would rather be doing than taking care of my sick daughter."

Tears dripped down both of their cheeks. There was silence for a moment until Jessi added:

"I feel like you got shit on, too. This isn't the life I wanted, for sure."

"It's not the life I wanted for you either, but shit happens, ya know?" Ruthie spoke with enormous tenderness, emotion still filling her throat. "Do you know the song 'I'm Gonna Love You Through It?' We are gonna love you through it, and we're gonna beat this thing too, darn it. We're all too stubborn. There are two statements that stayed with me since my childhood: "Where there's a will there's a way" and "With God nothing is impossible." And I do believe that nothing is impossible."

As fall gave way to Thanksgiving, Jessi remained in terrible pain. It was not obvious when looking at her. She masked it well, but her frustration was palpable. She thought she'd be in a lot less discomfort with the many types of treatments that she had undertaken.

On Thanksgiving morning, Jessi sat in the bed the family had reestablished in the living room. She watched the Macy's Thanksgiving Parade, the whirling dancers in bright costumes flying across the screen as she rested her head on several pillows propped behind her.

Casey was there with Sawyer and Cassidy, along with Aunt Nancy and Uncle Andy. Jenn was soon to join the group, but she was busy cooking at her house. Between Jenn and Nancy, the two of them had offered to prepare the Thanksgiving feast so Ruthie and Jeff wouldn't have to worry about making a huge meal followed by a kitchen sink full of pots and pans.

The mood in the house was not great. The new, younger oncologist was not turning into the savior they had hoped for. He was clearly not in favor of alternative medicine; he wasn't even curious about it. He also wanted to withhold Herceptin unless she took two other chemo drugs. They had debated what to do for a while but decided in the end that the side effects of doing all three chemo drugs together outweighed the benefits. They hoped to keep Jessi's body as healthy as possible so that it could fight off the cancer properly, and they had stepped up treatments to boost Jessi's immune system. They decided they were done with what they felt was "two steps forward, one step back." They had charted a course they were comfortable with and confident in, and Jessi had been practicing the new protocol since mid-October.

Jessi was still vomiting, but Ruthie and Jeff were hoping against hope that it still could be a good sign. What Jessi was bringing up continued to be thick and filled with mucous, almost red in color. Could it be dead cancer cells? They held their breath every day.

The biggest issue was pain. It was so bad that Jessi had consented to more radiation. The oncologist offered her targeted radiation, the conventional treatment to reduce pain. The FitzRandolphs hesitated at first because they believed radiation caused a reduction in the body's ability to produce red blood cells. Ultimately, Jessi decided the pain was unmanageable. She needed anything, anything at all, to make it go away. Ruthie agreed, and Jeff half-heartedly gave in. They knew that one possible side effect would be the need for transfusions to keep her red blood cells up. The human body needs red blood cells to stay alert and active and to deliver oxygen to tissues.

The radiation treatment came and went, but it hardly touched the pain and made Jessi's legs feel like Bambi's—wobbly and unsteady. She was on oxycodone but said it was akin to eating candy. It was not providing any relief either. Her discomfort was so acute that Jessi was reluctant to get up to go to the bathroom. She tried to drink less so her bladder would hold out longer. She was mostly confined to the bed, and her world had shrunk to that one view of the same living room, but she did have company around the clock. Ruthie had just requested and received her second six-week family leave from her job at Stoughton Hospital. She started sleeping on a blow-up bed next to her daughter, not wanting Jessi to be alone. Ruthie didn't care if her own luxurious, king-sized bed was just steps away. Her comfort was the least of her worries. And besides, Jessi was a much quieter sleeper than Jeff.

A new portable toilet was next to the bed. On Thanksgiving, Ruthie abruptly sensed that Jessi needed a break and shooed everyone into a different part of the open-air living area. Ruthie and her sister held up a blanket to shield Jessi's privacy. After a few minutes things were back to normal, at least as normal as you can be when your living room has become your daughter's intensive care unit.

Jenn came in holding trays of steaming food: turkey and mashed potatoes, gravy and cranberries. She had offered to host at their house, but Jessi was too immobile to make the trip, and so the personalized catering service came to Jeff, Ruthie, and Jessi instead.

Jenn looked a little harried as she hauled plate after plate up the stairs, the unusually warm November air swirling in every time the door opened and closed. It had been a crazy morning for Jenn, trying to get everything done in a timely manner. She was clearly attempting to pick up the slack for the rest of the family. Jenn's days were long—teaching first-graders for seven straight hours before returning to a house with her own kindergartner and preschooler. Casey's job took him on the road, and he still loved to have time to deer hunt and tend to his land, so Jenn was the only parent in the house more often than she wanted. The stress on everyone was clear. Each person wanted so desperately for everything to feel normal and right, and it just wasn't. If they could just get a sign that their medical plan was working—something, anything—it might keep them going. As they sat in the house on that clear, bright Thanksgiving morning, so many questions hung in the air. Would Jessi get better? And if so, when? What no one knew was that a change was coming, and soon. If Jessi had one of those black plastic Magic eight-balls so many of us played with as kids, it might have said, "All signs point to yes." Before Christmas that positive moment was going to make its appearance.

CHAPTER THIRTEEN

A Turn for the Better

Fall 2012

C an you imagine being in unfathomable pain, discomfort so bad
you can hardly move, and then—poof!—one day you wake
up and it's gone? Amazingly and unbelievably, that is exactly
what happened to Jessi. She had gone into the hospital shortly after
Thanksgiving with a racing heart and anemia; several units of blood were
pumped through her system, and she stayed for three days. On the last
morning, she woke up feeling great. The doctor came in and asked her
what her pain level was at, and she shyly told him, "Right now it's at zero;
I have no pain." She had literally witnessed a melting away of the searing
pain. Everyone was stunned.

Somehow, some way, something had worked. Her parents credited
Jessi's genes and willpower. Ruthie thought back again to her own mother,
who decided that she was not ready to give in to lymphoma. Ruthie's father
had also lived twenty years longer than expected after learning of a bad
heart.

"There's some quirky little thing I think that goes through our blood
that isn't quite normal," marveled Ruthie. "This last time in the hospital
the oncologist even told us she's probably the only known survivor of
chemo-induced HUS. It's been a year and a half, and her kidneys are as
good as they've been since the episode."

It's possible the Poly-MVA, Bob Beck protocol, and Rife machines also
contributed to the sudden decrease in pain, but no one knows for sure. All
they could tell was that the sociable and happy Jessi was back, and they

were over the moon. It had been a rough, rough November. Jeff called it the worst month of his life. Seeing his daughter in such incredible pain was gut-wrenching.

"I finally got to the point where I felt helpless as her caretaker. I honestly didn't know what to do next, so I called Ruthie and told her I needed her at home. She came. We agreed she'd take some time off and we would get through this together."

Now, Jessi was exhilaratingly pain free, and hope returned to everyone's mind. It seemed to reinforce everything they were doing and infused them all with renewed energy.

Over the next month, Jessi went Christmas shopping with her mom and finally got that pedicure she had had to put off. She baked and frosted Christmas cookies with her dad and even went out with the Verona Babes to a Friday dinner and movie. She then hit a Saturday lunch spot with another small group of friends. That Sunday she felt well enough to travel to Casey's house to watch the Packers game in his living room. All of this would have been unthinkable in the very recent past.

The Christmas shopping trip and pedicure day meant a lot to mother and daughter. They drove to Farm and Fleet looking for presents for Sawyer and Cassidy. Jessi still needed to use a motorized cart—she wasn't quite ready to stroll the aisles on her own—but she felt good, damn good, compared to just a few weeks before. They took their time perusing the toy section and picked out pint-sized hunting gear for Sawyer, who liked to look like his dad and "Jeepers" (as Sawyer called Jeff), and lots of cute dolls for Cassidy. At the nail salon, Jessi chose a green sparkly color, her favorite, and Ruthie went for red sparkles; when you put their feet together they radiated Christmas colors. It was almost as if some sort of holiday magic dust had been sprinkled by elves who had passed their way.

Meanwhile, Christmas Day rolled around. Casey, Jenn, and the kids came to the house along with Aunt Nancy and Andy. Brunch was served while the kids tore into their gifts and Jessi opened her items—a new comforter, a winter coat in her favorite shade of green, and an electric toothbrush. Jessi also had a surprise for her mom.

"She gave me my very first Coach product. I don't splurge on myself too much," admitted Ruthie smiling. "But Jessi has this wonderful pink

Coach watch, and every time she wears it I think it's so pretty. I just love it. She got me one exactly like that."

Knowing her father's love of hunting, Jessi bought him a pair of tall, camouflaged rubber boots to hike to and from his deer stand without leaving any human scent for his wary prey. They were all feeling cautiously optimistic and, at the very least, grateful that Jessi had spunk and energy back. Jessi and Ruthie talked about her taking guitar lessons or doing some scrapbooking on a new electronic device. They thought it might help some of the boredom Jessi had from hanging out in the living room all day. She was still sleeping a lot, recharging her body, but when she was up her mind was active and ready for a challenge.

On New Year's Eve, Jeff decided to take over cooking duties and made a dinner he was proud of: bacon-wrapped scallops, shrimp on a skewer, a carrot and pea casserole, and long-grain wild rice harvested near their cabin on Big Siss. Jessi ate heartily. Her appetite had come back at about the same time that the pain disappeared. None of the family was able to stay up until midnight to watch the ball drop, but they went to bed on the last night of 2012 with some hope in the frosty air.

Jessi was feeling so good she decided she was ready to move back downstairs to her own bedroom. The hospital bed in the living room would stay, but only in the upright position as a comfortable place to sit and watch TV. They decided to change the living room from the ICU feel to a "rehab center" and put up pots of new orchids around to make it cheery. Jessi was able to negotiate the two flights of stairs down to her own space to sleep, and she was thrilled not to hear her mother's tossing and turning or her father getting up at five in the morning with the dogs. Ruthie, however, had grown to really enjoy sleeping on the blowup bed next to her daughter. It might not have been the most comfortable thing in the world, but the pleasure came in feeling that she was there to protect Jessi—as much as she could—24/7. Being apart for the night was a good and natural thing, a positive sign, and of course Ruthie knew that, but it was also just a little difficult for a mom to let go. The first night they slumbered in separate rooms, Ruthie couldn't sleep at all. Her mothering instincts were on high alert.

Ruthie had another issue, too. Her leave at Stoughton Hospital was nearly up, and she had to go back to work, a prospect that she wasn't looking forward to. Every fiber in her body wanted to be home with Jessi, but she also knew the family needed the income. She tried to prepare herself for the return.

Things weren't perfect. Although the pain was gone, Jessi was hardly doing jumping jacks and described how she felt this way: "I feel good, but old. When I wake up in the morning I feel kind of sick. It takes a little while to loosen up a little bit, but as the day goes on it gets better. Mornings are a little rough, but I'm not going to complain. Compared to a month or two ago, it's like 100 percent better."

The good news about the pain was tempered by the latest PET scan, which looks at all organs, soft tissues, and parts of the body. Although the disease had not spread to her liver or lungs, the bone mets were still significant, and the doctors thought there might have been some progression of the cancer. Why her pain was gone was still a mystery, but it was a happy mystery as far as the FitzRandolphs were concerned. Maybe the alternative meds were starting to do the trick, slowly but surely.

In early January, Jessi and Ruthie made a special outing to Whole Foods to fill the fridge with fresh, organic produce. The outing turned frustrating when the one motorized cart the store provided was broken. Jessi was not able to walk the entire store on her own and wound up sitting in the car while her mother checked out. The family was gaining a new appreciation for handicapped accommodations, and Ruthie decided to write Whole Foods a note of frustration. The experience reminded them that Jessi was not yet ready to negotiate the world alone, and the FitzRandolphs were not going to rest until she was.

Ruthie had a new idea. She read about an alternative medicine that used some of the properties in marijuana to get at cancer cells. She learned that medical cannabis had powerful medicinal value when the leaves and buds of the plant were boiled and then reduced to produce an oil-like substance.

Supporters believe the THC and CBD components of the resulting product work to kill cancer cells while reducing pain and strengthening bones. It does this without producing the same high experienced when smoking marijuana. And you didn't have to worry about lung cancer from inhaling the toxins. As an added benefit, the oil had a nutty flavor and only needed to be used in miniscule doses because of the high concentration of healing power in the condensed substance. Speaking on the phone with a lymphoma patient who had used it with phenomenal success, Ruthie got excited and vowed to do her homework to find out how to procure some for her daughter.

Jeff, who had decided his next research project would be stem cell and bone marrow transplants, quickly switched gears and pitched in with the cannabis oil research. While the FitzRandolphs felt a lot of things they were doing were working, they also had an unstoppable commitment to look at every single cancer-fighting possibility. The cannabis oil appeared to be a promising treatment. The only catch would be finding a source for the oil. Medicinal cannabis was illegal in Wisconsin. The FitzRandolphs soon learned that most people who were using the substance were illegally growing the plants and making their own oil or lived in one of nineteen states where it was then-legalized. That wouldn't stop them.

The family's relationship with their new, younger oncologist was finally showing some promise, even though he wouldn't prescribe cannabis for them. On his recommendation, the family decided to move ahead with one more surgery: the removal of Jessi's ovaries so any hormones that might feed her cancer would be eliminated. They finally got approval to go back on Herceptin. The doctor agreed to prescribe medicine that would help Jessi with her hot flashes, a result of the ovarian surgery, and a bone strengthening agent. The family secretly believed that if they were successful in procuring the medical cannabis, neither of the drugs would be needed for long. In their minds, every medicine Jessi took compromised her immune system in some way. They were bound and determined to rebuild Jessi's immune system and use that as the initial building block to renewed health. They would be dogged in their pursuit of a clean scan.

"There are a lot of people who have somehow survived stage IV cancer. I know for Jessi there's a cure out there," summarized Ruthie. "It's up to us to figure out just what that is."

"You know how we are. We're not happy sitting here until she's back to 100 percent," said Jeff with conviction. Now they just needed to find a source for the cannabis.

CHAPTER FOURTEEN

Cannabis Oil

Spring 2013

The FitzRandolphs would do anything for Jessi, even if that meant handing over an envelope full of money at a restaurant in exchange for a drug run. Yes, it happened.

Ruthie had a nurse friend named Tori who was diagnosed with fibromyalgia and had used medical cannabis for years. Tori would often joke that she was born in the wrong generation, calling herself the perfect flower child. Now she offered to help the couple, who did come of age in the sixties but were never much into weed. And thus, a new journey began.

Tori told them about cannabis oil, a system of boiling marijuana to harness its powerful and natural health benefits. The family learned that there are hundreds of strains of marijuana and two are considered especially therapeutic: Sativa and Indica. Sativa is the strain that has anti-anxiety, energizing and euphoric properties; Indica relaxes and induces sleepiness. Both were said to contain healing properties if you could extract the THC, the beneficial compound of the plant. Now Jeff and Ruthie had to find a way to buy some fresh pot, even though they were living in the middle of a state where it was illegal.

Tori jumped to help. First she offered to fly to Portland, Oregon, where a person can legally purchase medicinal dope. If one could prove they had a real, legitimate problem—and Tori did with fibromyalgia—that person could see a doctor and get a "green card" for $200. That card would then give you the right to buy from a legal medicinal dealer. Tori still would have to drive it back to Wisconsin. Flying with drugs was illegal, and even in a car there remained the danger of crossing state lines with marijuana, but Tori would do it for her friends. The FitzRandolphs were happy to buy Tori's airfare and pay mileage expenses on the return route.

Yet the best intentions did not pan out. Tori wasn't able to take time off work. She didn't want to keep the family waiting, so instead she began investigating sources closer to home and managed to find one right there in Wisconsin. She could buy the FitzRandolphs a large dose of the plant's healing buds. They would then make their own oil following directions from a website. The dealer had two large sandwich bags full of buds. The first bag was a pure Indica strain called Blackberry Kush. The second contained a blend of 70/30 Indica/Sativa strains called Blue Dream. These two combined, weighing a quarter of a pound, would yield approximately fifteen grams of oil and would cost Jeff and Ruthie $1,300.

Within a week the deal was set, but there was another problem: Tori was working and unable to pick it up. Her friend, "Steve," offered to make the run and told Jeff to meet him at a national chain restaurant and hand him the cash.

Jeff walked into the establishment, located in a suburban strip mall, one afternoon looking for a big guy with long hair, as the boyfriend had described himself. Sure enough, there he was eating lunch. They sat together making small talk until he finished his meal. Jeff didn't want to be sliding a cache of cash across the table in a crowded lunchtime spot. They were also conscious of possible security cameras mounted around the interior, so Steve suggested they do the deal in the vestibule. They walked out together, where Jeff handed him the envelope stuffed with cash.

Now, Steve had to drive to the supplier and give him the $1,300 in exchange for the buds. He told Jeff he'd be back at their house in two hours. As Jeff said good-bye and drove out of the parking lot, he couldn't help but think, 'Well, this was a big leap of faith.' He knew Ruthie trusted Tori, and he did too, but a little question mark was a natural thing to creep into one's head.

"Here's this guy, I don't know him from Adam, and I'm giving him $1,300 in hundred-dollar bills. He could take a nice trip for all I know."

Back at the house, Jeff told Jessi about his drug deal, and they set about to waiting. And waiting. Two hours went by, then two and a half, with no sign of Steve.

"Should I get nervous now?" Jeff asked his daughter.

He was thinking that perhaps this wasn't good. Finally, three hours later, their anxiety was quelled when Steve called to report it had taken him longer than expected. He offered to still come to the house that night, but Jeff told him not to worry. It was late afternoon on a Friday, and Tori was planning to be there the next day to help the family boil up their first batch of oil. Jeff directed Steve to send the goods with her. Everything was set.

The FitzRandolphs double checked the supply list they had already purchased, an odd assortment of items: paint thinner, a rice cooker, pickle jar, candle warmer, plastic dishes, wood mortar, coffee filters, a funnel and empty syringes.

The next afternoon, their personal Ganja goddess was at the door right at one p.m. Tori had the haul wrapped in five plastic bags for transporting because the smell permeated her entire car. The overwhelming and distinctive scent now filled the FitzRandolph's airy home as they laid everything out and set about to work. The buds were the size of a cherry tomato with a rough pitted surface filled with spiny hair follicles. It was such pure product that there were no leaves or shreds. The buds were harvested at the precise moment to guarantee the highest concentration of THC.

The first step was to place those balls in a plastic bowl and cover them with a very thin layer of the paint thinner called Naphtha. Then the FitzRandolphs took the wood mortar and beat the buds to get the medicinal properties to bond with the Naphtha. Although the web directions recommended beating it for three minutes, Jeff stood at the counter pounding for ten. Determination was practically his middle name and he wanted to be sure he wrenched every piece of goodness out for Jessi. When he was done, the buds had broken down to a flaky powder, still wet from the Naphtha. Jeff, Ruthie, Jessi and Tori strained this, giving them a liquid that looked a lot like gasoline. Then, they put the funnel in the pickle jar with a filter over it, running the oil through the filter. This left the group with a small amount of liquid to place in the rice cooker. Because paint thinner is highly explosive and flammable, they used a rice cooker to warm it very slowly, thereby getting rid of the Naphtha, but eliminating any fire danger that would have come from a more rapid heating process.

After thirty minutes of cooking, the Naphtha was fully boiled off and now yielded a very dark liquid. This went into a small jar with a few drops of water and was placed on the candle warmer for three hours. Water boils out at a higher temperature than the Naphtha. When the water was boiled and there was only a clear surface that indicated that all of Naphtha was gone. Now, the only thing left was to suck it up with a syringe and cool it, effectively turning it into its final form: a dark syrup that resembled motor oil.

The way to ingest this was to place a small drop of oil on a piece of bread and eat it. And Jessi would do this for the next three months. She started slowly at a quarter gram (a drop smaller than the tip of a pencil) twice per day and gradually worked up to a full gram four times a day, the dose recommended for getting rid of cancer.

On that first afternoon, with their baptismal batch cooling in a syringe, the family decided to celebrate by taking a small amount of weed the old fashioned way. Using a pipe Jessi had left over from her party days, father and daughter lit up. Ruthie abstained, not wanting to compromise her job as the sole breadwinner. Tori had her own pipe. They all talked and laughed and spirits were brighter than they had been in a while. They had earned a night like this.

In Madison, Wisconsin, one of the nation's most liberal cities, you can own up to a gram of marijuana for recreational use. But the FitzRandolphs lived in Verona, six miles outside of the Madison city limits. Plus, they were sitting on about a quarter-pound of marijuana.

So if a police officer walked in?

"He'd haul us off to jail," chuckled Jeff. "But I would say shame on that police officer for walking in here. We're not harming anybody, we're not selling, and we have no interest in making money from the oil we've made. All we want to do is to cure our daughter of this damn cancer that she's got. If this is going to do it, the risk is worth it—very definitely the risk is worth it to us."

That doesn't mean they didn't have moments of worry. Ruthie was startled awake by a dream that she was drug tested at work, even though she wasn't smoking herself. She reasoned that traces might be found from secondhand smoke left over from the one occasion the rest of the house lit up. Luckily, no tests or extra questions ever came her way.

Over the next few weeks, Jessi took the cannabis religiously, and Jeff became a master at cooking buds into oil. Even though paint thinner was a part of the process, he felt confident Jessi was not in danger of ingesting anything harmful because it burned off. Plus, he would test each batch for safety himself with a drop on bread that he ate.

"I figured if it didn't kill me, it wouldn't kill her."

As advertised, the Indica definitely made Jessi relaxed and very, very drowsy. She slept for the first two and a half weeks nearly nonstop, and most of February 2013 was a complete blur.

"I didn't like it but I didn't hate it" was her summation. She hoped the tradeoff would be worth it. In March, she was awake a little more often but still felt that, sometimes, she was only half in the room. While Jessi adjusted to constantly having marijuana in her body, Jeff and Ruthie were thrilled by some immediate results. Jessi's blood pressure, which had once been dangerously high due to kidney failure, went down and stabilized. They believed her heart, damaged from chemo and radiation, would show signs of strength as time went on. Any lingering pain in her hip was greatly reduced. She ditched her walker most days and went to dinner with Jeff, Sawyer, and Cassidy at a Mexican restaurant the second Friday night she was on the oil. She even drove her own car to and from the spot, her first time behind the wheel in six weeks. When the kids came back to the house, Jessi played Wii video games with them in the living room.

The big test would be another bone scan in June of 2013 to look for regression in any of the bone mets. The website indicated that they needed to give the oil three months before realistically hoping for any improvement. If there were positive signs on the scan, they could decrease the dosage to a maintenance stage after that.

In the meantime, the FitzRandolphs turned down another round of chemo being offered by the traditional oncologist, whose only other recommendation was to go to hospice.

"He said the chemo drug might make her more comfortable—*might*— but it wouldn't affect her longevity. Why would we do that?" asked Ruthie.

In the end, they also decided to decline Herceptin. This was the drug they had been trying so hard to get Jessi's doctor to approve, and he had finally agreed to put her back on it after the surgery to remove her ovaries. But following the surgery, they thought about it some more and decided the downside potential for more heart damage wasn't worth it. They were happy with what they were seeing from the cannabis oil. Why reintroduce a mildly toxic chemical to their natural, plant-based therapy?

About two weeks into the oil treatments, Jeff tweaked Jessi's dosage. He started giving her the Blue Dream blend at noon and six in the evening and the Blackberry Kush at midnight and six in the morning. Jessi immediately became more alert during her waking hours, and her frame of mind was much improved. He reasoned that by mixing the strains daily, they might just be enhancing the healing effects. It was all a part of the fact-finding process.

Jessi continued on the Poly-MVA four times per day. She took drops of a new supplement, CoQ10, a coenzyme vitamin for heart strength, as part of the Poly-MVA protocol, did the Bob Beck treatment, swallowed immune system–building tablets called Laetrile (brought home from Mexico), juiced and ate organic foods, employed coffee enemas to remove toxins, and lay down with the Rife machine sending radio frequency signals through her body every other day.

"We think that the Rife works because she threw up halfway through a recent four-hour sweep on the machine. We think that's the body ridding itself of the dead cancer cells," said Ruthie.

The FitzRandolphs decided then and there that they were really and truly done with traditional cancer medications. When Jessi's doctor offered and encouraged her to use radiation on her hip, they declined. A new, miracle breast cancer drug called TDM-1 was being touted all over the media. It was Herceptin wrapped in a carrier drug that transported it directly to cancer cells and then was said to dissolve those cells. Jeff and Ruthie scoffed for several reasons.

"It'll give you three extra months to live—that's it, they admit that in their product build-up. And it only has three possible side effects: it may cause heart failure, it might toxify your liver, or, worst case scenario, it might kill you. Yet they call it the safest drug they've ever discovered? It's also $9,800 for one monthly treatment. It's just another way to make money. It's so bold-faced and blatant. I don't understand the oncology system. They obviously have no moral conscience. They have no fear, so they don't care," spit Jeff.

It would ultimately be Jessi's choice if she wanted to try it, but her parents were adamantly against it.

"It's so expensive because it's the first chemo drug with a carrier that targets the cancer cells. Well, guess what? Targeting cancer cells is exactly the way Poly-MVA works, and there are any number of other alternative treatments that do this, too. This technology has been out there for years, and here they are claiming this new super drug as if they've just discovered how to carry it to the cancer cells. It's a hoax. Plus, they have the nerve to call alternative practitioners charlatans. Guess who the real charlatans are!"

The family felt very, very comfortable with the direction they were heading. It was then that they decided against a return trip to Mexico for more immune system building. Jessi wasn't really up to flying anyway, but the bigger issue would have been transporting the Rife machine and all of her treatments—including illegal drugs—across the border. Maybe that would not be the best plan. So they sat tight in their lovely wooded home and waited for more of the good results they really felt were already happening.

The whole family got together for an afternoon visit less than a month after Jessi started the oil. Cassidy rode around in a plastic car, winding her way through the living room, onto the imaginary expressway in the dining room, and back down a country road next to the coffee table. Sawyer hitched a semi to a wagon and dragged a small Toys R Us load of goodies along the same path. They occasionally bumped into each other, and Jenn and Casey broke up a few angry sibling moments.

Jessi leaned back in a recliner near the windows, her legs hidden in a thick blanket. She was awake and alert for most of the lengthy visit, sometime watching the movie *Bridesmaids* and at other moments joining in the conversation or simply relaxing and watching her niece and nephew play. She seemed extremely mellow, but not anywhere close to what people would classify as stoned. Jeff brought her a smoothie from her favorite neighborhood café to wash down the oil, and she drank it heartily. She looked really good. She had all of her hair, wasn't bloated, was mentally sharp, and was feeling mostly comfortable nearly twenty-four hours per day.

"For the first time, I can honestly say we're doing everything in our power, and what we're doing is having a positive effect," said Jeff. "It took us a while to settle on all of those things. We've been playing around with different protocols since July 2012. Is she improving or not? Her strength is getting better, her pain is reduced, her blood pressure is stabilized, and her creatinine, which is a measure of her kidneys, is not far from normal. It has been high since her battle with aHUS. Her blood counts, for the most part, are very normal. The red blood counts she has a little trouble with, but we believe that's because of radiation. Just about everything that ailed her was a direct result of conventional oncology medicine trying to cure her."

Jeff and Tori continued to work together to find the best deal they possibly could. Tori's contacts were turning up multiple leads. A supplier from Kentucky could get them sixty grams of high-quality oil for $2,000, a much better price than the $1,300 they originally paid for fifteen grams of buds to turn into oil. She also found a supplier in Washington, DC, and sent Jeff the following e-mail:

> *Great news! Just got done jumping up and down over this, but details have to be worked out ...*
>
> *Two pounds of OG Kush (one of the BEST medicinal Indica strains) for ... $2,500! That's almost the entire treatment! Catch—the supplier is out of Maryland. He gets his supply from a DC activist MD. He's getting back to me with a time frame and details, but wow! That's less than half the street cost! The KY person is still willing to advise on extraction with alcohol if we don't buy oil from him. I'm going to go about checking the Maryland person out but either luck/fate/karma are looking down on us or ... I don't know. Ha-ha!*
>
> *Tori*

Call it whatever you want, the FitzRandolphs didn't care. It was definitely music to their ears, and Jeff sent this email to a friend:

> *Just think about it-$2,500 to get a two-month supply of four daily doses of a natural cancer-curing medicine versus $9,800 for one month's treatment of a chemo drug that will give you three more months to live if it doesn't destroy your heart, toxify your liver, or just plain kill you first. Need I say*

"No-brainer?" Oh, but I forgot, Jessi's insurance will gladly pay the cost of the chemo drug but wouldn't consider even a co-pay for the much cheaper, natural cure. Blows my mind.

The Maryland connection never materialized in the end, and the FitzRandolphs continued their clandestine meetings with Steve to provide the oil needed for Jessi's care. The pipeline was becoming increasingly difficult to manage because their local supplier could make more money selling in smaller amounts to his already established clientele. But they kept plugging along and, with Tori's help, were able to find enough product with only a few short lapses to Jessi's treatment.

As the weeks went on, they tweaked the strains. Jessi perked up so much she drove herself out to dinner with friends and made a trip to the grocery store by herself. The oil was making all the difference in the world, they believed, and the FitzRandolphs were beside themselves. They really felt they were on to something.

"I can honestly say I'm as encouraged as I've been in a long time about something actually working," summed up Jeff. Now, they just had to wait for the scan.

CHAPTER FIFTEEN

Perfecting the Alternative Protocol

2012

As the family became more and more comfortable and confident in their alternative treatments, they looked back and started to question the cancer routes they had taken early on. It had all happened so fast: Jessi telling them that day in the kitchen, the mastectomy, chemo, and a whirlwind of decisions they had to make almost instantaneously.

"I wish I could have had a five-year notice," sighed Ruthie. "That someone had told me, 'Jessi's going to get cancer in five years, so do your homework.'"

Instead it was like the bad dream many of us have endured: a monstrous pop quiz in high school or college where you barely even know the subject. With the benefit of hindsight, Ruthie rethinks their quick decision to remove Jessi's breast. Most women would automatically agree to this if it housed a cancerous lump. That's just what we do: we want to get the tumor out of our body, to feel clean again, But after turning to alternative treatments Ruthie is firmly in the court that the mastectomy was a mistake. She has an entirely different belief than the typical American: The lump can actually be a helpful tool to the patient.

"You can tell if the cancer is getting better or worse because you've got a lump there and that can be measured with a caliper. If they removed the breast, you don't have anything to measure. You lose that palpable gauge. Plus, when they go in and do surgery I think that frees up all the radical cells loose in your body. It stirs up the hornet's nest. They also take out lymph nodes, which are there for a purpose, to filter toxins out of your body, and now you've lost that natural protection."

There were other missteps. If they looked all the way back to when Jessi first went to the ER with a fractured rib and was told it was because of the way she coughed, they realized that they should have requested further investigation. Later, when she had mild back pain, they should not have let the oncologist pooh-pooh it.

"She and I both brought it up," remembered Ruthie. "When he heard it moved around a bit, he said that was nothing to worry about. He never looked into it, and we never pressed the subject. I thought 'Whew, that's nothing to worry about because the doctor didn't react.' I'm thinking I'm the nurse-mother that overreacts. I don't know why they didn't do a metastatic workup before taking the breast and the nodes. They absolutely should have looked at a bone scan. If breast cancer metastasizes, after the lymph nodes the bone is usually the next stop on the cancer agenda."

The FitzRandolphs don't agree on the German travel and treatments. Was it the right thing to do? If she had it to relive over again, Ruthie would have opted instead to go to Mexico right away. She came to believe that the clinic they would go to in Mexico addressed the body's own immune system response much more aggressively and also provided safer hyperthermia treatments as an option. Jessi never blamed the German hospital for her aHUS, and Jeff stood steadfast in his belief that the German treatments would have put Jessi's cancer in remission. He felt that there was too much uncertainty among the attending physicians at St. Mary's Hospital regarding what caused the aHUS to attach blame. In his eyes, there were simply too many possible causes to establish a definitive culprit.

As far as American treatment, they also would not have consented to so many surgeries and biopsies. In their opinion, each one creates new problems by revving up cancer cells. They believe the same of radiation. While it might help its one targeted area, it then sends those cells running away to find new burrowing spots elsewhere. The idea, as they see it, should be to treat the entire person to get rid of the cancer, not just chase the symptoms from place to place.

What they would have done from the very beginning instead, and what they would like other people to think about, is the following:

"Immune system building as well as alkalizing the environment in the body," explained Ruthie. "Cancer is sometimes hereditary, but there can be different things that cause it. I would have first of all tried to cut out sugar and white foods, alcohol, smoking, do the juicing, and exercise. I would suggest having a metastatic workup before considering surgery. In advanced disease, if you have a lump that you can palpate, you can monitor your progress. Check out websites for yourself and decide if some of the alternative treatments are for you."

Jeff's advice: "If you're diagnosed with cancer, immediately get a second opinion. Get that second opinion from a naturopath or a doctor who practices alternative protocols, or maybe both. Learn the options that are available for your treatment before you make a decision on what to do. Once the surgery is done and you're headed down that course, you've already weakened your immune system and started to compromise your ability to regain your health completely. Your first attempt should be to try to cure your own cancer by boosting your immune system, lowering your body's acidity level, eliminating all toxins currently in your body, limiting introduction of new toxins, and increasing your oxygen intake. This can be done relatively inexpensively by using the right supplements and changing your diet. I would recommend this protocol for six months before considering surgery while you ask your doctor to monitor the change in the size of your tumor.

"I wish I would have been better educated about alternative options when Jessi was diagnosed, but that's an unrealistic expectation on my part. None of her doctors ever suggested that if we were not happy with what they offered, we could go out and take a look at what the options are. It's typical of the way the medical world works today. It's engrained in people that what your doctor says is in your best interest and you don't question that. Don't be bullied. That's like the ostrich sticking its head in the sand, and ostriches are not known for being one of the most intelligent birds."

The FitzRandolphs truly feel that the big pharmaceutical companies in the United States have something to do with the way cancer is treated in America. The system failed them, they think. Drug companies are more interested in the profitability of their drugs than in whether or not they actually cure the patient's disease. The system treats the patient like a commodity to be used. The chemotherapy drugs on the market today are filled with toxins that not only kill cancer cells but kill healthy cells as well. The list of negative side effects is usually longer and more devastating than the benefits. But pharmaceutical companies keep producing them, and doctors keep prescribing them. Western medicine and the doctors who practice it don't really expect the majority of their stage IV patients to get well, and the facts bear them out. In the family's estimation, chemotherapy and radiation are self-serving placebos that kill.

"I am very disappointed in our system. I feel betrayed," reflected Ruthie. "Money talks. I've read that doctors get perks for pushing the drug company's products. The pharmaceutical company will sell product and get very, very rich. I fail to find the morality in that. I am just very disappointed and frustrated."

"I just wish they were a little more open minded" was Jessi's opinion of Western medicine. "I'm not angry. [My doctor] is just doing his job. He's doing what he knows."

"It's hard to fault him for doing that because when you go through medical school this is what you learn, what you're trained to do. Certainly no medical school is going to introduce them to alternative methods of treatment," concluded Ruthie.

Jeff puts it this way: "I have become very skeptical of many of the doctors we have worked with. They seem as though they are willing to help keep you alive, but not much more than that. They manage your symptoms but give no indication they would like to help you find a cure. God forbid you suggest something outside their comfort zone. If you do, most will turn on you like you are crazy. They are totally inflexible and unwilling to even consider that there might be a better way. Jessi's insurance company has paid hundreds of thousands of dollars providing stopgap measures prescribed by her doctors. If they believed in alternative options, the insurance company could have saved themselves and us quite a bit of money."

The FitzRandolphs do understand why most people would be reluctant to try alternative treatments if they had a loved one going through cancer.

More than one doctor told the family, at some point along the way, that going against the grain was unproven and even dangerous.

"Some experts will call these alternative practitioners 'charlatans that prey on helpless victims,'" said Ruthie. "I disagree because we saw so many people in Mexico and Germany with success stories. I can promise you this: Every doctor we have worked with [in those countries] has been just as professional and knowledgeable about their practice as the doctors we've worked with in the United States.

"In Mexico, there was a woman named Barb. She was diagnosed with stage IV breast cancer eight years ago. She went down there initially for treatment. Eight years later, she's still very much alive and she looks the picture of health. She does go down there every six months for her treatments. Jessi's tests showed a reduction in the size of the spots on her bones while she was having hyperthermia treatments in Germany, and then the aHUS reared its ugly head. There are so many living examples that it just baffles me that our doctors here think that nothing is proven. There is statistical evidence that shows cure rates using alternative protocols dwarf the cure rates for chemo and radiation. I think it's simply a lack of knowledge and a lack of exposure. I certainly don't believe it is because they don't care."

Ruthie feels that if American doctors struck out on their own and embraced alternative methods, they would be banned from the system. Jeff believes that Western treatments in general tend to mask or treat the symptoms without getting to the root of the cause. In doing radiation, for instance, a temporary fix may (or may not) be achieved in reducing pain, but it's a palliative treatment. Each successive treatment reduces the body's ability to restore and repair itself. As he sees it, alternative treatments present mountains of hope compared to the molehills American doctors offer their advanced-stage cancer patients.

Alternative therapies gave the FitzRandolph family something to hang onto in an otherwise bleak landscape and something to believe in.

"I will have no regrets regardless of the final outcome," Ruthie said in early 2014

"Alternative therapies have allowed us to live with this dreadful diagnosis with hope, anticipating a future, as opposed to accepting the inevitable fate, death."

Casey, the ultimate American hero, felt the same way. In his opinion, doctors might as well say this: "Come with us and you have a zero percent chance of living, or look into something else where you have a chance … but we won't offer it to you. Don't come to us for help. All we can prescribe for you is the stuff that's going to ultimately kill you."

Casey's gut feeling, based partly on being an elite athlete, is that the human body and cancer are both intricately complex things that don't have a right or wrong way of being treated. If something worked every time for everyone, we would all use it. Yet if we're in a gray area, why do we only look at the half of the gray we're taught and deny that other options exit? Such is the battle of conventional versus alternative treatments.

He strongly believes that more and more Americans will start to turn elsewhere for cancer treatments and not accept a death sentence. It won't be the medical system that leads the population; instead, the future will be the other way around. The ground swell will have to come from the cancer patients themselves.

However, the family recognizes that not many people can afford to do what they did. Most folks have to stick with what their insurance plan offers. So, in reality, change will be a long and slow process driven by patients and families pressuring the insurance industry. If and when the companies get on board with alternative medicine, the entire fabric of the medical world will change. The FitzRandolphs believe that it may be fear of that change that drives doctors to urge patients to avoid alternative treatments. Perhaps they fear that they may find themselves without patients because their conventional treatment protocols don't work.

Casey understands that other doctors might be worried about being sued in the current climate if they endorse methods that don't work. But he questions why they can't have a patient sign a release and absolve the doctor of any responsibility. Also, those same doctors could learn something along the way if they had patients agree to help test alternative treatments. If ten thousand people in the United States are diagnosed with terminal cancer and eight thousand of them want to try non-conventional routes, wouldn't that be a robust sample size to see if certain things work? Even if none of the treatments actually produced meaningful results, at least we would have a better understanding of how the protocols worked or which treatments worked better than others.

And if Casey were to be diagnosed with cancer? If it were early-stage, he might go the conventional route, but if it were in an advanced stage, after witnessing what his sister has experienced, the gold medalist would be much more inclined to drift in the direction of alternative. The first step for him would be turning his internal being into the cleanest, healthiest environment possible through food and drink. Then, as a big believer in visualization, Casey would try to rid his body of cancer through his mind. As he sees it, if you can visualize yourself getting better over time, it can happen. He doesn't encourage unrealistic expectations, he says. It's not a matter of 'If I think it's going to be gone tomorrow it will' but instead of imagining each bite of nourishing food as a powerful good guy going to battle and defeating the bad guys. He would put a thought into his mind about the size of the cancer and then see it shrinking bit by bit, methodically, over time. Visualization with conviction is a very combative hammer for a human being to hold in their own personal toolbox, he believes. The bottom line: the FitzRandolphs would never say it's over until it's over, even if every doctor on the planet told them otherwise.

CHAPTER SIXTEEN

Life after Gold

Spring 2006

I t might be tempting to think that Casey's life moved happily along on autopilot after the Olympics, at least until the day Jessi gathered her brother and Jenn around the dining room table to share her startling breast cancer news. To an outsider, Casey's personal life likely resembled paradise. He was a golden boy with a beautiful wife, two healthy children, a new career, two farms to retreat to, and that shiny thing from the Olympics around his neck to share at his many speaking engagements.

Reality looks a little different. Casey and Jenn are human beings with real struggles like all of us. They endured their own set of hardships that ranged from a difficult birth to a splinter in their relationship that nearly drove them apart.

First, there was the job situation. Casey retired from speedskating at age thirty-one but was far from real retirement with three decades of work still ahead of him. Many Olympic athletes forgo college because there are no college teams for their sport. College would, to say the least, have gotten in the way of reaching his full athletic potential. Casey focused solely on speedskating after getting halfway through college. He never earned a degree and was now almost a decade behind his peers in the workforce.

Luckily for him, two businesses that had sponsored his speedskating career offered him a chance to jump on board. He wrestled between working in insurance or public affairs, finally settling on a career in business insurance, first with Wausau Insurance and later with a Madison company, M3 Insurance. Business insurance proved to be a great opportunity, but there was a huge learning curve for a guy who admittedly didn't even know what property and casualty insurance was. Insurance language looked like Chinese to Casey. He felt behind and scrambled to get up to speed, taking classes to get licensed and later entrenching himself in continuing education courses for years. It was a trial by fire, not easy for a guy who was used to being the best and having things come quickly for him. Plus, working in the real world was a reversal in the way he structured his life.

"You go from being able to physically exert yourself on a day-to-day basis in order to find satisfaction and control, to having to sit down and think 95 percent of the time. That's a huge change, and all of a sudden not using your body as much chemically changes you too."

Speedskating is also a black and white sport where the clock doesn't lie.

"I had success at the ultimate level, which I can't ever duplicate. How can you proclaim that you are the best in the world at selling insurance, as a matter of fact? You can't."

Casey suddenly felt as if he were living at the mercy of other people's opinions and decisions and he wasn't used to it. How was he to measure success? Everything about this new civilian lifestyle took time to adjust to, and he struggled to find his place. Jenn did not have that issue, as she happily landed a full-time teaching position to pursue her passion at an elementary school.

The couple did recognize from early on that they wanted children, and before they knew it, they were staring in wonder at the pink lines on the pregnancy test. This was all happening right after Casey had retired from the sport and entered the working world. It was a lot to take in all at once, but they were both thrilled to be expecting.

Fourteen weeks later, the ultrasound showed something startling. There were two round sacs. Jenn herself had a fraternal twin sister, and her eyes grew large looking at the monitor. She was clearly seeing the same thing happening in her body. Both excitement and shock rippled through her. Yet it didn't last long.

"When the technician started panning across, she saw the second baby was only a fraction of the size of the first. They figured it stopped living at about twelve weeks. The technician told me it happens for a reason; the fetus must have stopped growing," said Jenn.

Jenn's mind had gone from having one healthy baby to twins back to just one in the matter of three minutes. She gave herself a very brief mourning period for the baby that wasn't and turned her attention to the baby that was. She read every pamphlet she could and matched her diet to the development of the fetus. If the baby was growing eyes that week she would load up on carrots, joking that she didn't care if she turned orange. Casey and Jenn had discovered early on that the surviving baby was a boy, and as the time grew closer they wrestled with names, finally inventing a *Survivor*-type game where each was permitted to vote some names off the island. Through this system, the young couple whittled the finalists down to three: Caden, Camden, and Sawyer. Three days past her due date, on January 10, 2007, Jenn woke up first thing in the morning to find her water had broken in bed. It was time.

Ruthie, Jeff, and Jessi joined the couple at the hospital. Jenn was in contact with her father and stepmother by phone. She progressed rapidly, and the doctors thought she would have the baby by noon, but then things changed. The little one stalled, and she pushed for four straight hours. At one point the nurses couldn't find his heartbeat. There was a brief moment of fear until they placed the heart rate monitor up the birth canal and attached it right to his head. Then the steady pulse of the heart came through. Still, the doctors told her that if she didn't get the baby out soon, they would need to perform an episiotomy or C-section. Nurses from the NICU waited around the perimeter of the room on standby as Jenn continued to labor, almost spent. Finally, the doctors declared they needed to go in and get him. It seemed that those were the words that Jenn had been waiting for. She asked for one more chance and delivered on the next push. The baby inched his way out only to give them another shock.

"There was no cord to cut. It had separated during the labor," Jenn explained. "The doctors didn't know at what point it had come unattached, so they were really concerned that he had lacked oxygen for too long."

Imagine the terror for first-time parents. The doctors scrambled to run some tests and look him over while Casey and Jenn held their breath with trepidation. Thankfully, it didn't take the medical personnel long to come back with the best possible news: he appeared healthy and perfect.

Now Jenn and Casey had to name their boy. They each whispered their top choice into the nurse's ear, and she laughed.

"You both picked the same name!"

He was Sawyer, a perfect little creature with the grayish eyes newborns have and a small patch of fluffy blond hair. The warm bundle was placed in Jenn's welcoming arms even as the doctor continued to work on her. She needed to birth the placenta.

"I was on the phone with my dad telling him I was holding the baby. I looked down, and the intern had just pulled her arm out! It was literally covered with blood up to her elbow. I said, 'Dad, I think I need to call you back.'"

Usually, the doctor can guide the placenta by pulling on the intact cord. Without one, it was much more of a challenge. Finally, the intern was able to retrieve the life blood that had nourished Sawyer for nine months. If this were a hundred years ago, what might have happened to Sawyer and to Jenn? They shuddered to think of it. The couple felt as if God had smiled upon them, providing Sawyer the lifeline he needed just long enough.

"Between losing one fetus early on and then Sawyer getting through (alive and healthy) on what we considered a miracle," reflected Casey. "I mean, how is the cord not attached? Were we one bump away from delivering a dead baby?"

Instead, Sawyer was both alive and healthy. That's why another incident just nine days later took them completely off guard. Casey had agreed to watch Sawyer. Jenn was looking forward to her very first alone time. She poured a glass of wine and sank gratefully into a warm bubble bath. Ahhh … she exhaled and shut her eyes. Her head leaned against the back of the porcelain as she enjoyed the stillness of the house and contemplated reading a magazine. Never one to shy away from winter activities, Casey had taken baby Sawyer out for a walk. They were planning to raise him as an outdoors kid anyway, so why not start now? Casey put the little guy in a fleece snowsuit and hat, plopped him into the Baby Bjorn front carrier, donned his own parka, and wrapped that around both of their fronts. It was a cold January day in Wisconsin, well below freezing, and the new parents wanted to make sure their baby stayed warm.

"I'm in the tub, completely relaxed. Probably a half hour has passed, and I hear them come back. Suddenly Casey screams 'Jenn!' He comes racing upstairs, boots and all, panting, and I think to myself, 'Casey doesn't panic.' Then he says 'Jenn, Jenn, he's not breathing!'"

She vaulted from the tub as Casey pulled Sawyer from the Baby Bjorn. They laid him out on the counter in the bathroom. The baby was as still as could be and looked to be sleeping, but he was not breathing. He didn't even flinch when they undressed him.

Panic rushed through their very souls, but something in Jenn told her that Sawyer was simply overheated.

"Get me a washcloth," she commanded with amazingly calm authority.

Casey lunged for the cabinet and grabbed a washcloth. Jenn shoved the cloth under the faucet, drenching it in cold water, and then pressed the cold, dripping cloth against Sawyer's bare chest and forehead. Within a few seconds, he opened his eyes and startled awake, crying his newborn cry. The two parents looked at each other, their hearts pounding with relief. Little Sawyer seemed to be the victim of a near heatstroke in the deepest part of January. Out for the walk with his dad, he had gotten too hot in his layers of fleece and down next to his dad's chest. Another disaster with Sawyer was averted.

But the baby who had a few rough starts turned out to be a wonderful boy and a tiny imprint of Casey, interested in hunting, fishing, and the outdoors. He could spend an entire weekend working with his dad and his grandfather, "Jeepers," on the farm and walk around as happy and fulfilled as any little boy could be.

Yet, as any new parent discovers, the adjustment to suddenly having a dependent is not an easy one. Gone are the days when you can sleep in late or go to a movie on a whim. Everything you do, all day long, revolves around the well-being of this tiny creature. Your own wants and needs, including exercise, time with friends, and lazy mornings with your spouse, get thrown out with that first bundle of dirty diapers. Jenn stayed home for nine months before she returned to teaching in the fall. The transition to motherhood was wonderful and amazing.

"Sawyer and I settled into a nice routine of morning and afternoon walks along with social time with neighbors and friends. With all the transition in our world, having Sawyer forced me into settling down and having a day-to-day routine. But being a full-time mother, teacher, and wife, and being able to do all the roles and do them well, was hard. I'm a type-A personality and I wanted to do them as well as I envisioned. Casey was trying to find a new career. It made it hard. He wasn't around a whole lot. We tried to figure out what our roles were as parents without forgetting about each other."

Casey's change to this new life was amplified by the fact that he had been hardwired for so many years to think about himself first.

"One of the traits that allowed me to be the best at what I did was being self-centered, and Jenn didn't realize how difficult that is to change. Neither did I, to be honest, as I still am fairly self-centered. I do a lot of good things for other people in the world, and I have a good heart. But when I'm not trying to make a positive difference in our community and country, I tend to focus a lot on what Casey is doing and on Casey's goals and dreams and priorities. I think she thought … we both thought … that would go away after I was done skating."

"Not go away," corrected Jenn. "Just balance out or shift to be family focused."

Instead, they sometimes found themselves at odds over who would do what, who might get some time to themselves, and whose career needs were being met. Then along came baby number two.

The pair had hoped and planned for another child. And a baby girl entered the fold. Cassidy was a wonderful baby, but having two children under the age of three, two full-time careers, and many additional commitments on the side took their toll. Jenn could only get twelve weeks off for maternity leave this time. Those three months whipped by, tossing them back into the daily grind before they knew it. It was a highly challenging period for their marriage and nearly sent them to the breaking point. Casey felt overwhelmed. He started seeing a counselor and then brought Jenn in to talk as well. She agreed willingly, as she was feeling fully committed to the relationship and to seeing it through.

"I believe you marry one person in your life and that's who you're with through thick and thin."

For his part, Casey wasn't so sure. Was marriage really supposed to be this difficult?

"It got to a point where I had to make a decision. Was I going to leave or not? There was a day I remember being at the edge of the cliff."

"I remember that day," said Jenn. "I went to school, and one of my girlfriends, before the kids came in, said 'You don't look good.' I said 'No, I didn't sleep much last night,' and she asked why. I told her, 'Casey's leaving me today. I think he's packing a bag right now.' Within five minutes, I had three teachers in giving me hugs and saying, 'Do you need to go home? We'll cover your class.' I said, 'No, no, no. I need to be here. I can't be thinking about this all day. I just need to get through the day and keep my mind off things.'"

They hadn't had a fight the night before, just a somber talk where Jenn let him know exactly how baffled she was by his uncertainty.

"Why are you being so stupid?" she told him. "Things really aren't that bad around here. I don't know what other life you want to live. You have a wife who's taking care of your two children and taking care of you. How hard do you really have it around here?"

Jenn paused as she recollected this three years later, her eyes filling with tears. She wiped the corners and went on.

"I just wish marriage counseling would tell you what it's really like. When you get married, it's all roses, right? 'We're so happy for you.' No one talks about the bad and the ugly. That sometimes you'll be so angry with each other that you're going to say things you never thought would come out of your mouth to this person that's supposed to be your best friend."

"You know what they should tell people?" said Casey. "They should paint the most horrible picture in the world so your relationship has nowhere to go but up. People are not wired to happily come home to the same person every day for fifty years, period. You try living with your best buddy. It's going to be the same way. They're going to grate on you, and there will be times that you will be sick of that person. You would be sick of *any* person. In hindsight, I wish I'd been better prepared."

In the end, Casey slowly came to a realization. It took a while and a lot of deep self-reflection.

"I remember thinking the grass must be greener somewhere else. But then I reminded myself the grass always looks greener when you're not looking at it through your magnifying glass. I weighed this, and it was a tough period for us for close to two years, from Cassidy's birth to Jessi's diagnosis. I finally decided that I didn't want to leave my family. I wanted to be with Jenn, raise our children, and move forward together as a team."

"We still want to punch each other once in a while," said Jenn.

She faked a few punches toward his shoulder as they sat close together on the couch, his hand on her knee.

"Yeah we do," agreed Casey with an appreciative chuckle. "But the good news is now we talk about the challenges associated with marriage. We acknowledge them."

This rocky patch that walloped them was exacerbated by the incredible stress of Jessi's diagnosis right in the middle of it. To go from stage II to IV in the matter of months, to be told that your little sister is dying? It was a back breaker for Casey.

"There was a period, I didn't even tell Jenn all of it, but I actually went in and took a small dosage of anti-depressants. I remember having a real hesitancy, thinking we're too drug dependent as a society and I don't want to rely on a drug to be happy in my life. I got them and didn't take them for a while, but then I gave in. I took half the suggested dose for about three months. Then I weaned myself off and have never had a desire to take them again. It wasn't something I was proud of, but in hindsight I think it actually helped because I literally couldn't sleep without them. My anxiety and stress levels were through the roof."

Casey also leaned on his faith to help him through this shaky stretch. Jeff and Ruthie were not regular churchgoers, but as Casey got into his twenties, he felt a calling to a higher power. He was baptized as a Seventh Day Baptist at the age of twenty-seven, as was Jessi. During the ensuing pivotal moments of his life, be it the Olympics, the fork in the road of his marriage, or his sister's battle with cancer, Casey felt he could turn to God for guidance. He would later speak to kids for the Fellowship of Christian Athletes and Athletes in Action about faith, making good choices, and forgiveness.

He felt this connection with God most when outside with nature. It was the final piece that brought Casey back from the dark place he sometimes visited. An outdoorsman for as long as he could remember, Casey had always wanted land. He had bought the 180-acre family farm from his grandparents shortly after returning to Wisconsin in 2006. It was a place of cherished memories. Casey and Jessi had gone there so many times for Thanksgivings, watching *Charlie and the Chocolate Factory* and waiting for the grownups to return from deer hunting. The only downside was that this farm was located one and a half hours north, near Wisconsin Dells. Now that he and Jenn were back to being bonded as a stronger couple, they looked around for a second farm closer to Madison. They wanted one they could retire to.

After they had been searching for a while, a friend mentioned the possibility of a farm southwest of Madison being for sale. This farm was bigger, nearly three hundred acres, so they teamed with a longtime friend, who became a silent partner, and went in together. Casey and Jenn owned two-thirds of the farm and the partner one-third. They leased ninety acres to a farmer who planted corn and soybeans and promised to treat the land right, but Casey's main goal was to turn it into a wildlife haven that would attract all kinds of creatures, especially deer. He wanted to have his very own place to enjoy the bow hunting he loved so much and also for the simple pleasure of observing the wildlife that called the farm home. So he, Jenn, Jessi, Jeepers, Sawyer, Cassidy and many friends set about planting 18,000 trees to create new travel corridors giving animals food and cover. They planted all kinds of food sources and even dug small ponds for drinking water for the wildlife. Casey bought a tractor and tended to every part of his new land. It nourished him right back.

"It was a lifesaver, almost literally. Having a partner in life and two kiddos is awesome, but the farm allows me to recharge, rejuvenate, and regain perspective on our place in this world. Both farms have been a huge stress reliever, places for peace, and they allow me to be able to deal with life. Not that my life is that hard or harder than anyone else's, but it would feel overwhelming at times if I didn't have a place to get away like that."

Casey travels to one of the farms at least once a week. He plants and prunes and waters, and then he sits in his deer stand. During the season, he shoots mainly does in an effort to control the population and also to bring venison to his family. They almost never purchase store-bought meat products. They all enjoy the venison, turkey, pheasant, waterfowl, and fish he brings home from his expeditions. They call it the most organic, freerange meat you can find.

While Casey's rejuvenation comes from getting dirty and driving a tractor, Jenn finds enough satisfaction in the everyday things in life: a clean kitchen, the laundry put away, the quiet of her classroom after the kids have left. She always dreamt of being a mother, and her endorphins kick in when she's driving her kids to and from events and then watching them be successful at whatever they're doing. She sometimes gets up at five thirty in the morning to fit in exercise, as she would be hard-pressed to have time later in the day.

"A family weekend is rejuvenating for me," added Jenn.

"I cherish family time, but it doesn't necessarily recharge me like a weekend or a full day at the farm would, with or without them," admitted Casey.

The couple has very different tastes, but together they survived a highly charged and stressful time in their union and stayed a duo. The kids continued to grow, and Casey and Jenn turned their attention to parenting. Like many adults, they could look back on their own childhoods and draw out things they admired and things they wanted to change from the way their parents raised them.

"My childhood was very intense," said Casey. "It was all or nothing. Go get your dreams. If you believe you can, you will. We, and you, will do whatever it takes. Well, lo and behold, it worked! But you also then have learned behaviors and a mentality that sticks with you after you retire from sports. I always have been a dreamer, and that's a good and bad thing. That trait that won me a gold medal makes me kind of restless, always wanting more and better—more land, a bigger deer, is the grass greener outside my marriage? I should make more money. I can't sit on the couch very well. It's hard for me to be content with any aspect of my life because I always visualize bigger and better.

"From my perspective with our kids—for every action there's a reaction, and the pendulum probably swings a little more in the other direction—but I want to make sure our kids are comfortable in their own skin and have a relaxed confidence. Sawyer is already a type-A personality—he gets nervous and anxious. With him, we really try to be positive. When he plays sports we just try to discuss one key thing to focus on after pointing out the really good things he has done. We really want to make sure it's a good and fun experience."

At Sawyer's age of six, Casey had already declared his intention to be a gold medal speedskater and had become a state champion for his age level. He was spending all of his free time circling Vilas Park Lagoon near the monkey cages. The family was making regular trips to Milwaukee to find ice time at the Pettit Center. His course was already being set. Now, as a father, he sees things differently.

"I want them to be happy and content. We talk about being good people, trying our best and enjoying life. If we do this, the rest will fall in place."

So they'll keep Sawyer and Cassidy involved in local activities. They'll spend weekends either at the farm or on a lake. They'll take the kids outdoors in any weather, limit electronics, and have them participate in activities they enjoy. In those ways, they're parroting how they both were brought up. But Jenn teases Casey that he was spoiled, and he admits he probably was, albeit with the caveat of hard work.

"We just want our kids to enjoy the simple things in life, like eating a raw stalk of asparagus sitting on a ridge while having a picnic and watching the sunset, the birds, and the bugs," said Jenn.

"At age thirty-eight, I feel like I've worked for thirty years, I feel like a fifty-eight-year-old in terms of amount of years I've put in to a career. My body feels the effects. I'm seven years into my second career now at thirty-eight, and I wonder if I had started in my twenties and put half the effort into a professional career that I did into speedskating, where would I be now? Would I be making a quarter of a million bucks or half a million bucks, and we wouldn't have the stress that we have now about finances? (They made a conscious decision to use Casey's skating money on the farms but live day to day off their day jobs). You pay a price to pursue your dreams."

So, taking it all into account, would he go back and change any of the past? Casey took a long time to answer this. He looked down and thought, as if he were flipping through a photo album that contained single snapshots of every important moment of his existence. His eyes were far away as he pondered the question.

"No." He paused. "But it's so hard to answer. If my childhood had been different, then my perspective on life would be different as well. The bottom line is— the experiences were great. There were a lot of perks. There were some cons, but being able to say I was the best in the world at what I did is something almost no one can say, and I'll take that as a source of pride to my grave. That ... is priceless to me."

CHAPTER SEVENTEEN

A Summer of Hope

2013

Jessi and her parents decided to wait on another scan until the end of the summer of 2013. They hoped to give the cannabis oil as much time as possible to hopefully work some magic in Jessi's system. But the results they were seeing from the outside were nothing short of astounding. Jessi had more energy, slept better, and had a hearty appetite. Most amazingly, they watched her pain level go from a ten to a zero when sitting and a two when walking around. She ventured out to see *Oz* with a friend one night, hit a lunch spot with a group another day, made plans for a pool party at the house in honor of her birthday, bought tickets for *Wicked* in downtown Madison with her mom, and even scheduled a trip to Wisconsin Dells, the water park capital of the world, with Casey, Jenn, and the kids. She decided she was up for the lazy river and would watch her niece and nephew tackle the big slides. She also drove herself to her brother's house and helped Jenn entertain the kids one night when Casey was away. Jessi, Jenn, Sawyer, and Cassidy watched the singers croon on *American Idol*, and then Jessi and Jenn stayed up talking after the kids went down for bed. The two had grown closer since Jessi's diagnosis. Back when Jessi was the partier and Casey and Jenn the straight-laced ones, the two women hadn't been extremely tight. Now Jessi felt completely comfortable hanging and relaxing with Jenn.

Jessi's eyes were bright and clear as April turned to May. While she adjusted to the medical cannabis, she had been sleeping nearly nonstop at times. But now, they seemed to have hit on the right strains, and she felt a new rhythm, sleeping maybe ten hours per day and sunning herself on the back deck when the Wisconsin weather would allow it. She had a stack of favorite magazines nearby—*US* and *People* being her top picks, no more Stephen King—and she was feeling happy, energized, calm, and on a healing path, all at the same time.

Her new appetite was a delight for all to see. She freely admitted that she was eating everything in sight, including her favorite snack food, Honey Nut Cheerios, straight out of the box. Her blood pressure remained down, and she was able to go shopping with her mom at Whole Foods again. This time they found a cart that worked for her to ride in, although she thought she was close to being able to walk the whole store on her own. She looked downright vibrant and healthy and felt it, too.

Jessi had an appointment with a new primary care doctor who was well known in Wisconsin after making appearances on public radio and television and having a column in a local paper. To the family's great joy, he was also the first doctor to fully support the alternative mission. In fact, the doctor told them he would do exactly the same thing in their shoes, adding that conventional oncology had gone nowhere in decades in terms of advancements or success rates. It was refreshing and validating to actually have an American doctor on their side. Before they left the office, he typed out a letter stating that he endorsed Jessi's use of medicinal marijuana for her cancer treatments. It would not keep the family out of jail if their marijuana use was discovered, but it provided them with comfort just the same. He also told the family he was right there with them, agreeing that cancer treatment was all about big business and money.

Jessi's spring of 2013 was a time of hope. The family had put close to ten pots of fresh orchids in the living room next to her main reclining chair. Brightly colored purples and pinks sprang up from the potting medium and wood chips, making the room cheery and colorful. The pots rested on a glass table near a window. Ruthie noted that Jessi herself was like those orchids, blooming and becoming more awake, beautiful, and alive every single day.

During this time, the only downside for Jessi was going through early menopause due to her ovaries being removed. She would sweat but then get cold, sometimes all at the same time. A blanket near her went on and off dozens of times per day, and fans whirred all around when she got the sweats. But she could get up and move about the house freely, fixing her own food or using the restroom with no help. She decided to sleep on the hospital bed in the living room again, but only because the best television in the house was right there; negotiating stairs would not have been a problem. Ruthie, being the supermom that she is, pulled the blow-up bed out of the closet again and parked herself right next to Jessi's bed. Mother and daughter had a slumber party each night as they stayed up watching a favorite show or talking. Ruthie would end the evening with a kiss to Jessi's forehead and the words "I love you." Having her mother sleep next to her had once annoyed Jessi, but now she said it was "actually kind of nice."

Jeff did not have to make batches of oil himself anymore. Tori was able to find them a better deal from a man in Kentucky who created the oil in larger quantities and then shipped it ready-made. The cost was about half of what they had been paying, and it was already cooked and ready to ingest. So now boxes of syringes filled with the dark liquid were arriving via the US Postal Service at their doorstep. Good thing the oil didn't have a smell and the FitzRandolphs were never found out. The oil was shipped vacuum-packed in boxes that had once held VHS tapes when they were popular. Tori had an extra step to take on this adventure. She had to prove to the Kentucky supplier that she was not law enforcement to get him to trust her. To do this, Tori needed to fly to Colorado and have some of the Kentucky man's friends meet her and get to know her. The whole thing was quite an underground operation, and the FitzRandolphs thought the fact that cannabis wasn't legal for medicinal purposes was ridiculous. They were grateful beyond words to Tori and others who were helping them procure what they saw as Jessi's best chance against the insidious cancer.

The biggest news around the house had nothing to do with Jessi's treatments. Ruthie lost her nursing job.

"I was basically forced out," she explained. "I think I was about the eighth person to be forced out in the last five or six years. I was accused of a couple of different things. Number one, I've been late to punch out at times and have been warned about that. So, the next time I was running late, I punched out on time but actually charted until eight. I was accused of being devious, trying to hide it. I didn't realize the labor laws prohibited working after punching out. People come in early or stay late on their own time very often. Yet that was the straw that broke the camel's back. I was called into the HR office, and they told me I could resign or be fired ... what would I like? So I resigned."

Ruthie felt anger towards the nurse manager, who she felt had a pattern of firing people. Jessi had actually been the star of a video for the hospital about breast cancer, and she knew a number of the nurses personally after they all went to a Milwaukee Brewers game together by bus. Yet a few late punch outs were enough to justify sacking her mother? The whole family was upset.

Ruthie was told, "Your patients love you, their families love you, and your coworkers love you, but ..."

Ruthie was still working part time at Agrace HospiceCare, but she decided to take most of the summer off and consider full-time work again in September. They sent a letter to the president of the hospital, stating Ruthie's side of the story, but mostly tried to move on.

This meant Ruthie was around the house more often, which was a huge positive to an otherwise negative situation. Ruthie relished her time with Jessi even as she tried to soften her anger and disappointment toward the hospital.

Jessi loved having her mom's nurturing hands so often. "She's better at caring. Dad does a great job, but men seem to need so much praise when they do one little thing," joked Jessi.

Ruthie applied for unemployment, as she was only getting eight hours per week of work at Agrace. She lost her health insurance when she resigned, and she and Jeff walked around with no insurance for months.

"It makes me a little nervous. Jeff spent six days at the farm climbing up hills, turkey hunting. I mean, he could have had a heart attack. Anything could have happened."

Jeff said he wasn't worried about it. Still, they began the tedious process of paperwork and research to get themselves health insurance. Jessi was still covered by the insurance she had signed on with before she even got cancer. But money was tight, really tight. The FitzRandolphs put their house up for sale. The sprawling home was beautiful, but it cost a lot to maintain and had numerous rooms to keep clean. Even with Jessi still in the fold, they felt they were ready to downsize and thought about apartments somewhere in the Madison area. They even considered moving to the family farm in Mauston, where Casey needed a caretaker. There was also chatter about something as exotic and adventurous as another country. Costa Rica, anyone?

"We could have beautiful summer conditions all year round and live real cheap," mused Jeff.

"We've thought about everything," added Ruthie. "Wisconsin ranks third in worst places to retire, according to a survey."

"But it would be tough to move away from the grandkids," Jeff and Ruthie said almost simultaneously.

Still, the thought of sprawling land, a lake, warmer weather, and cheaper living conditions made a place like Tennessee also appealing. All options were open, and they had the summer to figure it out.

Jessi was looking forward to a summer of real-life experiences, not hospitals, doctors, or the chair in the living room. She was going to a spa in the Wisconsin Dells for a massage and planned to travel with her parents to and from the farm when she could. Loads of friends would be coming for the pool party as she turned thirty-six.

It was a waiting game for the scan, but all signs pointed to some really good things happening in her body.

"I never expect anything. I'm hopeful—that's the word to use. I don't like getting my hopes up because I usually get let down. I've learned to be a little guarded," reflected Jessi.

Jeff was more direct: "We want the doc's jaws to drop."

"I'd be thrilled, of course," added Jessi. "I'd want to throw it in their face, but I wouldn't. I'm just not like that. I'd just love to tell the other doctors that they really need to open their minds and do some research on alternative options."

If everything went as well as they hoped, they would be able to decrease the heavy dose of marijuana to one gram per day, and they even thought of setting up a hydroponic tent to grow their own buds. But they decided it wasn't the best idea to have a marijuana greenhouse going if they had realtors and potential buyers walking through the house.

Jessi's birthday pool party was a huge hit, and Jeff posted about it on CarePages.

Jessi Turns 36
June 5, 2013
8:34 a.m.

Jessi celebrated her thirty-sixth birthday with close friends and family last Sunday. It wasn't just another ordinary birthday party ... it was one that wasn't supposed to happen. Yep, her doctors told us two years ago that there was no more that they could do for her, and they recommended we admit her to hospice for end-of-life support.

How foolish. In spite of the fact that they have worked with her for nearly three years, they didn't understand they were dealing with a "gamer" who was not about to give up. They also didn't realize, in spite of multiple meetings with the family and multiple trips to Germany for hyperthermia treatments, that we would leave no stone unturned in finding an alternative cure for her cancer. Sadly, they greatly underestimated our family's spirit.

It's true we have exhausted several alternative options, but recently we seem to have hit on a protocol that has energized Jessi. After a particularly rough stretch from October through early December, we have seen a continued improvement in her health. Admittedly we struggled most of last fall trying to find the perfect mix of alternative treatments that were right for her. She simply wasn't able to tolerate the first couple of therapies we tried, but eventually we settled on a series of protocols that were compatible with her taste buds (stomach) and easy enough for her to use in her somewhat compromised state of health. We attribute her recent improvement to the multiple treatment options that she has used on a daily basis since December, with the addition of one treatment we started in February.

The introduction of two grams of cannabis oil daily to her existing protocols signaled some very significant changes in Jessi. Her appetite came back, and she has been able to gain back some of the weight she lost last fall. Her energy level has increased significantly. Her mobility is much better, and she *has noticed a considerable reduction in her pain level. But the most significant change is in her mood. She has become bright, bubbly, and much more positive about her condition. She seems much more determined to defeat the demon that remains in her body, and recent improvements suggest that she is making steady progress to that end. She engages in light conversations, and occasionally we will have discussions about subjects that were taboo as recently as last year. She just seems to be much more open-minded and at peace with herself.*

All of this is of course great news for Ruthie and me. We continue to support her current initiatives every way that we can and are hoping to spend a couple of weeks with her at our cabin in northern Wisconsin over the Fourth of July. We were there over Memorial Day, and Jessi tolerated the increased activity level very well. As usual, she outfished me every time I took her out.

We'll be sharing more regarding her newest alternative treatment protocol later this summer, so please check back for more news. And, of course, we remain eternally grateful for your support and prayers for Jessi. The protocols are working, but the power of your prayers gives all of us additional strength to fight on and ultimately defeat the demon.

God Bless,

Jeff

Ruthie also had a plan that involved church. They weren't big churchgoers, going maybe four times per year, but Ruthie felt a need to say something to the heavens above.

"You can only say please, please, please God so many times before you say thank you," said Ruthie. "I think that's important."

And at that moment they felt they had a lot to be thankful for.

CHAPTER EIGHTEEN

Ups and Downs

August 2013

The fish were biting and the world seemed right when the family went back to Big Siss shortly after the CarePages post in June. They called it the best trip in the world. Jessi was in good spirits and moved around the cabin with ease. They spent lazy days on the boat soaking up the long-awaited Wisconsin sun and settled around the table together at night to enjoy the fish they caught. Mother, father, and daughter talked and read and basked in the pleasure of time together. Jessi continued to take the oil each day, and the whole group felt they were really on to something positive. Jessi enjoyed the cabin so much she wanted to go back in August. But just two days into that journey, things started to go badly.

She felt worn down—lethargic, really—and she had constant diarrhea. The closest emergency room was in tiny Hayward, Wisconsin, a city known internationally for the Birkebeiner cross-country ski race, muskie fishing and Lumberjack World Championships, but otherwise a quiet Wisconsin outpost. Feeling that she needed to be checked anywhere, they drove to Hayward. The doctor came back with a quick diagnosis: her liver enzymes were dangerously high. He told them, with shocking certainty, that every indication was that the cancer had spread to her liver. That's when the "Miracle on I-94" (as Jeff called it) began to unfold.

The threesome decided to get Jessi back to Madison as quickly as possible in search of more veteran and reliable medical care. An ambulance would have cost eight thousand dollars, so they made up their minds that Ruthie and Jessi would drive it. This was all happening at ten at night. The trip would be five hours, landing Ruthie and Jessi at a Madison hospital at three a.m. Intrepid soldiers that they were, they pressed on. It turned out to be a pure hell ride for Ruthie. Jessi was unbearably sick in the seat next to her, constantly throwing up, so much so that Ruthie kept thinking they might not make it to Madison. Ruthie watched every exit to see where the next hospital was, and she was choking down tears trying to control herself the entire way. Jessi finally fell into a fitful sleep. They pulled into St. Mary's Hospital in the middle of the night, and that's when the miracle part happened.

"They did labs in Madison, and her liver enzymes were hardly elevated at all," marveled Jeff. "She was cured on I-94. She went from cancer to no cancer."

No one could figure out how or why she would have had such elevated numbers in Hayward and almost no trace of a problem in Madison. There was nothing but a stressful car ride in between. Even an ultrasound of the liver turned up nothing in Madison. Doctors gave her some fluids, and after hours of rest she was on her way—back up to the cabin, where Jeff and Ruthie provided constant TLC until the lethargy and diarrhea finally subsided.

The fall of 2013 seemed to have many similar stops and starts. Jessi continued on a good stretch, hit a bad patch, recovered and felt great, and then had a few days or a week of being either really tired, nauseated, or in pain. One of the main problems, from the family's point of view, was procuring enough medical cannabis to keep the oil flowing. Based on recommendations from sources who had experienced success with higher doses, Jessi's daily dosage had been doubled in the summer. The marijuana suppliers they had weren't able to consistently provide the amount of product needed for the higher dose.

They wanted to get her to two grams a day, and they had trouble finding someone who could supply it in a state with a heavily Republican governor and no chance of legalizing marijuana anytime soon. Jessi would have to endure stretches without the oil while Jeff pulled money out of the family's retirement account to purchase what he could.

She struggled. Lower-back pain flared up, and her right hip bothered her and made her less and less mobile. In October, another bone scan showed more mets. There was a significant spot in her right hip and one in her lower back that was impinging on her spinal cord. The doctors suggested targeted radiation, which they assured would consist of limited sessions in targeted areas. They also told Jessi that paralysis was a real possibility if they didn't stop the spot near her spine from growing. Not being able to get enough cannabis and wanting to relieve her pain, the FitzRandolphs agreed. So they did the radiation, though it was not their first choice.

As fall progressed, Jessi continued to experience on and off pain, and another check of her liver enzymes showed that the Miracle on I-94 had not lasted as long as they had hoped. Her enzymes were elevated again. However, there were also a huge number of positives that they attributed to the oil: her kidney and heart functions were normal—this after having been diagnosed with congestive heart failure and stage V (the worst stage) renal failure in the past—and her sleeping and eating were better.

"We've cured everything but the cancer" is how Jeff summed it up.

Because of the liver enzyme elevation and new confirmation of spots on the liver, they were back to discussing chemo drugs. Kadcyla was a new one similar to Herceptin. It was supposed to target HER2 proteins and not have nasty side effects, including the loss of hair. The family agreed to try one treatment, but Jessi felt sick afterward, and they struggled with whether to continue. Jessi's spirits were down after hearing of this latest progression to the liver. She had some difficult days and lashed out in anger.

"It's understandable," sympathized Jeff. "Who wouldn't be angry?"

It was a trying time in the house. Jessi's health went one step forward and two steps back. But, showing her grit, after just two days of being really angry and down, Jessi found her fight again.

"Overall, she handles this just beautifully," her father said.

In the meantime, they took a long, hard look at everything they were trying and decided to scale back. When they examined the big picture, the one protocol they felt was truly making a positive difference was the marijuana. Poly-MVA was expensive, and the tests showed negligible results. The Rife machine and Bob Beck treatments likely yielded some good results. It seemed to them that Jessi's kidneys, heart, appetite, and pain level had been at their best after they started the oil. They decided to dive fully into the deep end with that. And thus began another journey for Jeff.

Montana is a long way from Wisconsin, but it was another stone to turn in their battle for Jessi's life. Jeff was told of a dealer who specialized in the exact strains of marijuana they needed to fight cancer. Medical cannabis is legal in Montana, so without hesitation, off went Jeff, alone in a car. The travel alone would be $1,400 for gas, food, and lodging. Each pound of pot was going to set them back $3,600, and he also planned to add a hydroponic growing system for $2,600. But what was money, really? It was just a means to an end, and their end was getting all of the cancer out of Jessi's body as soon as possible. Jeff spent a day on a pot farm with the growers, learning all about how to nourish the rich, green plants. Then he loaded up the back of the car and prepared to drive home. There was so much marijuana in his little Mini Cooper that the whole thing reeked. He covered the stash with a blanket and drove with his hands at ten and two on the wheel, nervous because he was a notoriously bad driver, prone to speeding or drifting from one lane to another. It was incredibly stressful for him to cross state lines with enough pot to put him away for years. He went through a speed trap entering South Dakota from Wyoming where the speed limit was inexplicably reduced from seventy-five to sixty-five miles per hour. The state police had people pulled over practically every hundred yards for half a mile. Keeping his eye on the odometer and his mind on Jessi, Jeff plodded along at the exact speed limit, counting down the minutes until he was back in Verona.

Then he hit a deer. *Oh, shit.* It was more of a graze, really, and did not connect with a huge impact, but still his mind raced. Would there be underbody damage he'd have to address? Would he be at an auto body shop trying to explain away the smell permeating from the backseat? Would he need to get a police officer involved if the car started to break down? Jeff pulled over and examined the situation. Thank God, it didn't look bad. It was another highway miracle, truly. He got back in and continued driving, listening for any strange clicks or whirs that might signify problems. There was nothing but the sound of his engine, the silence of the night, and thousands of stars overhead. Saying a prayer, Jeff pressed on.

Safely back in Wisconsin, Jeff finally had enough of the precious buds to keep the family supplied for a good, long stretch. He had been able to buy oil made by the dealer as well. He unpacked the hydroponic growing system and examined it. The whole thing would require a plumber, fans, lights, and a vent to the outside, but they would be self-sufficient, and the system would cut growing time from 10–12 weeks to 7–8 weeks for a batch. He was happy. They had plans to get Casey's friend, a plumber, over to help them start the process of setting it up in the basement. There was a negative, however: They were still trying to sell the house.

Just a few weeks after the Montana road trip, the FitzRandolphs experienced a scary moment. Ruthie came home from work at eight in the morning and called out Jessi's name. Nothing. She went searching, only to find her daughter in bed in a near-comatose state. Jessi was not coherent, and her breathing was shallow. Ruthie couldn't communicate with Jessi about what was wrong, so she raced her off to the ER, where the diagnosis was something they did not expect: pneumonia. There was fluid in her lungs even though she wasn't coughing. A few days later, with a stay in the ICU and proper treatment, Jessi was back in her own bed once again. By now, the FitzRandolphs were accepting every ER diagnosis with a skeptical nod and a grain of salt.

And so continued the yo-yo of hospital and home, hospital and home. And like a yo-yo, the ever-amazing Jessi rebounded quickly. She was up and eating, feeling better, and back to herself mentally. They all exhaled again. Thanksgiving was approaching, and they looked forward to a family holiday. Jessi took up scrapbooking and talked of wanting to spend a week at the cabin at Christmas. Friends came by, and Jessi had the desire to get out with them once again. But then came another flick of the wrist on the yo-yo.

Right before Thanksgiving of 2013, Jessi was feeling quite nauseated. The family decided to take her in for fluids and a check. Ruthie was working the overnight shift at Agrace and trying to catch a few hours of sleep during the day when she wasn't caring for Jessi. In her sixties, when many others were retired, Ruthie needed to put in these kind of hours to pay for the cannabis oil and everyday living expenses. That day before, Ruthie had worked a fourteen-hour night shift and slept in a vinyl hospital recliner while various tests were run. When she was awake her only concern was Jessi's well-being. The FitzRandolphs couldn't figure out why Jessi's stomach kept bothering her. It was an unsettled time, frustrating and challenging.

"It's impossible to get into a rhythm, and that's the hardest thing," said Ruthie. "That's what we're looking forward to. Last winter, when it was cold, she stayed in a lot, and it seems she does a lot of healing during those winter days. She had more good days than bad last year."

Now, they just wanted to get her home and try to find that groove again. Casey and Jenn were hosting Thanksgiving this year. The whole family hoped to go, but they weren't sure if Jessi would be released on time. Her stomach seemed a bit better since arrival, but she wasn't out of the woods. They got their answer the next day.

"Leaving the hospital!" Jessi texted a friend. "Going to stop at Casey and Jenn's for a bit."

Fluids and rest had once again done their trick. Jessi's stomach settled down, and she began eating. She slept well and was able to walk herself to the bathroom using just an IV pole. The family was whole on Thanksgiving night, taking in a feast and once again thanking God for dodging a bullet.

CHAPTER NINETEEN

Heartbreak

Winter 2013

Christmas of 2013 saw Jessi and her parents exchange some very meaningful gifts. Over the summer, the FitzRandolphs had hired a professional photographer to take a series of family photos in the front yard, and Jessi surprised Ruthie and Jeff with framed prints of her favorites. In the photos, Jessi is wearing a pink and white top, her cheeks are sun-kissed, and her teeth glisten in a wide smile as she sits on a rock nestled between the two of them, with trees to their sides and bright green grass beneath their feet.

Ruthie presented her daughter with a ring that had belonged to her, an eternity band. Jeff had taken the ring in to a jeweler and had it polished and set with a new series of diamonds. An eternity ring has the same series of stones all the way around the band, with no discernible beginning or end. This gift symbolized so much more than just a ring; it was meant to portray to Jessi the beautiful circle that life takes, how there is never really an end. We simply travel in circles, meeting new people, visiting new places, and knowing we will all be reunited at some time.

Ruthie had to work the night shift on Christmas Eve, arriving home just in time to welcome Casey, Jenn, and their family for the day. She managed to stay awake for their Christmas tradition of quiche, blueberry muffins, and gift opening but fell asleep immediately after the three-hour gift-giving session was completed. New Year's was equally quiet. Jessi's good friend Justin was having a party, but Jessi had been experiencing too many roller coaster days on the health front.

"I've been feeling pretty good other than nausea, which comes and goes but seems to come a fair amount," she described it. She dressed for the party in her usual fashion, but when it came time to leave, she was feeling nauseated and weak. As a result, she stayed home for New Year's Eve.

By January 2014, the FitzRandolphs were flush with oil from multiple suppliers as the word of their need for product to produce the oil had spread. They also had their own marijuana plants budding in soil near their home's large south- and west-facing windows on the lower level. They were in plain view of all who entered the residence, but no one seemed to take anything other than a passing glance at the plants and the modest aroma they gave off. It was as if there was an unspoken respect for the things the FitzRandolphs would try for their daughter. They still had not set up the hydroponic system and weren't sure they would now for two reasons: they seemed to have found a supplier who could meet their needs at a reasonable price; just $35 a gram for cannabis oil. And they still were thinking of selling their house.

The major problem on the health front was that Jessi couldn't keep the oil down with all of the stomach trouble she was having. She simply wasn't getting anywhere close to the recommended dosage of two grams per day.

"Jeff would give her the medicine. By now we had advanced to filling an empty capsule with half a gram of oil, and Jessi would take four capsules a day, one every six hours," stated Ruthie. "It was more palatable for Jessi as opposed to taking it on a slice of bread."

"It's frustrating being on and off the marijuana," said Jessi who, like her parents, wanted to remain on a steady protocol they all believed in. She feared the stopping and starting meant she was not getting enough into her system.

Then, in mid-January, things suddenly began to take a drastic turn downward. The family saw the yo-yo they had been on for four years crank into hyper-speed. The highs and lows were coming at a pace that was hard to fathom. Jessi would feel pretty good and be settled at home for a week or more, only to experience sudden extreme nausea, fatigue, dehydration, and even respiratory distress and be rushed to the hospital for fluids and or a blood transfusion. She spent many nights in St. Mary's Hospital, back in the suite she had become accustomed to, which also accommodated a bed for Ruthie. One such night, in February, was nearly fatal when her hematocrit, the count of red blood cells, dipped well below the normal 12–16 range to 6.5 and the rapid response team was called in.

"I recall the incident vividly," Jeff remembered. "Ruthie was working that night, and Jessi and I agreed that Ruthie should go to work and we would go to the ER. Her oncologist wanted her to get the red blood cell transfusion sooner rather than a day later, when it had been originally scheduled. After we spent a short period of time in the ER, the medical personnel got her hooked up with the blood transfusion and then moved Jessi and me to a more comfortable room in the hospital but not our usual suite.

"We settled in and talked for a little while—nothing very deep, just plans about what we were going to do at the cabin next summer and how we should have a bet on who would catch the biggest fish. Knowing I had no chance didn't seem to matter: when Jessi caught fish, her already infectious smile grew to a kind of taunting challenge: Come on, Dad, top that one!

"At about four thirty in the morning, as I was sleeping in the chair next to her bed, Jessi woke me up. She said she was having trouble breathing and was in pain. Nurses were summoned and performed the recommended treatments for the discomfort Jessi was experiencing, but nothing worked. Jessi continued to complain that she couldn't breathe. The doctor was summoned next and confirmed she had more fluid on her lungs than earlier that evening. A full rapid response code was issued, and soon Jessi's room was filled with three doctors and five nurses. The diagnosis came swiftly: Her heart was overloaded trying to keep up with the rest of her body."

All Jeff could do was stand by Jessi's bed, confused. The nurses comforted him, and he called Ruthie at work and suggested she come to the hospital as soon as possible. The staff took Jessi to the intensive care unit, where they could monitor her more closely and assist her breathing mechanically. Jeff was relegated to a patient family lounge to wait for more word on the fate of his daughter. Ruthie arrived, and the two sat in the family lounge as Jeff tried to explain what had happened and what he had been told. Finally, Jessi gained control of her breathing and laid her head back on the hospital pillow to sleep. The family was told again that she had experienced another congestive heart failure exacerbation. This frightened them deeply, although they continued to believe that strength of spirit would help Jessi once again.

"She has the Whitinger genes that give her the ability to heal her body against all odds. I would expect the next echo [echocardiogram, a heart monitor] to be improved, just because she's Jessi," said Ruthie a few days later.

The family had reluctantly agreed to try yet another new chemo drug that wasn't supposed to cause all of the side effects of some of the other drugs. Jessi's oncologist thought it just might help slow the progress of the metastases. But things had only worsened, and Jessi seemed to reach her lowest points after taking it. Her system appeared to be too delicate to tolerate even these newly approved chemo drugs, and Jeff and Ruthie were afraid another dose might kill her. Even more frustrating for the FitzRandolphs was that the cannabis oil moved further to the background as the family struggled to get Jessi to a state where she could tolerate it daily.

"We want to get back to the things we believe in but from which we've strayed," said Jeff.

While they continued to battle for Jessi's life, volleying between home and hospital, sports fans around the world were getting ready for the 2014 Winter Olympics. Jeff, Ruthie, and Jessi planned to watch the Olympics nearly nonstop. It was in their blood, and yet being a part of the action, and Casey's gold of 2002, seemed like a different lifetime. To think of what had unfolded since then was heart-wrenching and sickening. Weren't they a happy, healthy American family back then, where the biggest choice they faced some nights was where to go for dinner? Now they spent more time in a hospital watching Jessi labor just to take a breath. It was shocking.

The family was tentatively planning another fundraiser in Madison for early April. Jessi's friend Bowen Best was going to help organize it again. Their first event, Fighting4Fitz, had been a huge success and provided the family with funds to make the trips to Germany that had shown so much potential for healing Jessi. This time, they had their eyes on the Majestic Theater in downtown Madison and hoped to enjoy a daylong schedule of bands and a silent auction. The money raised would be a welcome gift for the family as they continued to drain finances on treatments. Plus, the event would provide a much-needed chance for relaxation and fraternization with friends. But as winter lingered on in early 2014, Ruthie saw Jessi having so many setbacks that the fundraiser was pushed back while they labored to keep Jessi on track. Ruthie soon found herself taking on a different mindset when she looked at her daughter.

"Today, our focus is more on the here and now," she explained. "The Trans-Siberian Orchestra comes to town every year, and we always think, 'It's too expensive, maybe next year.' But this year, we just went. None of us know if we have a tomorrow. We're living for the moment, and we have had no regrets."

Jessi found herself gravitating toward faith, something she had never been much interested in before. She believed herself to be an agnostic based on conversations she had with friends throughout the years. But now, in addition to the eternity ring, Ruthie and Jeff bought Jessi a new Bible for Christmas.

"It warms my heart," said Ruthie, who was also deepening her own belief in spirituality. "I know I'll catch up with her if she passes before me. That is very comforting to me. One night, Jessi was alone and feeling down. She got out some pamphlets given to her by the hospital chaplain and started reading."

"I felt calm. It helped settle me," Jessi said.

As the calendar turned to March, things got even worse. The family couldn't build up Jessi's dosage of oil to two grams a day. Now Jessi was throwing up the undissolved capsules as soon as she took them. As a result, they had to depend on the drugs they so dearly despised in order to fight Jessi's discomfort. Ruthie's CarePages update was filled with discouraging news.

> *More Bumps in the Road*
> *March 7, 2014*
> *9:57 p.m.*
>
> *Jessi is back in the hospital again. A couple days ago, she started having vision changes. She was more sensitive to light and sound. Her vision deteriorated to the point where now everything is very blurry. When describing what she saw when looking at her dad yesterday, she said, "I see a floating chin." This makes the simplest of tasks challenging. TV is not enjoyable, nor is being on her computer or cell phone.*

Even feeding herself and walking are difficult because her coordination is way off.

She was admitted to St. Mary's Wednesday. She had a CT scan of the brain that same day which was surprisingly negative. Following that, she had two MRIs of the brain, with and without IV contrast. They were markedly abnormal, showing many minute spots that appear like mini-strokes although much smaller. The MRIs showed multiple areas of hemorrhage in the brain as well, again very tiny spots.

Once again, she has everyone here baffled. The doctors have never seen anything like it, not even the neurologist. In an attempt to find out what is causing these spots, she had a trans-esophageal echocardiogram to see if there is anything around the heart that might be producing any tiny particles that could be causing these spots in the brain. That was basically unremarkable. I'm not sure what is next. A lumbar puncture was scheduled for this afternoon but then cancelled due to risk of bleeding.

Jessi enjoyed a visit from Casey, Jenn, Sawyer, and Cassidy tonight. I think she will be up for more visitors soon. She had cabin fever before she even got here. Haven't we all! Please feel free to be in touch with me by text if you want to visit. I am taking a leave of absence from Agrace to try to get us through this latest bump in the road. I am hoping to make another post tomorrow with an update and plan to include a photo of an amazing work of art from a wonderful relative. Thank you for your support, love, and prayers.

Ruthie

Five days later, in the middle of the night, Ruthie posted her most emotional note up to that point.

March 12, 2014
12:42 a.m.
Another day is winding down. Jessi just had a dose of IV Dilaudid for back pain caused by the spread of cancer to her bones. She is sleeping right now and looks so peaceful

and content—and young. Just lying quietly in bed, she looks like the picture of health. She is still sporting freckles from last summer's sun.

This journey has brought Jessi and me so close together. There are no barriers, no walls. For that, I will be forever grateful. We continue to struggle with the why questions and "what next." We had engaged Agrace Palliative Care just prior to this admission to help manage symptoms and direct her care.

Jessi hasn't had much of an appetite but thought a porta salad from Porta Bella sounded good tonight. One bite into the salad, Jessi looked up and asked me, "Mom, am I dying?" I answered as honestly as I could and told her it didn't look good. We cried together and hugged for the next thirty minutes until we were both exhausted. I can't begin to explain what it feels like to watch this cancer get its grip on my daughter, taking one little piece after the next.

Jessi wants to continue to fight this "darling" of cancers. We talked about a plan, and at the top of the list she is asking for prayers for a miracle. The medical interventions are no longer working well and Jeff and I are running short on alternative treatments to try as well.

We are hoping for discharge tomorrow (Wed.). Jessi has enjoyed so many visitors—family, friends, the Babes. Thank you all so much for your love and your supportive messages, and Jessi particularly thanks you prayer warriors for your prayers for a miracle.

Ruthie

People started calling, e-mailing, and posting comments immediately. Sixty-one comments arrived on the CarePages website in just a few hours. Most people were praying for the miracle Jessi requested, and the family was warmed by the incredible outpouring of love for Jessi. But it was clear that everything was headed in the wrong direction. Several doctors and specialists at the hospital had a long talk with the family. After the meeting, Jeff was so choked with emotion that he excused himself to go home. He was simply overwhelmed with every feeling associated with grief, including shock, sadness, and anger. His daughter—his beautiful, spunky, strong daughter—was close to the end. He drove to the house in tears, gathered the dogs, and went straight to bed in the middle of the afternoon. Wrapping his arms around the pups, he sobbed. Ruthie stayed at the hospital at Jessi's side. Jeff was amazed by her strength.

Jessi was discharged and returned home after a few days. Her recovery had stalled, and further tests were not providing any answers. She remained confused, disoriented, restless, and clearly in pain. Her vision was nearly gone due to the mini-strokes, and she had lost all of her appetite. Her weight was at its lowest, and she was unable to stand independently. She complained of her hands being numb and took to slapping them in an attempt to get the feeling back. It also became nearly impossible to reason with her; Jessi would forget conversations just minutes after they happened and couldn't recall things she had just done. Taking her oil in capsules was out of the question. The only alternative left was to administer it as a suppository, but that option was quickly discounted. Jeff and Ruthie had a heart-wrenching talk and came to the conclusion that it had to be time for hospice. It was the most difficult decision of their lives.

Still very disoriented, on Sunday, March 16, Jessi was told by her parents that they were going to take her to Agrace HospiceCare for symptom management with the plan to return home once she stabilized. But once Dr. Kim Kinsley, the physician at Agrace, examined Jessi and then looked into Ruthie's eyes, Ruthie knew there would be no fairy tale ending to the story this time.

"I knew in my heart that Jessi was in her final days, but it somehow still caught me off guard," Ruthie stated, tears streaming down her face.

"She would not have wanted to live like that. That, I know. I'm glad she didn't have to be uncomfortable like that for very long," she added.

So, Ruthie and Jeff made arrangements for their daughter's end-of-life care. They simply wanted to see her comfortable. They now knew she was dying and quickly agreed with the doctor's recommendation that Jessi be given heavy pain and relaxation medications. She slipped into a deep sleep almost immediately. For the next couple of days, Jessi stayed asleep in the bed in room seventeen. Ruthie would not leave her side. Jeff ran out only to quickly feed and let out the dogs. Both parents slept on the pullout couch, and Casey and Sawyer also spent an unexpected overnight.

Casey, Jenn, and the kids had come over after work for a short visit, but father and son felt so drawn to Jessi that they camped out. Without pajamas or toothbrushes, Casey borrowed surgical scrubs to sleep in and forced his frame into a reclining chair until he woke up uncomfortable at four thirty in the morning. Sawyer slept wedged between his "Jammers" (Ruthie) and "Jeepers" (Jeff). That night was St. Patrick's Day, and while many people were sleeping off an evening of drinking green beer and partying, Casey pulled out the laptop and reflected on his sister as he wrote his first CarePages entry.

> *Hero*
> *March 17, 2014*
>
> *Today is all about luck. It's St. Patrick's Day, after all, and while we FitzRandolphs are actually not Irish, we are thinking about our luck on this seventeenth day of March, 2014.*
>
> *At first glance, it's horrific. As I sit by Jessi's bedside typing, she sleeps—what appears to be comfortably—in the hospice bed to my right in Room Seventeen at Agrace HospiceCare here in Madison, a place she entered yesterday afternoon to be most comfortable. Jenn just took Cassidy home to get some rest. Sawyer stayed and is straight ahead, just past my feet, sandwiched between Jammers and Jeepers (Ruthie and Jeff) on the twin-sized pull-out couch. The noise machine which sits on the window sill to my left, along with the beautiful family portraits we had taken last summer on the steps of 6434 Sunset Drive, has drowned out any hallway noise as well as any thoughts my family had distracting them prior to finally succumbing to exhaustion.*
>
> *Sawyer and Cass, at ages seven and five, learned yesterday that "Aunt Jessers isn't doing very well" and that "she might not be with us here much longer because her body is really tired." "We are going to go in to tell her how much we love her and give her hugs and kisses," Jenn and I said. "But you*

know, we can talk to her anytime because she'll be up in heaven looking down on us after she leaves." Jenn and I spoke with them individually, not having a clue what to expect. Both had the same reaction. They stared straight ahead for a few seconds and then broke down crying. So we cried together, told them it's perfectly okay to feel sad or mad or wonder why. And then we came in to visit Aunt Jessers.

A lot has changed in the past week. Even the past couple days. And each time we see her we feel she is closer to being called home to be with Him. It is, to be honest, an internal conflict between not wanting her to leave and wanting her to leave so she can enter eternal peace. One second it is gut-wrenching to look at my thirty-six-year-old little sister lying next to me in this state and environment, and the next I am reminded of this unparalleled and unexpected journey she has led us all on.

Because we are also very lucky. It's been almost four years since they diagnosed Jess at stage IV and almost three since she was sent home from the hospital to die because there was "nothing more we can do." Since that time we have learned that Jessi is, to our amazement, the strongest one in our family. We have seen a strength the likes of which this older brother can literally not comprehend. We have witnessed a loved one go from fourth-in line to leading our family by example. And, perhaps most amazingly, we have been privy to witnessing an unwavering optimism rise and flourish that we cannot yet fathom, yet will forever aspire to follow.

For these reasons, we could not be more grateful of what her journey has unveiled for us.

Casey

PS: If I may make a prayer suggestion, please join me in praying for Jessi's continued comfort and belief, our folks' continued strength, and Sawyer and Cassidy's ability to process their feelings. These are the areas we can most use the strength you have been so generous in giving :-).

A steady stream of visitors arrived over the next two days. Every one of the six Verona Babes came, some more than once, as well as a slew of other friends, Aunt Nancy and Andy. Agrace HospiceCare is one of the most beautiful and peaceful places to see a life end. Jessi's room was huge and welcoming, with everything done in warm shades of brown wood. A bird feeder hung outside of her window; chickadees, a robin, and finches not yet in summer color visited the feeder every morning. The room had a few tasteful paintings on the wall, and the only noises were the soft hush of people in the hallway or Jessi's iPod gently crooning her favorite songs when Ruthie put it on shuffle at a low level. The FitzRandolphs brought a favorite orange fleece blanket from home to keep Jessi warm, and they lined family photos along the windowsill. Agrace provided a teddy bear and tucked it under Jessi's arm.

Jeff, Ruthie, and Casey allowed each visitor as much time as they needed alone with Jessi while the rest of the group walked across the hall to a private kitchen and dining area. There was an alternating flow of tears and hugs mixed with stories. Everyone had a funny memory: the time Jessi and her friend, Julie, hitchhiked to Lambeau Field to see a Green Bay Packers game with no plan for a ride home and the time Jessi washed every single piece of fruit even though it wasn't necessary to cleanse each individual piece of sliced cantaloupe or watermelon. The nostalgia was both heartwarming and heartbreaking as their wonderful Jessi was slipping away.

She never regained consciousness at Agrace. While she slept, it was difficult to tell she was sick. Her shoulder-length brown hair was in pigtails, she wore a black and white striped long-sleeved shirt, and her face was smooth and unblemished, with still nearly-perfect skin at the age of thirty six. The eternity ring was on her left hand. In another setting, one might think she could be taking a nap, just about to hop up for a night out.

Ruthie and Jeff showed incredible strength greeting and comforting each distraught friend or family member, but mother and father also teared up every single time they pulled a chair next to their daughter's bedside. Ruthie would stroke Jessi's hair and kiss her forehead, murmuring, "You look so pretty, sweetie," and "I love you." Jeff held her arm or her hand. Jessi slept on. She was not being given fluids or nutrition, and the telltale signs of her body failing were starting to show, like amber-colored urine as the kidneys slowly shut down.

Sawyer was allowed to stay back from school one day to be with Casey and his grandparents. He spent much of this day crawling onto the bed and throwing his tiny seven-year-old arms around Jessi or snuggling next to her, his body only half the height of hers. Sawyer even slipped his small hands under the orange blanket and rubbed her feet. The contact from her nephew was the one time Jessi's eyes fluttered open, but only for an instant, and then she was asleep again. A few times she appeared to give a slight smile to Sawyer's touch.

On March 19, 2014, at five thirty in the morning, Jessi's respiratory pattern changed, and she became restless. Ruthie, by then sleeping on an air bed directly at Jessi's side, jumped up to attend to her. She pushed the nurse call button and asked that Jessi be given more medication to help keep her calm. Most of the time, morphine would be the first drug given, but Ruthie requested Dilaudid because she knew from past experience that it worked better for Jessi. No one questioned her.

By seven, Jessi was clearly in discomfort. She moaned softly and was struggling for air. This woke Jeff. She twisted uncomfortably in the bed. Her eyes were still shut. Ruthie knew the signs that someone displays when they are close to death; restlessness and change in respiratory status are among them. Ruthie called for the nurse again, and Sonya Liboy, one of Ruthie's favorite night shift coworkers, responded. Ruthie asked for even more of the heavy-duty pain meds. She couldn't bear to see Jessi in any distress.

And then, Ruthie did what any loving mother would do: She held Jessi's hand and offered a few words of encouragement. "Oh, sweetheart, this is the hardest thing I've ever had to say, but you have suffered long enough. It's time to go to Jesus and be free. I will miss you so much, and I love you dearly. Dad and I will be okay and will take good care of each other. Jessi, you are so beautiful. Be at peace with yourself as you travel to your new home."

The restlessness stopped, and Jessi settled back into a peaceful position. The combination of her mother's message and the additional medication seemed to calm her. She took three or four last deep breaths and then ceased breathing.

Jessilyn Kae FitzRandolph passed at seven fifteen in the morning with the two people who brought her into the world on either side of her, each holding one of her hands, sobs coming from their throats and tears streaming down their cheeks.

Casey, who had not been there at the moment Jessi passed, arrived at Agrace a short time later with Jenn and the kids. He described it when he took to the computer late that night.

> *A Star Is Born*
> *March 19, 2014*
> *11:30 p.m.*
> *Jessi's Followers,*
>
> *It has been a long day, so this will not be long nor probably eloquent. At seven this morning our folks called to suggest Jenn and I and the kids hurry to Agrace to say goodbye to Jessi. Fifteen minutes later, with Jenn and the kids and I still in route, she left for heaven with Mom and Dad by her side, holding her hands.*
>
> *I don't have the energy to paint you an accurate picture of our day, but we want you to know that Jessi's journey here is over and her glorious journey has begun. As hard as the past week has been, today felt, at times, like the eye of the storm and, at others, like the calm and rainbow immediately after.*
>
> *We are heartbroken. We miss her dearly. We will struggle as we process and prioritize the good with the bad and the ugly, trying to be okay with His timeline for her. And we will undoubtedly lean on you for your continued support now that she has left us, perhaps especially now that she has left us.*
>
> *But we have started the process of peeling back the grip that cancer had bestowed upon us. It is ugly, as you know, and is hard to take deep breaths as you navigate days and weeks and months and years while it squeezes someone you love. And so, while cancer succeeded in taking her body, we are finding significant solace in the fact that it never took her spirit, not even for a day and not even for one single minute. We find great comfort for ourselves and great comfort and*

pride for Jessi in knowing that it did win a battle but got its ass kicked in the war.

For those of you who have never been through this, I don't expect you to understand. I would not have myself as recently as a week ago. And yet now it is so clear.

And it is so cool too, really. It is just so rewarding to think about how dignified, how calm, how optimistic, and how in control Jessi remained until she left—not to mention how beautiful. The other night I mentioned in my post how she grew and blossomed as a person and leader during her journey. But, even as her older brother, I must confess that she looked as beautiful on the outside as she is on the inside. So the vain part of me is even proud of her for that. (Anyone that knows how important fashion was to Jess knows it was fairly high on her priority list as well.)

So I found myself smiling as I cried on our procession out of Agrace. I couldn't help it. She looked so beautiful and so at peace. And her face was an obvious reminder of how cancer had actually made her better while trying to make her worse. For this, I give thanks to both God and Mom and Dad.

So it is with heavy hearts but high hopes that we ask you to pray, again, for Jessers as she is welcomed at The Gates today. Ask for a pleasant ride and for it to be all that we hope it will be. But also know that, if this calmness that has come over me today is any indication, her big brown eyes have never been bigger than they are right now as they take in the unworldly view she has now been granted. And her smile has picked up right where it left off.

Casey

PS: I would be remiss if I did not acknowledge the role Agrace Hospice played in our family's physical and mental comfort during our stay. I could write a short book on all the ways they made our week more tolerable.

The processional Casey referred to is Agrace's way of showing respect to a patient and his or her family. When someone passes away, people nearby—nurses, staff members, and family members of other patients—pause what they are doing and stand in the hallway. Quietly, they stand at attention as the body passes by, with the person's face sometimes exposed and other times completely covered. Usually, family accompanies a loved one as he or she is slowly wheeled through the hallways to the front door. Someone might whisper "I'm sorry" or reach out to touch the hand of a grieving family member, but otherwise this is a quiet ritual that means the world to those who have just lost a loved one. For a few moments, normal activity stops to acknowledge their grief. There could be perhaps twenty to thirty people watching a processional, but for Jessi's, the nurses asked the FitzRandolphs to hold off for a few moments.

"I couldn't figure out why," said Ruthie. "Then we learned that they were getting organized."

At least 150 people lined the halls, from nursing staff, doctors, and social workers to administration.

"Everyone, I think every single person in the building, must have left their work stations to pay their respects. It was incredible," remembered Ruthie, her eyes misting over. "I've never seen anything like it."

The FitzRandolphs chose not to cover Jessi's face for the processional. "I put a little pink lipstick on her lips and a little blush on her cheeks. I think she would have liked that," said Ruthie. "And she looked wonderful, just so beautiful and peaceful. She somehow maintained her color, which is really unusual because typically the color drains from someone who has just passed."

In fact, Jeff and Ruthie noticed that Jessi seemed to defy the odds, looking lovely throughout the breast cancer and hospice.

"Jessi had liver mets. My mom had lymphoma with liver mets, and she was jaundiced from time to time. She also retained fluids that would accumulate in her belly and joked that she looked like she was nine months pregnant. It was difficult for my mom to breathe with this extra load on her small frame. Jessi had the mets, but her skin never paled, and her color was just beautiful." Ruthie smiled. "Jessi was also fortunate in that she never had the abdominal fluid."

It was especially difficult for all of the adults to watch seven-year-old Sawyer and five-year-old Cassidy handle the death of their Aunt Jessi.

"I've never seen two little kids experience such grief. It was just painful. I didn't think that they would get it, but they totally, totally got it," said Ruthie. "The social workers were quite surprised at Cassidy's reaction— she's just barely five years old—and Sawyer's reaction, too, how distraught they both were."

As excruciating as Jessi's death was on the family, they were also relieved and comforted that she did not have to suffer or stay in hospice too long.

"For as many roadblocks as He threw at us—He being God—and as many challenges as He presented us with, at least in the end He allowed her to go quickly, fairly painlessly, and relatively peacefully," said Jeff. "If she had hung on in such pain and distress for another month or six weeks, it would have been terribly hard."

In some ways, this felt like affirmation. As mind-boggling as her death was, it seemed that it was Jessi's time. God was calling her, and she was accepting it and allowing her body to shut down. Still, it was gut wrenching to experience. Back at home, Ruthie slept in Jessi's bed the first few nights to feel closer to her daughter, with Jessi's prayer shawl in her arms, sobbing until she finally fell asleep.

The FitzRandolphs waited nine days for the funeral to allow everyone time to make or change travel plans. People were coming from as far away as Pennsylvania, Florida, and Colorado. And many of Jessi's closest friends with young children were on spring break and traveling to Florida; some hastily made changes to their itinerary. The venue chosen was Blackhawk Church, a worship space west of Madison so large it dwarfs a multiplex theater. Yet the entire reception area overflowed with people. Jeff, Ruthie, and Casey stood on one end of the receiving line that snaked the lengths of several football fields. They had planned ninety minutes to greet guests, but three-quarters of the line never moved more than a few feet forward. There were just so many people. Everyone had a story, tears, and a hug to share with the FitzRandolphs. The pastor was finally forced to interrupt the line to begin the service, with condolences to be continued afterward.

"There's no way in a million years we expected that kind of turnout for the visitation," said Jeff. "We were originally going to do a one-hour visitation, and Casey called and said, 'You have to extend this.' So we decided on an hour and a half, and we still couldn't come close to seeing everyone. People came from all walks of life—from our speedskating past, Ruthie's workplace, Casey's friends, co-workers, and neighbors, and, of course, people that knew Jessi. We learned more about our daughter in one day than we ever knew."

Flowers sat brightly in vases and pots all around the church. Most notably, there were Jessi's favorite, orchids. Many family members and friends wore green, her color of choice. A video montage on two huge screens showed images of a young Jessi and Casey at the lake, all the way up to the most recent shots with the Verona Babes, taken only a few days before Jessi entered Agrace. Two of her parents' favorite spiritual songs were performed by a duo from the church's ministry group.

Jeff and Ruthie mostly wanted personal remembrances, so the service was dominated by stories, each inspiring a mix of laughter and a wave of fresh tears. Casey spoke, his words echoing the CarePages posts he wrote from his sister's bedside. He wanted everyone at the service to know just how strong she had been through the entire ordeal and what that meant to him. She was the fourth in line in terms of birth order but led their family all to a higher place in the end.

"He had never seen such a profound change in a person as in Jessi during the last four years—really, the last few on the medical cannabis, especially," said Jeff. "She impressed her brother, and that's not an easy thing to do. She had a profound impact on him, and that's going to affect him the rest of his life."

"She was my little sister," Casey reflected later. "But through her battle with cancer, she displayed a strength, grace, perseverance, and a confident calmness that really impressed and inspired me. She taught me things about life that have made me a more sensitive and loving person. She also gave me a new perspective on life. If my little sis could go from bed to chair staring death in the face, with the unwavering confidence and morale that she did, how could I not consider my life's trials and tribulations anything other than trivial?"

The Verona Babes each took a turn talking about their dear friend, their messages spawning a wide variety of emotions. Some recalled humorous stories, things Jessi had done in the crazy, fun moments of her life. Others reflected on Jessi's laughter and playfulness. All were heartfelt and deeply appreciated by the FitzRandolph family.

Jeff and Ruthie approached the podium last, expressing thoughts and reflections about their beautiful daughter and thanking people for coming to celebrate her life. They reflected on how her life had seemed to take on a glow over the last two years. Finding Pastor Matt and Blackhawk had changed her life, as though a candle had taken permanent residence within her spirit. They wanted Jessi to be remembered for burning brightly, and the closing music would echo that theme.

As the guest singers performed "Go Light Your World," the Verona Babes helped every one of the hundreds of mourners light a candle in the darkened chapel. The congregation lifted their candles simultaneously, a glittering lake of twinkles in honor of Jessi.

After the benediction, Pastor Matt led the entire congregation outside to a concrete patio area. Casey had arranged for a white, wicker box to be waiting. Sawyer and Cassidy, in their best clothing, approached the box tentatively, holding on to their parents' hands. Jenn helped them open the top.

Four powder-white doves flew out, rising quickly into a gray March sky, starting in one direction before reversing course all at the same moment and disappearing into the clouds. The eyes of hundreds of mourners watched them go.

CHAPTER TWENTY

Seeking a New Normal

Spring 2014

The first few months after the death of a loved one are often the most difficult. The flurry of planning the funeral has ended, and everyone else goes back home. You are supposed to get back to somewhat of a normal life, including work, household chores, and day-to-day living. But now, there is just a hollow emptiness where that amazing person used to be: the chair they sat in, their clothing still in the closet, the dog looking around for the missing piece. Everything was a reminder of Jessi, especially because she had been living at home for so long.

"We did real well through the service," reflected Jeff. "There was so much to do to get ready that we didn't get a chance to properly grieve. But the Saturday after the service both of us spent most of the day crying and finding it very difficult to get out bed. It just kind of hit us on that day. We were alone for the first time. It was very painful. That's when the realization that she was really not going to be with us any longer set in."

There wasn't a moment Jeff and Ruthie weren't thinking of Jessi and missing her so much it sometimes made their knees buckle.

"We'll be doing something normal, like straightening up the house or going through some books or reading online, and come across a picture of her or an e-mail she sent us. It throws you totally off-kilter," said Jeff, about a month after her passing. "And you sit there and dab at your eyes for ten, fifteen minutes, maybe a half an hour. Then you try and pull yourself together and get back on with it."

The couple's routine had also gone from the daily, repetitive—and sometimes grueling—regimen of Jessi's care to nothing. The marijuana plants sat untouched in their pots. There was still unused oil in the pantry. The Rife machine and Bob Beck paddles remained stoically in the living room until Ruthie and Jeff put them in a closet. Where once Jeff would have been on the computer researching, planning a fundraiser, or getting Jessi some food, medicine, or another blanket, he now found himself adrift in a house that was eerily quiet.

There was, however, no shortage of visitors.

"I think the Babes must have promised Jessi that they would make sure we were okay," said Ruthie with a smile. "They have stopped over a number of times, bringing us lunch and dinner."

"We'll sit and visit, talking about the fun times, the good memories, and that's positive. It lifts everybody up," added Jeff. "Jessi's good friends Justin, Erick, and Libby came over. Erick loves to cook, and he made a huge pan of homemade lasagna. They stayed for a couple of hours and chatted, and we got to see Libby's baby girl."

In fact, so many friends wanted to stop by that the FitzRandolphs joked they could have stacked people on top of people on top of people one particular Friday. They appreciated every single gesture but also knew they had to pace themselves.

"We try to limit the number of people we see on a daily basis. As much as we enjoy seeing everybody, we still need our own space and our own time to grieve and to think about how we want to come to grips with this," said Jeff. "We're going to go through a fair amount of pain and consternation for probably a period of a year at least, until we go through one full cycle of all of the holidays, celebrations, summer trips to the cabin, Easter egg hunts, Thanksgiving dinners, and Christmas at our place. Until we go through that cycle one time without her it's going to be very, very difficult."

Ruthie had made what she called a misstep in the grieving process. She went back to work too soon, mostly thanks to her misinterpretation of salary rules.

"If you lose a child, they give you a one-week bereavement period with pay. When I looked at that I thought, 'Well, that must mean that I should be able to function after a week.' So I went back thinking I should be able to do this," Ruthie said.

With that in mind, just seven days after her daughter passed, Ruthie put on her scrubs and tried her usual overnight shift. It didn't go very well. Agrace was as sympathetic and wonderful as ever, putting Ruthie in a different wing so she was not required to walk past the room where Jessi had been, but it was still incredibly hard. Ruthie hadn't had time to process Jessi's passing, and she was assigned twenty-eight patients that night. Coworkers would stop to hug her and talk, which was heartwarming but mentally exhausting. She had trouble focusing and, if not for the help of Ricki, a certified nursing assistant, might not have been able to complete her duties.

"Ricki was able to pass oral meds on to patients," said Ruthie. "Without her, I would have been just overwhelmed."

When Ruthie dragged herself home the next morning, it all hit her again. She cried for five full hours before finally succumbing to exhaustion. The FitzRandolphs decided she needed a true break from work. Jeff filed paperwork for short-term disability, which would pay 60 percent of her salary for twelve weeks. Every grief counselor, pastor, and specialist they saw said it would take at least three months before one might be expected to have a head for work. For now, just focusing at all was a challenge.

"I can't read a book," said Ruthie. "I want to get into bed and read, and I can't read. I don't remember the last time I watched the news."

There was no question Ruthie had a strong desire to eventually go back to work, just not yet. "I love my co-workers. I got a check in the mail from them for $465, which they collected among themselves just to help out," she said.

Jeff helped Ruthie to understand that she needed to truly give herself time, not go by someone else's calendar or a paper that says you get one week of bereavement pay and that's it. And she definitely needed not to feel bad about it.

"You know, it's exactly like discovering you've been diagnosed with cancer. It's something you've never experienced before in your life, so you're clueless. You don't really know what to expect or how to deal with it, so you make the same mistakes you make when you're first trying to treat your cancer. We made all of those mistakes with Jessi at first, too," he concluded.

Two weeks after Jessi's passing, the two were having a very hard time with day-to-day living, but Jeff felt he had a vision. He put it down in a CarePages entry.

> *A Shower ... a Vision ... Healing!*
> *April 4, 2014*
> *12:09 p.m.*
> *It's been one week since we celebrated Jessi's life with so many family and friends. This morning I finally climbed in the shower shortly after ten a.m. That's very late for me—I'm usually a five-thirty-a.m. guy. But this shower would prove to be a very unique experience. About half way into my shower I started thinking of Jessi, which is not terribly startling in its own right since that's about all either Ruthie or I have done since March 19. But the thoughts usually make me start to tear up before I can really get a grip on my emotions.*
> *This shower was very different. First I saw a field of green grass with white lines dividing it into sections. Then I saw a beautiful blue sky with not a cloud in it. Next I felt a very slight breeze blowing against my damp body. But it didn't give me a chill; it brought me peace. Then Jessi, in her Verona soccer jersey, shorts, pads, and shoes, was running on that beautiful green grass and, you guessed it, kicking a soccer ball. This was not the typical vision one might get when trying to visualize something they want to happen. This was so vivid, I believed if I had been forty years younger I might be able to join Jessi on the field and maybe even steal the ball.*
> *It passed fairly quickly, but it did give me pause to think about what to write to every one of Jessi's supporters after the celebration of life service we had for Jessi last Friday at the BlackHawk Church in Middleton. Our family was overwhelmed (to say the least) at the support provided by family, friends, clients, neighbors, and many other people who have touched us in many different ways throughout our lives. Jessi and Ruthie found BlackHawk Church after several years of searching for a local church that could really relate to*

our family. Their first up close and personal experience was with Matt Rusten, the pastor who would help us celebrate Jessi's life. Matt explained biblical passages in ways that we could understand, ways that allowed us to relate to what the church represented, and we all fell in love with the church.

The visitation and service were not without their share of complications. First, we never anticipated so many loved ones coming to pay their respects to Jessi and our family. We did add thirty minutes to the visitation at Casey's request, extending it to ninety minutes, but we really needed another full hour of time to be able to properly greet all who came to show their love of our family.

If you were there and we weren't able to share time with you before the service, we are truly sad. I think it was our loss not being able to share just a few fleeting moments with people who felt strongly enough about their bond with our family to come to pay their respects. I want you to know that we really tried to keep the line moving, but we saw so many people who had such interesting stories to tell about their relationship with our family that we wouldn't think of not sharing those memories.

We would, however, like to thank each and every one of you for taking time from your busy lives to come to honor Jessi's memory. She was touched by many and loved by many more. Everyone there was fighting with the question, "Why take Jessi, who had so much to offer?"

This is one of those questions that just simply has to be trusted to the hand of God. I certainly don't understand why he would choose to take my daughter when there are so many alive who are struggling just to stay alive from whom he could have chosen.

But my thought process the last several days has been that heaven accepts many people from many walks of life. So, every once in a while you need to find a really beautiful person on earth who might be able to help teach and preach to those who reach heaven with heavy hearts and maybe a *little baggage. I believe Jessi was one of those people. With other family members of strong faith already there, she could lead a team of pretty powerful Christians who want to find peace and love among all mankind. That group of people can spend their lives on earth putting the care, peace, and health of others over their own needs.*

That is one of the most comforting thoughts I've been able to come to believe in since we lost Jessi. It's the basis on which I build my recovery. The grieving, tears, and just "blah" feeling in general have consumed most of my time in recent days, but each day the positive thoughts come through a little more clearly than the day before. If I continue to have visions of Jessi when I shower, I'll start showering a dozen times a day. The pain in my heart will never go away completely. Actually, I don't want it to. But I owe it to myself and to Jessi to regain a positive outlook on my life and come to grips with the fact that I will always feel some pain. I must also realize that it is a positive pain, that it reminds me of beautiful times in my life shared with Jessi. That's a pain I can live with as I move forward and pour out that part of me which was reserved for Jessi into my relationships with Ruthie, Casey, Jenn, Sawyer, and Cassidy. The future brings a little extra love for each of them and more healing for me.

Eventually, my beautiful daughter, we will be together again.

Godspeed,
Dad

PS: Jessi, I pray that my shower visions only go one way, just to spare you the embarrassment. Love You, Dad

In the coming weeks, Jeff and Ruthie took everyone's advice related to healing. They saw a psychologist and met with a chaplain from Agrace. They tried to exercise and socialize, but there were still plenty of days where getting out from under the covers took all of their mental strength.

"Your life is going to be different now. You have to find a new normal because that old normal doesn't exist," said Jeff. "We're searching for focus and a new normal, and all of those feelings are rolling around in your head all at one time."

Some say there is no greater pain than losing a child, and Jeff and Ruthie were feeling it acutely every moment. They had tried so hard to keep their daughter alive, and they did so for years beyond what conventional medical professionals has expected. But in the immediate aftermath of Jessi's death, it was a challenge to find comfort in anything.

As the weeks began to pass, in many ways the sadness deepened. Their shoulders drooped as the permanency of the situation fell like a relentless rain. Despite his touching moment in the shower, Jeff discovered he had miscalculated his own mourning period.

"I expected to grieve seriously for two to three weeks, to have things be not totally normal for another two to three weeks, and then be able to just kind of pick up and move on with my life, never totally forgetting Jessi, always having her there beside me, but at least being able to function at what I thought was my normal. And now I realize that there's no way in hell … no way in hell that that is going to happen."

"A lot of people ask us about anger. I've never been angry. I am disappointed with myself for not being able to come up with a way to save her life," reflected Ruthie.

"I never felt angry with God for taking her. Jessi had her angry moments. She wondered if it was payback for something she did. She never, ever thought this disease would take her life. I tried to reassure her it was just bad luck. I'm more sad than angry. I'm just sad and devastated. I would give anything to see her again, even—even just for a short visit." Ruthie's voice broke as a sob entered her throat. Jeff gently jumped in.

"I was actually pretty impressed with the way Jessi handled her anger, coming from where she came from. Before she was diagnosed, she was pretty much agnostic. To grow to where she did as a Christian over the last two years and to deal with the disease the way she did was nothing short of amazing. I would expect an agnostic to be angry all the time and just wonder, 'Why me? What is going on? Why do I have all the bad luck?' There are a lot of angry people in the world today. But Jessi wasn't one of them. She processed things in her own way and, as we all found out, was a lot stronger person than we ever gave her credit for." Ruthie wiped a tear away and added, "She didn't want anyone else to hurt. She didn't want our family to hurt for her, the Babes, or her brother and his family. I think she kept it together for everybody else's sake, too. I think the bottom line is she really never, ever thought that this disease would take her life."

Jeff was able to find a great degree of comfort in knowing he had helped his daughter live nearly three years beyond the day a conventional doctor told them to give up, but Ruthie still had a hard time seeing it that way.

"She and I were always going to figure out a way to beat this thing. It was never going to get her. Part of me feels I failed her, but we tried just about everything. I don't know what else we could have tried."

As they look back, the FitzRandolphs differ a bit on what they think worked and what didn't. Both are strongly in the camp that alternative medicine is far superior to conventional oncology for advanced-stage cancer, but Jeff's opinion is that Germany, where Jessi underwent wholebody hyperthermia from late 2010 until mid-2011, was getting her on a healthy path.

"She was sailing through the German treatments, and we were seeing progress. We were seeing halos around the cancer tumors in her bones, suggestions that she was healing, and then she got this God-awful aHUS. One in a billion. The doctors think she's the only known survivor of chemo-induced aHUS. Without that disease, I think there's a very good chance she'd be with us right now and she'd be in remission. But she got the disease, so she fought that and couldn't really fight the cancer at the same time. The doctors gave up on her and told us she had a couple of months to live. They suggested hospice and told us to make her comfortable while she was alive. We said thank you very much, and we brought her home and looked for other alternatives and found some. By God, they improved her quality of life, and they gave her a few more years of life.

"The medical cannabis was also huge, and that gave me hope that we might be able to turn this thing around. But we weren't able to get as much of the stuff as she needed and do it on a regular basis. If we had, we may still have been able to save her. It was so on and off because it was illegal, which made it a challenge to locate regular reliable sources. Another one of the ironies was that we finally found a local source that was affordable and could provide us what we needed, but it was too late."

Ruthie laments the fact that she didn't have more wisdom and education from the very start of the cancer journey. She never had enough time to do extensive research, but why would she have started the process earlier? Who expects their child to get cancer? Still, Ruthie wishes she had the knowledge to question more from the beginning.

"They [the oncologists] absolutely should have done a bone scan upon her original diagnosis, especially after she was found to have a fractured rib three months earlier. Then, I probably would not have recommended the mastectomy. If it's in her bones, why take off the breast? If I had known about the marijuana, I would have done that right away. I doubt I would have done any conventional chemotherapy because, you know, when you do conventional chemotherapy, the likelihood is the cancer is going to come back and come back with a vengeance, so why do it? I would have strongly considered and probably have done the Bob Beck protocol, and I would have started the Rife machine treatments immediately. I think I would have gone to Mexico before Germany because they were more about the immune system."

But Jeff still believed in the treatments in Germany. Seated across the living room from his wife of forty two years, he piped in:

"Germany and Bob Beck. I don't think we would have needed the Rife, although I do believe in the technology. I don't believe we would have needed the trips to Mexico. Dr. Joyce, Jessi's nutritionist, was all about eating right and building immunity. So, those things would have gotten her on a good road to health. And, if anything else, I would have supplemented the oil as needed for the rest of her life to keep her stable. That would have been my solution."

Both parents agreed they wished Jessi had been able to tolerate the alternative Cellect powder protocol, but it was not to be.

The house already had a different feel to it as Jeff and Ruthie sat reflecting. Gone was the hospital bed and all of the medical equipment in the living room. The chairs and couches were rearranged to fill the space. The three dogs, including Jessi's special pup Kirby, roamed back and forth to whomever had an open lap, but there was a cavernous feeling in the room, except for one bright corner where the FitzRandolphs had now added to the flourishing array of orchids in all shades of pinks and purples.

"We've become very attached to orchids." Ruthie smiled, thinking of her daughter's love for these delicate and cheerful flowers. The stalks stood tall against the windows, at least a dozen plants grouped together to make a colorful splash. On a white shelf next to the orchids rested a sturdy, green marble box. Inside were Jessi's ashes. Ruthie got up at one point to rearrange the box and a few knickknacks and pictures next it. On any given day, Ruthie would find herself gravitating to the box.

"I give her a kiss every morning and night," said Ruthie.

Ruthie and Jeff discussed what they would eventually do with Jessi's ashes: perhaps putting some into a locket, perhaps spreading some, perhaps burying them, or perhaps keeping her ashes with them forever.

Meanwhile, the FitzRandolphs decided to make a concerted effort to sell the house. With Ruthie taking a leave from work, they could use the money. And perhaps it was time for new memories, although it was going to be very, very difficult to leave.

"Maybe a whole new start wouldn't be so bad. I don't know," pondered Ruthie. "In a way, I really don't want to leave because we have so many memories. But if we could find a cute little place with a new start and yet with a lot of memories … I think I could deal with that."

Ruthie spent hours cleaning and organizing to try and put the house on the market, but there was one area that was almost crippling: going into Jessi's room.

"The first couple of times I went in, I couldn't stay. I just broke down."

Still, Jessi had a huge wardrobe of clothes that needed to be dealt with. First, they allowed the Verona Babes to take anything they wanted. Each reacted differently: Some said they would love to wear something of Jessi's but a few felt that they couldn't. One Babe, Erika, took a scarf and wrapped it around her neck.

"She said, 'Oh, it's so warm, and it smells like Jessi,'" said Ruthie with a smile. The scarf went to Erika; for everything else, they brought in a woman from a consignment shop. Jessi's clothes were always upscale, hip, and trendy.

"One of her few joys in the last year or so was buying clothes, so when she was healthier she could go out and look like a million bucks. And she did look like a million bucks, but she ran out of time to wear it all," said Ruthie, sighing.

As time passed, Jeff and Ruthie took baby steps toward their new normal. They hosted Sawyer and Cassidy for a sleepover, what Jeff called "one of the better days we've had since Jessi passed." The kids were rebounding faster than anyone else, absorbed by school, sports, and just being children. Casey had a hard time going back to work but was thrown into a schedule of speaking engagements that probably helped take his mind off of things.

Ruthie started to feel that there was one unexpected benefit to the horror they had endured, and it involved her job.

"I think I'll be a better nurse. When I see a patient who's having a rapid change or increasing symptoms, I don't care if there's a meeting that I'm late for. That patient and that family deserves to have my attention immediately. That's where my priority will be. I know how it feels."

Back at the house, Jeff and Ruthie struggled to make sense of it all.

"I still feel her presence. You can't touch it, feel it, or see it, but it's there," said Jeff. Ruthie was still waiting for such a feeling, and that bothered her.

"I haven't had it, and I was the one closest to her," she said with a touch of sadness.

"I just tried to reassure her that Jessi was taking care of the easy ones first and working her way up to the most difficult one," responded Jeff, looking with tenderness toward his wife.

During moments of intense grief, memories would sometimes wash over them like a wave, but other times it was almost too much to bear to picture Jessi at a different stage of her life.

"The really hard part is keeping the memories alive. I don't want to lose them, but they're so painful at the same time," said Ruthie, crying.

"Every time you fill out paperwork for life insurance or anything— put it this way, I haven't sent back many that haven't been pretty well tearstained," Jeff added.

"I absolutely believe I will see her again. In the last seven months, I have come to believe it very strongly. Prior to that I wasn't sure," said Ruthie.

This chapter of their life had never been part of the plan. They weren't supposed to be grieving the loss of a child. They weren't supposed to be packing up the house and figuring out what to do with their thirty-six-year-old daughter's things. They were forced into this, and it was just not fair. Jeff looked back on the past forty years, a journey that began when he spied Ruthie moving into her new apartment. Two babies, two houses, countless vans, many dogs, an Olympic journey, a gold medal, the peaceful years, the grandchildren, the horror of cancer, and an untimely death all followed.

"If we'd been offered the choice to have one child be one of the best in the world and the other child die, or have two children just live more average lives, we would have taken the latter for sure. We have experienced the highest of highs and lowest of lows. But life has to go on. It's up to us to accept and adapt," Jeff said resignedly.

Part of moving on meant donating the hydroponic growing system and the remaining marijuana plants to Tori, their first supplier. She was now active in developing hybrid brands of medicinal marijuana to help both cancer patients and children with seizure disorders. In the summer of 2014, Tori was already assisting six patients with different types of cancer—ovarian, breast, lung/bone, pediatric leukemia and a nerve disorder that causes tumors to grow called neurofibromatosis. All had been sent home to die by conventional practitioners. Tori and her partners were developing a rich soil for testing and breeding different strains of marijuana. The eventual goal was for the seeds to flourish without the use of chemicals and to also yield just the right strain for each patient. Tori's team planned to offer an easy-to-follow guide. Each person would know the genetics behind the plants, understanding how and why the marijuana grows and works and being educated on the exact amount of THC/CBD in each strain. Patients would be then counseled on the perfect strain of Mother Nature's medicine to treat their particular disorder. It would all happen in one beautiful piece of earth in Wisconsin.

Jeff and Ruthie had just been told the name of this new plot of land.

It would be called something very special.

It would be called:

"Jessi's Garden."

Epilogue

Novelists are lucky: Their books have a definite ending. The bad guys are killed in a hail of bullets, the monster is slain, the monarchy is tumbled, the enemy is crushed, or the hero and heroine live to fight another day. Our story doesn't get that nice, neat closure. In real life, it just doesn't happen that way.

Now, I'm the first to appreciate a good novel, and must admit that I might not still have my sanity today without Stephen King (go figure?), John Sandford, and John Grisham. But I've learned in writing our book that what they write about is pure fantasy. And winning gold and dying from cancer is anything but!

And those guys have to set up a sequel, their next novel. I don't expect we will write another book any time soon. This one was too draining. It was too real when I would get up every morning and mix Jessi's alternative cancer cocktail of Poly MVA, CoQ10, and grape juice. Then I'd squeeze out a rice-sized bead of oil onto a small piece of potato cheese bread from the Silly Yak Bakery and give both to her with her morning capsule of Laetrile. It was too sad when I would watch her sit in her chair daily and hope the one-hour Bob Beck magnetic paddle treatment would ease her pain. It was too frustrating when I would boil a concoction of distilled water, organic coffee grounds, and chamomile to make her daily coffee enemas. Geez, who should have to take a daily enema to rid her body of toxic killers? It was too devastating to watch her spend two hours daily on the Rife machine while praying the radio frequencies coursing through her body would kill those resilient cancer cells in her bones.

It was so emotionally draining that when I would lay my head on my pillow at night and cry myself to sleep, I would ultimately replay Casey's

Olympic gold medal–winning performance over and over in my mind to calm myself enough to allow sleep to come over my body.

I would find the time I got to spend with my grandchildren a reprieve from my daily regimen rather than just an opportunity to enjoy the two bundles of joy Casey and Jenn had blessed us with. They are so beautiful, so innocent, so naive, so fragile, and so vulnerable. Why should I pray every time I see my grandchildren, "Dear God, please don't allow this hideous disease to ever touch Sawyer or Cassidy?"

This is our book, our story. We hope you take what you can from it. I'm sure it will leave you with some questions. Why did Jeff push so hard, how could Ruthie spend so many hours for so many years taking her children to practices, and why didn't they try this or that? Why, why, how?

I can tell you this much: Take time to relish the good times. You've earned them. And don't ever stop trying. Don't ever accept no for an answer. In tough times, search your soul for answers, talk to your spouse and your children, seek outside advice, and turn to the computer and the vast world of knowledge it opens up to you. And most importantly, trust your instincts—they rarely lead down a dead-end path. More often, they'll open your soul to a new universe of information and knowledge.

Today, our lives continue to evolve. We continue to grieve, heal, grow, and hope. If you take one thing away from reading our book, let it be "don't ever give up hope."

It is also important for you to know what our children learned at an early age: "Believe and you will achieve." And know that, fortunately, it is never too late to learn a valuable lesson: to leave no stone unturned.

Teach your children well.

Godspeed,
Jeff (and Ruthie)

Afterword

This book would not have been possible without the contributions of many talented and caring people. First, to our author Jessie Garcia, who treated Jessi as her own sister and immediately became part of our family as she interviewed us for our book. To say that this book would never have been published without her is an understatement. She prompted and prodded, albeit it ever so gently, as the dynamic that was our lives ebbed and flowed. She encouraged us and cried with us. God has provided us many gifts in our lives, and she is truly one of them. Editors Laura Kearney and Becky Waugh Klinke brought amazing insight and sharp eyes to the project.

We have also attempted to recognize our family, friends, and supporters who significantly influenced our lives on the following pages. I'm betting we have forgotten someone along the way. If so, please forgive. It's not for lack of trying to remember all of the wonderful people we have known in our lifetimes. It's more likely that we simply ran out of time while scouring our written documents, photographs, and failing memories for loving people we've known.

The idea for this book was originally to recognize Casey and his twenty-two-year journey to winning an Olympic gold medal. It took a turn, which ultimately gave our book considerably more substance, when Jessi was diagnosed with breast cancer during the summer of 2010. It was a sometimes beautiful, often painful, but always important process for our family.

So we end by thanking Jessi herself, who agreed to open up during the most difficult stretch of her life in the hopes that her story would have meaning for others. We love you, dear Jessi, now and forever.

Here are some of the people who have shaped our family's lives:

Ivan and Virginia FitzRandolph
Jim and Trudy Whitinger
Merodie Bocher
Jeff and Nancy Bocher
"Nanners" Whitinger
Andy Anderson

Verona Babes:
Becky (Waugh) Klinke
Michelle (Mauel) Manzetti
Jessica (Michalski) Winthieser
Erica (Freng) Olson
Amy (Schellpfeffer) Niementscheck
Erin (Murphy) Brooks

Jessie Garcia-Marble
Bonnie Blair
Dan Jansen
Eric Heiden
Libby Cichy
Justin Dorrow
Eric Russell
Bowen Best
Mike Holewinski
Julie (Veloff) Helmer
Pastor Matt Rusten
Pastor George Calhoun
Dave Cruikshank
Marc Pelchat
Sean Ireland, Mike Ireland, Jeremy Wotherspoon, and our Calgary team and family.
Ryan Shimabukuro and our Salt Lake City team.
Bunk and Elayne Riley
Mike Crowe

Guy Thibault
Nick Thometz
Lyle LeBombard
Lori (Monk) Goff
Susan Sandvig-Shobe
Mary Doctor
Bob Corby
Greg and Laurie Wilkinson
Joe Gilles
Rich Lepping
Donna Sollenberger
Scott Arndt
Pete Settle and Caroll College family
Dr. Shaw
Dr. Tyre
Diane and Grant Gintz and family
Jon and Sue Cruzan
Tori LaChapelle
Greg Moriva
Robert Steil and Family
Andrei Beisinger
Fred Benjamin
Brad Goskowicz
Gene Sandvig
Tim Meyer
Agrace HospiceCare
St. Mary's Hospital
Dr. Roy Kim
C&N Photography
National Mutual Benefit
M3 Insurance
Madison Media
Fachklinik
IBM Hospital, Mexico
CarePages Supporters (all 791 visitors who left over 1,600 messages)

Made in the USA
Lexington, KY
27 January 2016